Pine Barrens: Life and Legends

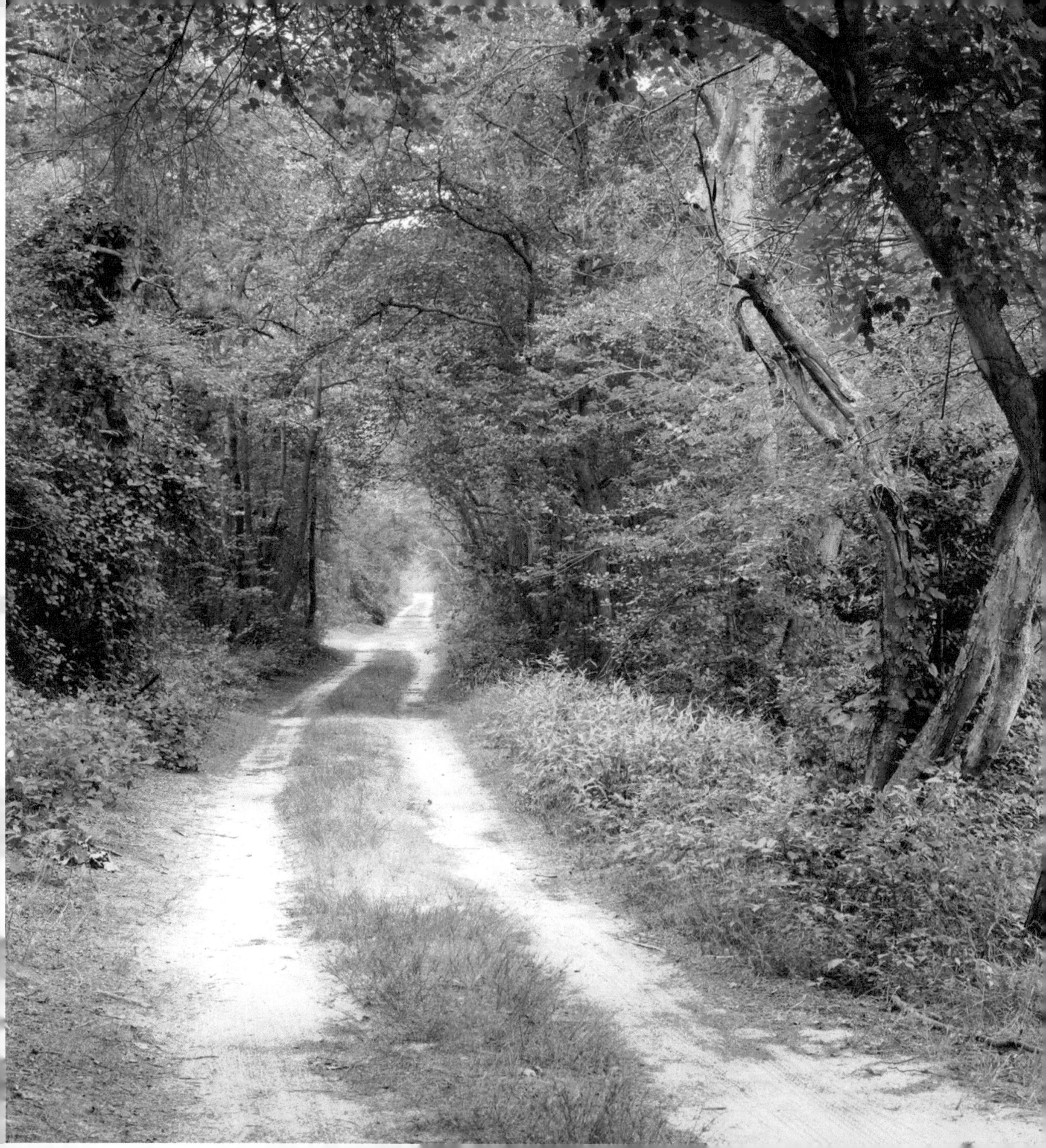

Pine Barrens: Life and Legends

An exhibition co-organized by the Noyes Museum of Art and the South Jersey Culture & History Center

January 30 - September 13, 2015

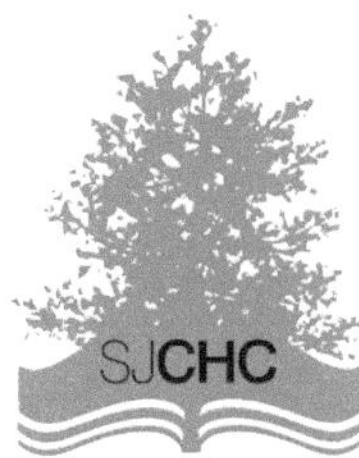

A publication of the South Jersey Culture & History Center

This publication is issued on the occasion of the exhibition PINE BARRENS: LIFE AND LEGENDS on view at the Noyes Museum of Art of Stockton University, Oceanville, New Jersey, from January 30 to September 13, 2015.

This exhibition was co-organized by the Noyes Museum of Art and the South Jersey Culture & History Center.

Published by the South Jersey Culture & History Center

blogs.stockton.edu/sjchc/

Tom Kinsella, Director SJCHC, & Paul W. Schopp, Associate Director SJCHC, *editors*

Dorrie Papademetriou, Director of Exhibitions & Collections, The Noyes Museum

Saskia Schmidt, Director of Education, The Noyes Museum

Eric R. Anglero, *exhibition photographer*

First Edition

ISBN 978-0-9888731-4-8

Road to the Bogs, Whitesbog Village, Pemberton, Burlington County, c. 1935.

(Frontispiece) A two track sand road through a canopy of arched trees – if photography had been at hand, this image might have been made 300 years ago in the Pines. It dates to the 1930s at Whitesbog, but roads of this sort continue to lace the Pine Barrens. Joseph Elliott, photographer; from the Prints and Photographs Division, Library of Congress.

In the Woods, Mill Road in the Cedars, Lower Bank, Burlington County, c. 1906.

Before automobiles, people moved through the Pines on horses, wagons, watercraft and, after their advent, trains, but most often on foot. Here a well-dressed young woman, perhaps a summertime visitor, stands beside horse and buggy. She is out for a ride in the Pines. Courtesy of the Paul W. Schopp Collection.

Foreword

In April 2013 Dorrie Papademetriou, Director of Exhibitions & Collections at the Noyes Museum, asked whether I was interested in helping the museum mount "an exhibition based on the folklore/culture and curiosities of the pinelands." I was interested, and thought Stockton students would be too. The result is *Pine Barrens: Life and Legends*.

Most citizens of New Jersey have a passing knowledge of the Pines and of the Jersey Devil, its most famous legend. Here we dig a bit deeper, presenting an overview of Pinelands history, describing common ways of life, and sampling the rich oral traditions of the place, most notably those recorded by anthropologist Herbert Halpert.

The Pines remain vibrant, both environmentally and culturally. We have accordingly paired historical commentary with contemporary artwork inspired by the Pines. Though some multimedia installations could not be duplicated in print, most of the exhibition is reproduced here along with additional materials that enhance the whole. We hope you enjoy this sampling of the Pines.

Tom Kinsella

Director, South Jersey Culture & History Center

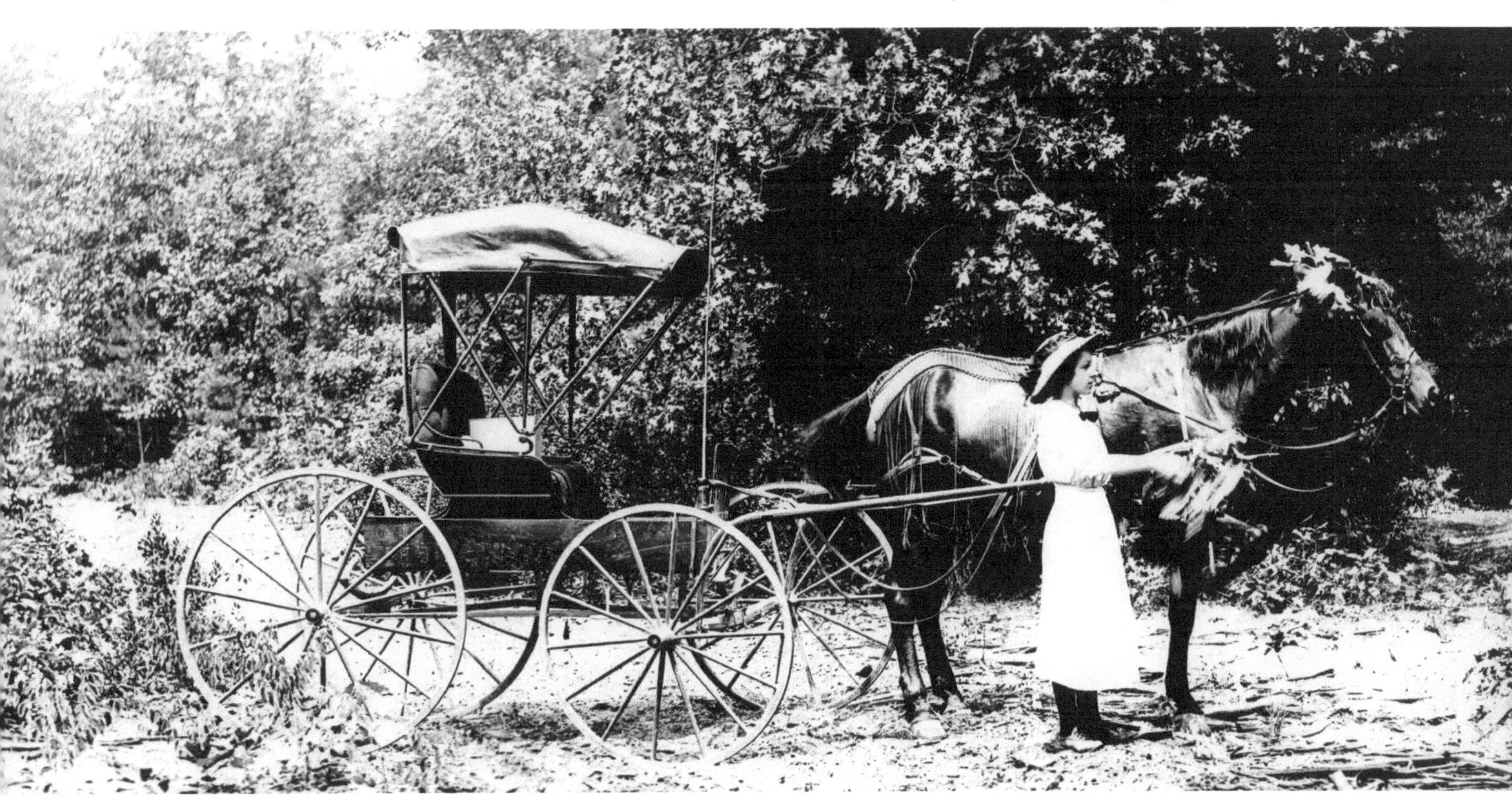

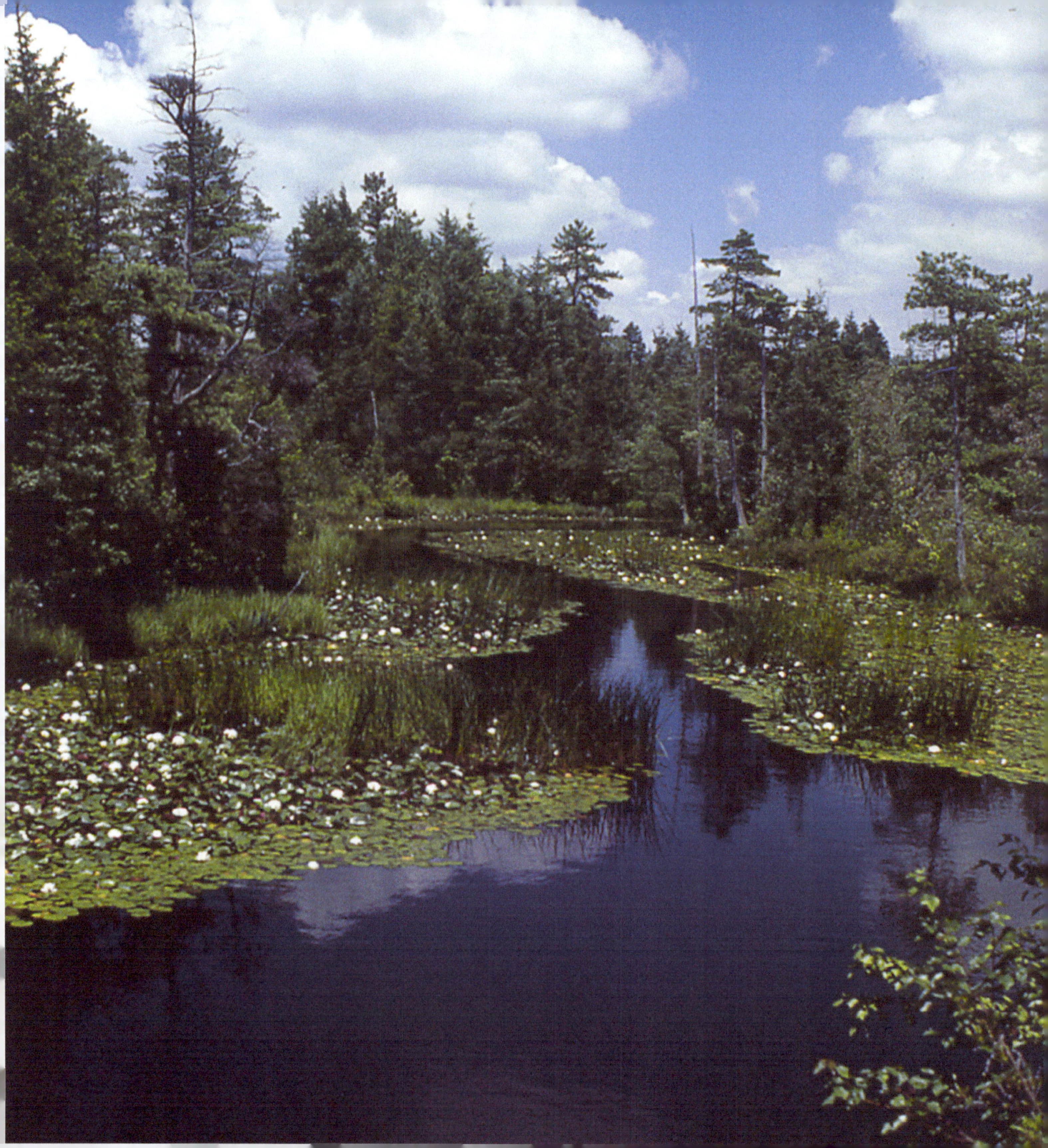

Contents

View of the Upper Wading River, Burlington County, 1984.

A distinctive feature of the Pines is water. Below ground the Kirkwood-Cohansey aquifer holds 17 trillion gallons. Above ground, the relatively flat geography of the Pines is crisscrossed with streams and rivers, most flowing east to the Atlantic. This is the view of the upper Wading River at Burnt Bridge south of the Chatsworth cemetery showing the stream channel dominated by *Nymphaea odorata*, Fragrant White Waterlily. Ted Gordon, photographer, July 1984.

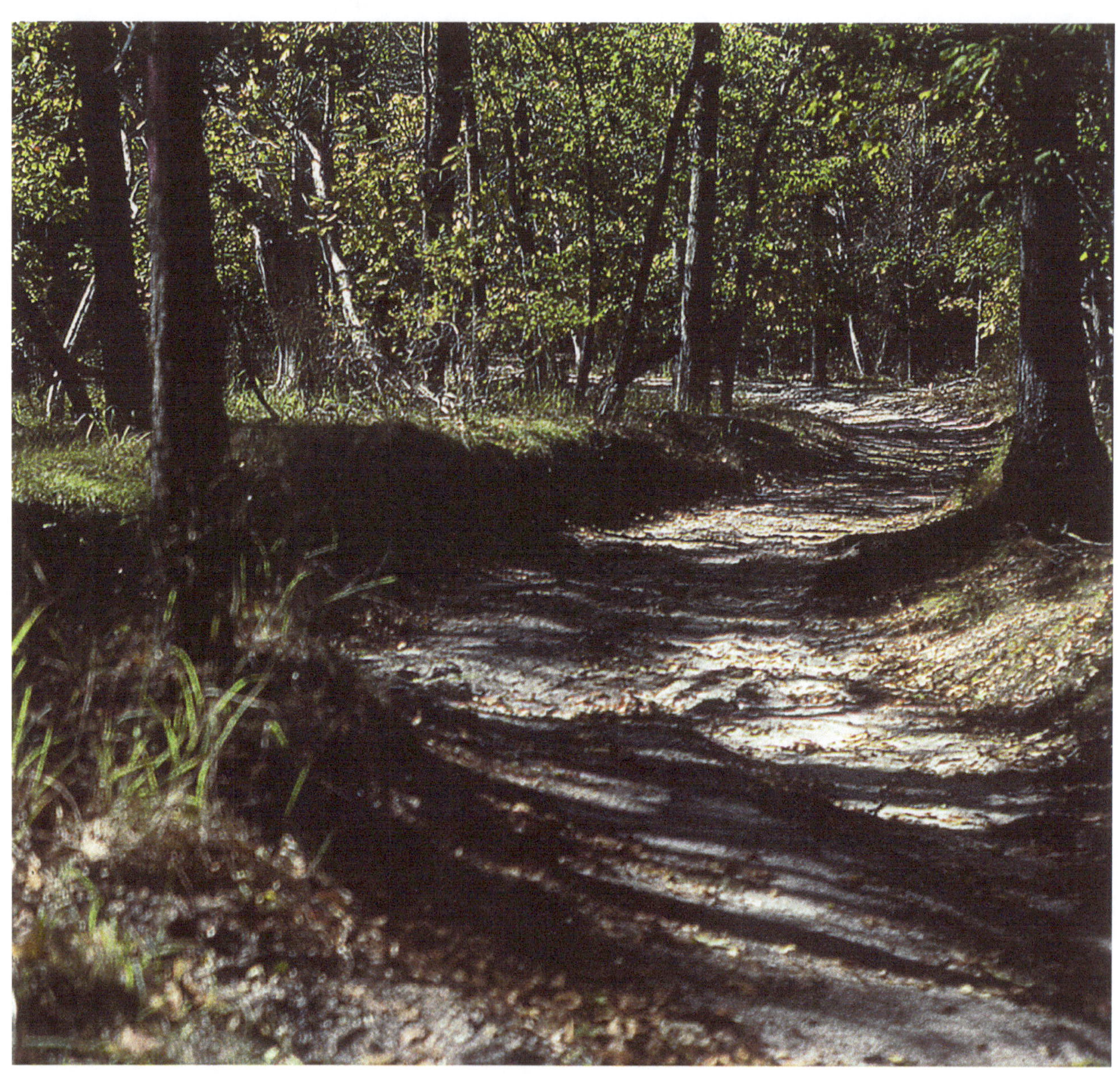

Road from Harrisville to Martha Furnace, Burlington County, 1995.

Residents of the Pines laid out their earliest roads atop Native American trails. All were blazed with respect for the land, as the best road is not always the straightest. Ted Gordon, photographer, October 1995.

Pine Barrens: Life and Legends

For a very long time the New Jersey Pine Barrens have been a world apart. Native Americans moved through the region, following the seasonal harvests of berries, nuts, fish and game. European settlers, beginning in the late seventeenth century, developed varied occupations within the Pines, nearly all based upon its natural resources. Communities grew up around industrial bases that are now largely gone. Life was not easy, and made few rich, yet neither was it barren. Generations of families were born, lived honest, hard lives, and died, but not before passing their values and way of life, and quite often their folklore and legends, to succeeding generations.

Life in the Pines progressed at a pace out of step with nearby industrial and urban centers. Even so, in the second half of the twentieth century, as the energy and wealth of the Delaware River Valley and North Jersey threatened to erode and homogenize the area, a wonder transpired. The Pinelands were recognized as a place apart – a place that should be preserved. And so within the most densely populated state in the Union, the first national reserve was created in 1978, 1.1 million acres of protected ground.

Today the natural beauty of the Pines, designated by the United Nations as an International Biosphere Reserve, is open to all who wish to experience it. The cultural history of this unique area – deeply rooted in and influenced by its unique landscape – deserves attention as well. Legends arose in the Pines that entertained generations of residents. As the contemporary art in this exhibition suggests, this special place continues to inspire.

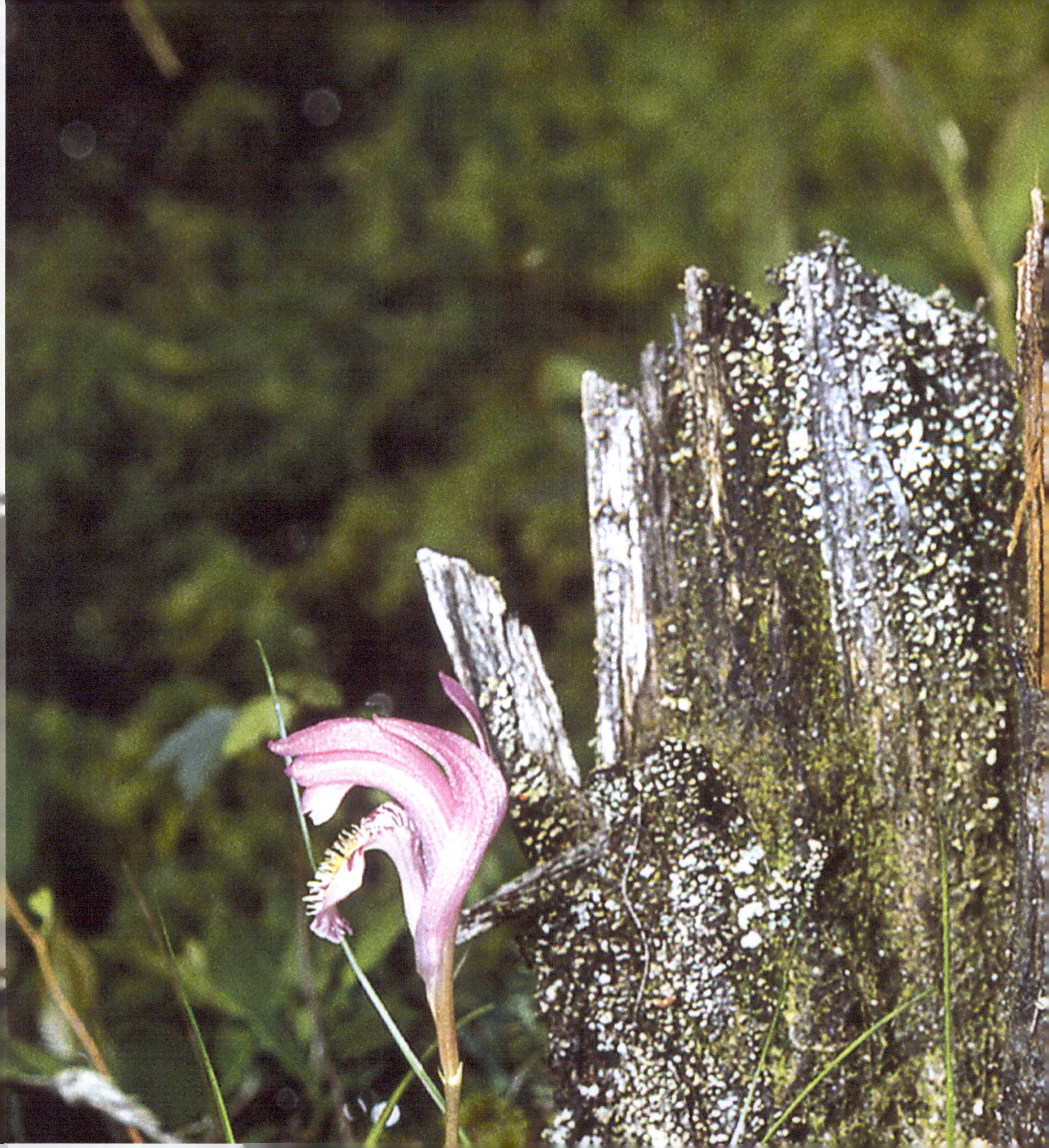

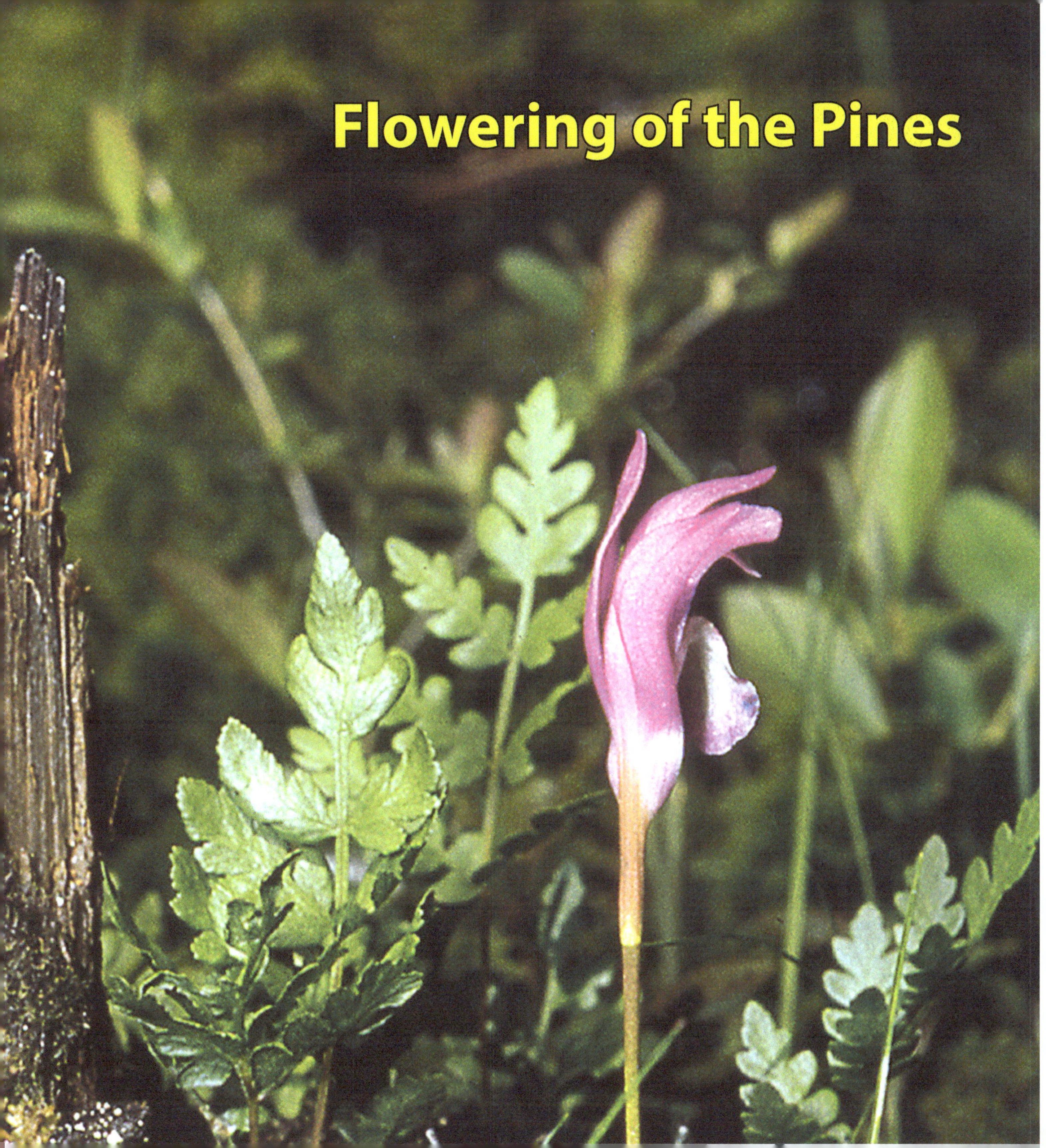
Flowering of the Pines

SALE OF LANDS.

WILL BE SOLD

AT PUBLIC SALE,

On Thursday the 17th day of October next, at the Inn of Joseph Cooper, in the Upper Township, in the County of Cape May,—the several Tracts of Land hereinafter mentioned, situate in the township of Weymouth, in the county of Gloucester, formerly belonging to *Seth Hand*—

1. One-half of 300 Acres, Woodland and Marsh, known by the name of the "Mickle Property."

2. 106 Acres of Cedar Swamp, known by the name of the "Benezet Swamp."

3. One-fourth part of a Saw-Mill and Mill Seat, on Gibson's Creek; called Steelman's Mill.

4. 40 Acres of Woodland, adjoining lands of Joseph Ingersoll.

5. 85 Acres of Woodland, on Turkey-Hoe, joining lands of John Williams.

6. 85 Acres of Land and Marsh, on Gibson's Creek.

7. 25 Acres of Land and Marsh, in Ragged Point Tract.

The subscriber is authorized to sell the same under the Insolvent Laws of New Jersey, being the Assignee of the above named Seth Hand. Sale will commence at two o'clock, P. M.

The Creditors of said Seth Hand, are desired to meet at the Inn above mentioned, on the day of sale, at one o'clock, P M. to settle the terms of sale.

A more particular description of the property, and the terms of sale, will be given on the day of sale.

JEREMIAH HAND.

Middle township, Cape May, Sept. 16. 90 ts.

Encountering the Pine Barrens

SIXTY PERCENT of New Jersey's geology is classified as Coastal Plain. This includes the eight counties of South Jersey plus the northern counties of Mercer, Middlesex, and Monmouth. The *Inner* Coastal Plain, ten to fifteen miles wide, drains west into the Delaware River and north into the Raritan Bay. The *Outer* Coastal Plain, more than twice that size, drains east into the Atlantic and south into the Delaware Bay. This geological feature makes possible and is dominated by the Pine Barrens.

As pioneers first pushed into the Barrens, they faced a formidable landscape with sandy, gravelly soils filled with pine and oak forests, vast swamps containing large white and red cedars, savannas, small ponds known as spungs, and a variety of other geological features. They were met by a rich ecosystem of plants and animals well adapted to the difficult terrain but not well suited to common agrarian practices.

The intrepid souls who first entered this environment did so for economic reasons: cutting timber, making charcoal, or producing naval stores from the pine trees. These pioneers began an era of natural-resource exploitation that led to the development of iron, glass, and paper industries in the Pines – and the exploitation continues today. Other early settlers watered and grazed herds of cattle in the savannas scattered throughout the Pines, exploiting the readily available water flowing from the great aquifers underlying this strange landscape. They soon found that in many areas wild blueberries (huckleberries) and cranberries abounded and thus new agricultural pursuits developed.

SALE OF LANDS, Weymouth Township, Atlantic County (Gloucester), 1822.

No McMansions or commercial properties were for sale in eastern Gloucester County during 1822 (Atlantic County separated from Gloucester in 1837). Woodlands, marshes, cedar swamps, and a sawmill are the valuable commodities. *Washington Whig*, Bridgeton, New Jersey, September 30, 1822.

ARETHUSA BULBOSA, along the Batsto River near Quaker Bridge, 1970.

(Preceding page) Dragon Mouth Orchid, on a sphagnum hummock within a light gap in a cedar swamp along the Batsto River. Ted Gordon, photographer, May 1970.

Living Close to the Land

SIMILAR TO the Native Americans before them who had engaged in the "seasonal round," residents of the Pines came to live close to the land, adapting life to the diverse, if rugged, offerings of the Pines. The goal of early agriculture in the Pines was household subsistence. Traditionally, residents merged two activities: gathering from the natural bounty of the woods and cultivating crops suited to the sandy, acidic soil of the Barrens. Occupations were seasonal.

In the spring, inhabitants gathered sphagnum moss, known for its absorbent qualities and sold in great quantities to florists. It is still widely used in the gardening industry. Residents grew small gardens of cool-weather crops early in the season. By June and July, wild blueberries (huckleberries) had ripened for harvest, and locals took to the woods, beating the fruit into baskets (made in the winter) hung around their necks. Cranberry harvest succeeded blueberry, from September into October. Late in this fall period, deer hunting began, with residents often serving as guides for out-of-the-area hunters. In winter, seasonal decorations were collected – holly, laurel, mistletoe, pinecones – and grave blankets assembled from local greens. Winter was also a time to move into the woods, without the depredations of mosquitoes, gnats, and ticks, to cut cedar, cord wood, and pulp wood.

In the 1850s, towns on the margins of the traditional Pines – Hammonton, Vineland, and Egg Harbor City – began large-scale farming of vegetables and fruits for which they remain famous today.

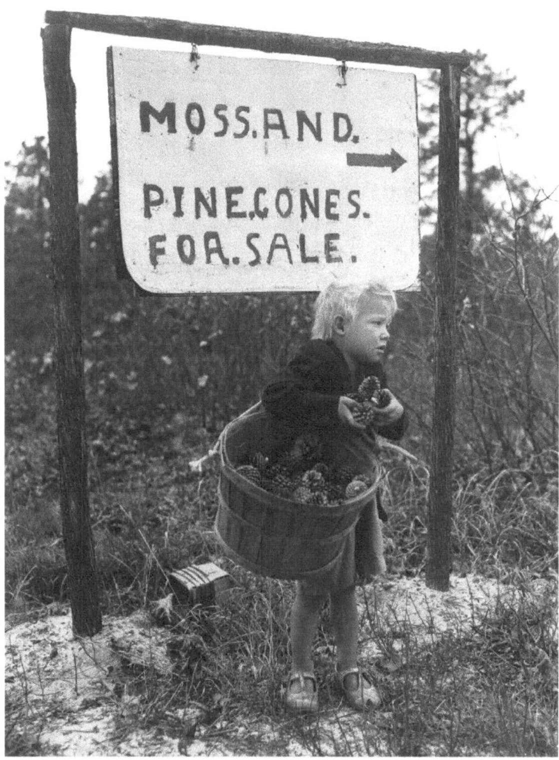

GIRL WITH PINECONES

Young and old alike contributed to seasonal harvests. A young girl, in a Piney version of a lemonade stand, has been pineballing and stands expectantly, waiting to sell to visitors to the Pines. The bulk of such pinecones were sold to florists in Philadelphia and New York. William F. Augustine, photographer, courtesy of the Pete Stemmer Collection.

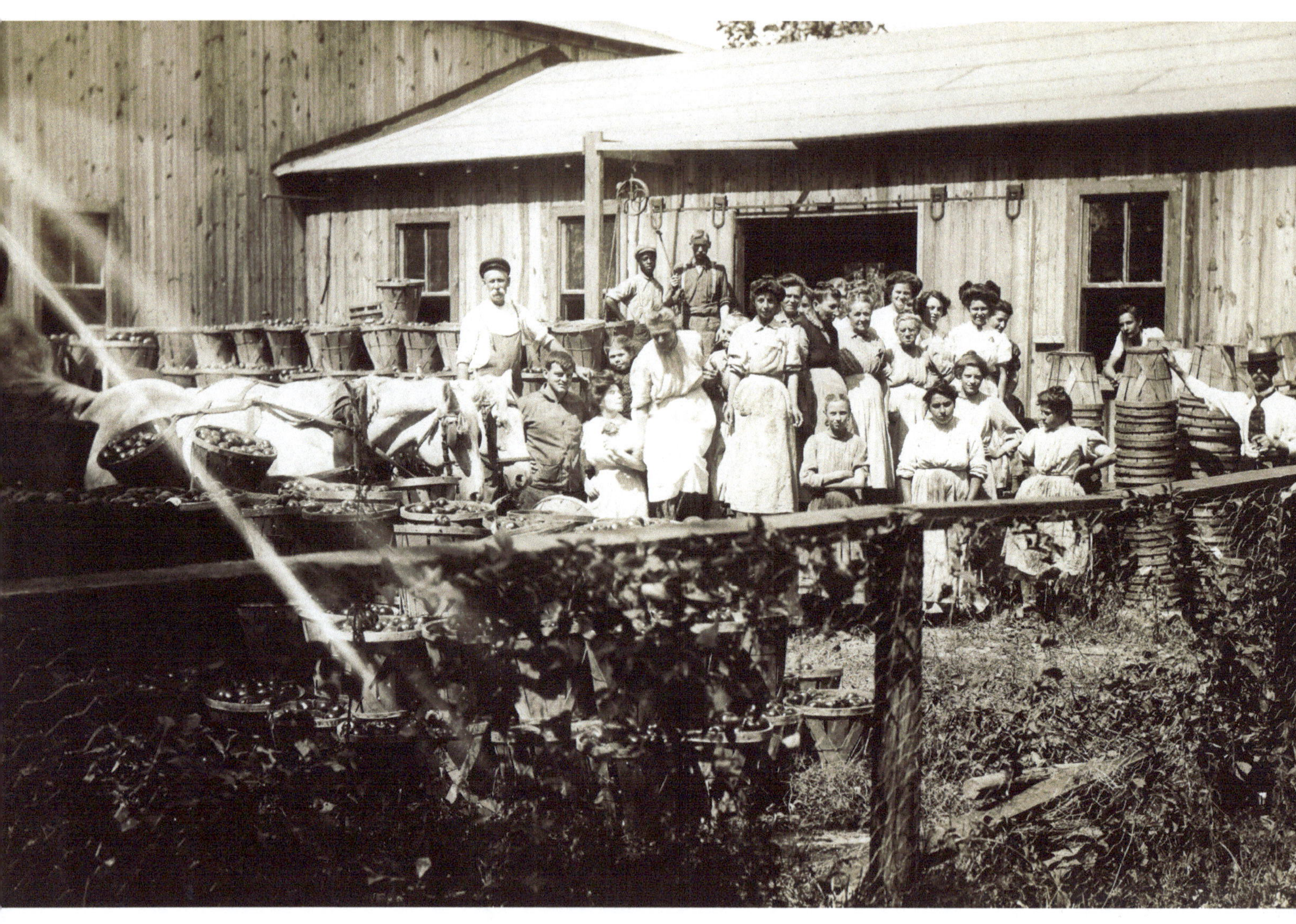

Harry May & Company Canning Factory, Egg Harbor City, Atlantic County, c. 1915.

Harry May & Company employed 23 people in 1915 and it appears all of these workers are standing in the canning factory's receiving yard, located at the northeastern corner of Beethoven and Cincinnati avenues. Tomato canning was a huge part of this cannery's business and baskets of red Jersey beauties can be seen in the yard waiting for processing. Courtesy of the Paul W. Schopp Collection.

Itinerant Berry Pickers

Indigenous to swampy areas, cranberries were cultivated in the Pines starting in the 1840s. The cranberry boom in the succeeding decades resulted from improved growing and sorting techniques. By the early twentieth century, harvesting required large numbers of pickers. While locals were often involved, itinerant workers arrived to work the bogs as well. Whole families often comprised the work gangs: grandparents, aunts and uncles, parents, older children, younger children – all had a hand in berry picking.

Many of these itinerant pickers, numbering in the thousands, were Italians who lived in South Philadelphia during the winter months, working in a variety of unskilled or semi-skilled jobs. During the harvest season, families first worked the South Jersey strawberry fields, starting around mid-May, lodging in rough tenements provided by the growers. By late June, they moved to Hammonton to pick blackberries and then raspberries, and to take part in the tomato and pepper harvests. Finally, in September and October they picked cranberries. The job was laborious, picking berries by hand and carrying full baskets or boxes from the bogs to bushelmen, who loaded the fruit onto wagons. But with a low cost of living at the fields, and working as a unit, families could earn enough during harvest season to allow them to live comfortably in Philadelphia, earning lower wages until the next season.

By the 1930s, day laborers from Philadelphia were trucked to and from the fields, but with the introduction of wet harvesting to New Jersey in 1960, harvest payrolls dropped precipitously. Most Jersey growers today use the wet harvesting method to gather their crops. Workers are still needed, but not in the quantity formerly required.

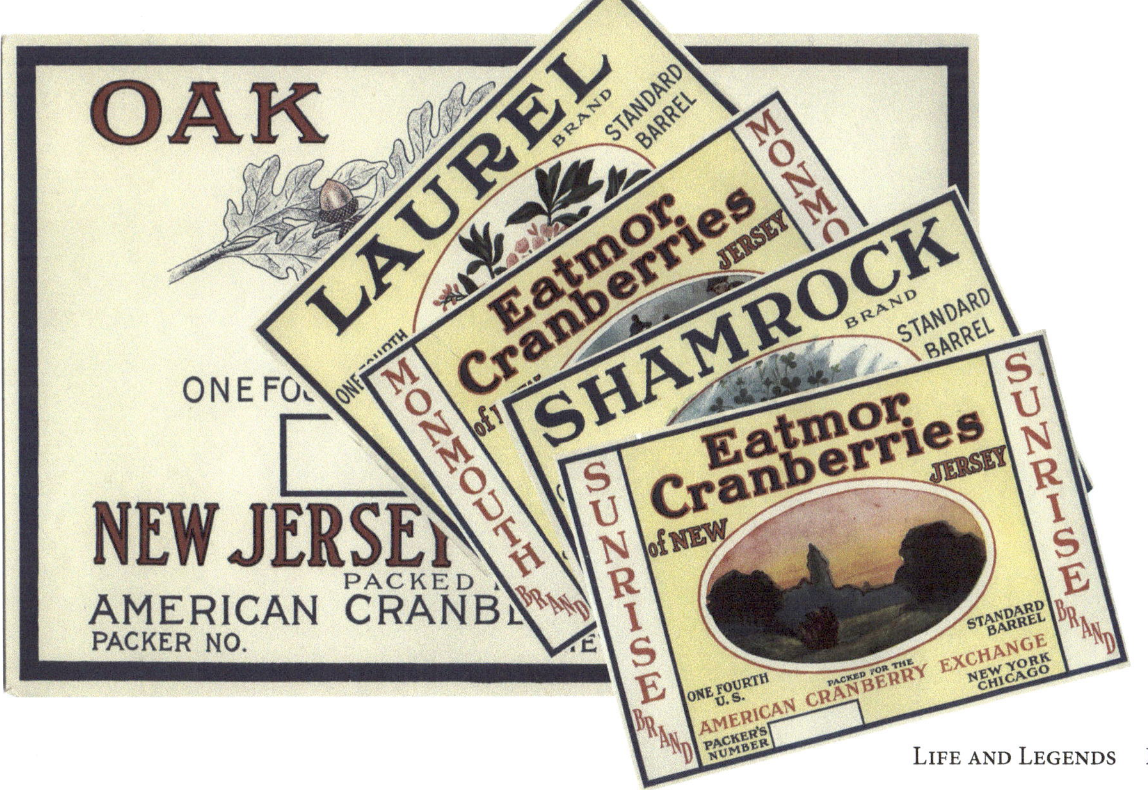

Salvin Nocito Carrying Cranberries, Whites Bog, Browns Mills, Burlington County, 1910.

Five year-old Salvin Nocito carries two pecks of cranberries over a long distance to the "bushelman." Lewis Wickes Hine, photographer, September 28, 1910; from the Prints and Photographs Division, Library of Congress.

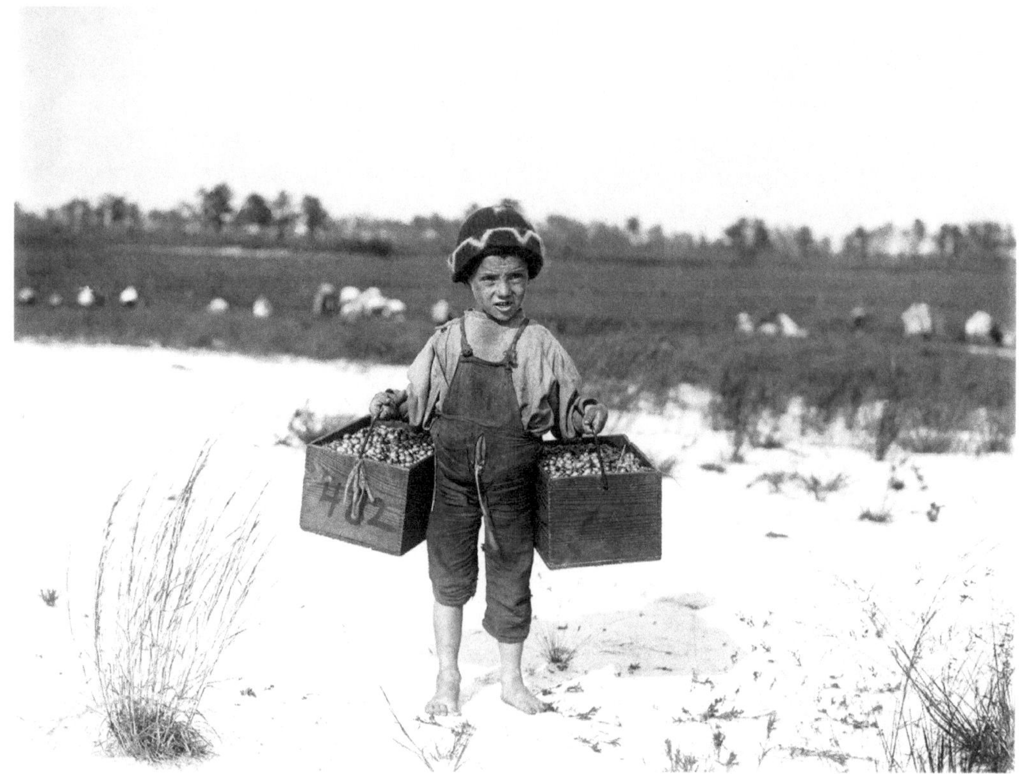

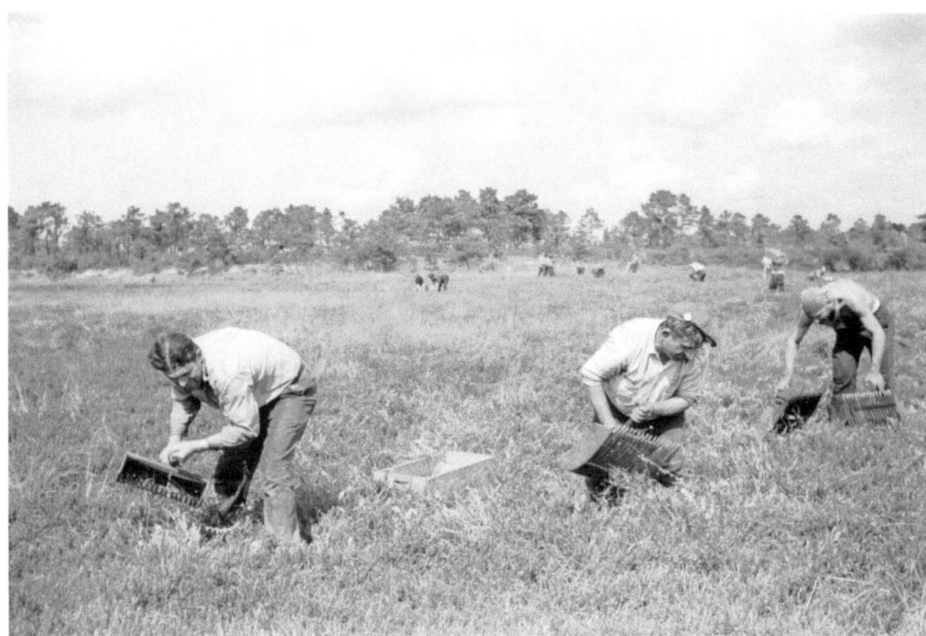

Men Scooping Cranberries, Burlington County, New Jersey, 1938.

Most harvesting was done quite literally by hand. Scooping was used when haste was necessary. These men are harvesting the older vines. Arthur Rothstein, photographer, October 1938; from the Prints and Photographs Division, Library of Congress.

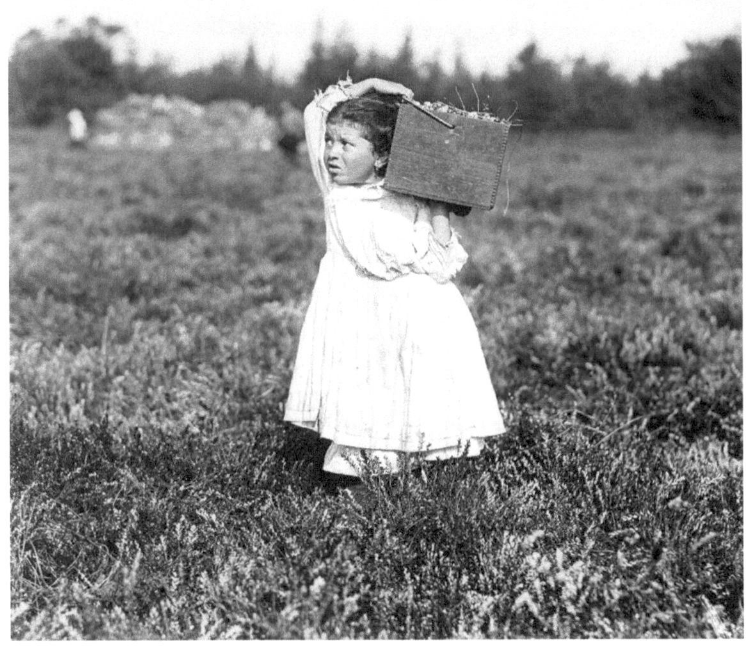

Jennie Camillo Carrying Cranberries, Theodore Budd's Bog, Turkeytown, Burlington County, 1910.

Jennie Camillo, eight-years-old, lived in West Manayunk, outside of Philadelphia. Four weeks into the school year and Jennie's family was slated to harvest for another two weeks. Her look of distress was caused by her father's impatience over her stopping in her tramp to the "bushelman" at the photographer's request. Lewis Wickes Hine, photographer, September 27, 1910; from the Prints and Photographs Division, Library of Congress.

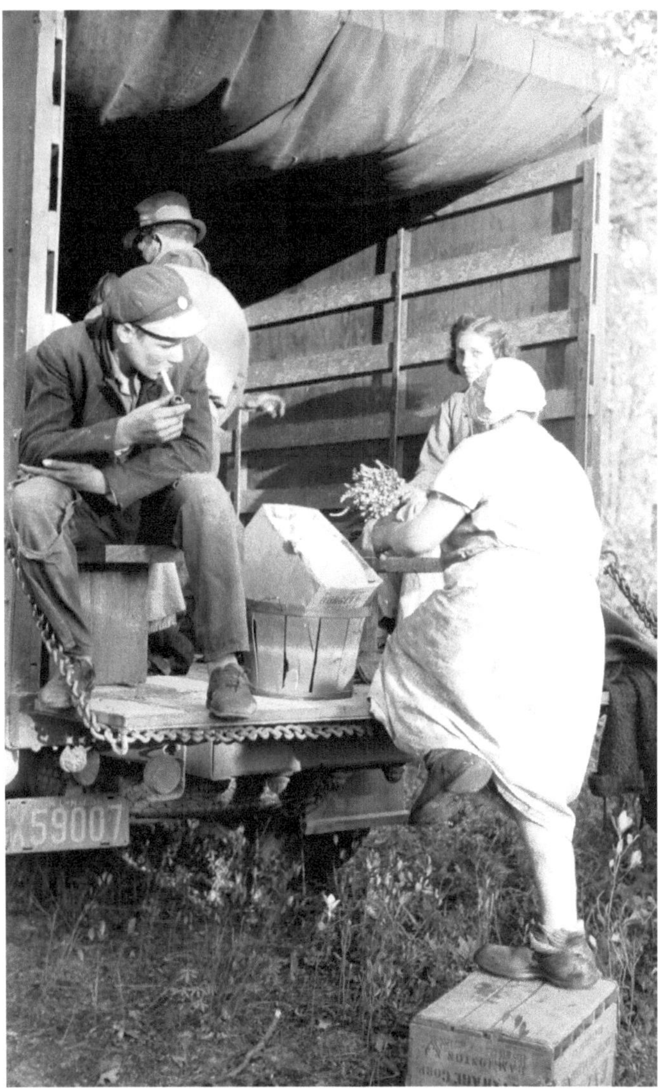

Heading Home, Burlington County, 1938.

Cranberry pickers of all ages clamber aboard a truck that will carry them back to Philadelphia after a day of harvesting. Arthur Rothstein, photographer, October 1938; from the Prints and Photographs Division, Library of Congress.

Dr. James Still

Cross-Roads, Burlington County, New Jersey

SELECTED CURATIVE HERBAL CONCOCTIONS

Salves, Tinctures, Poultices, Ointments, Powders, Teas, Tonics, Drops, Plasters

- Bayberry Bark Snuff: *for headache or migraine*
- Bitters: *as a restorative*
- Sassafras Roots: *for piles*
- Strengthening Bitters: *for dyspepsia, liver complaint or consumption*
- Soda Water or weak Lye Bath: *to reduce a fever*
- Sudorific Drops and Catnip Tea: *to produce perspiration and reduce fever, for sleep and for rheumatism*
- Diaphoretic Powders: *for fevers*
- Diaphoretic Powders with Catnip Tea and Laudanum: *for sleep and sedative*
- Emetic Medicine: *internal cleansing*
- Hartshorn (carbonate of ammonia), Gum-Arabic, Loaf Sugar, Mint Tea: *for low excitement or prostration*
- Lemonade: *for fevers*
- Vegetable Physic: *for fevers*
- Vegetable Emetic and warm Boneset Tea: *given as emetic when fever does not respond to other treatments; induces vomiting*
- Vegetable Preparations: *liver disease*
- Alkaline Wash for Bathing: *for fevers*
- Elm-Bark Poultice with Yeast: *for mortification of a limb and inflammation or erysipelas of the head and arm*
- May-Apple Root: *as a purgative (in place of calomel)*
- Peppermint Tea with Saleratus, sweetened with White Sugar: *for vomiting*
- Sudorific Drops contain: *opium, ipecac, saffron, camphor, Virginia snakeroot, and pleurisy root, all bruised, suspended in diluted alcohol.*

ALL COMPOUNDING, CONCOCTING, DECOCTING, AND PREPARATION DONE ON PREMISES

STILL HERBAL BROADSIDE.

This broadside, drawn from plants and remedies mentioned in James Still's autobiography, *Early Life and Recollections*, lists ailments and treatments that would have been familiar to late nineteenth-century residents of South Jersey.

Medicine in and from the Pines

HERBAL MEDICINE has existed as long as man has inhabited the earth. Millennia of trial and error have resulted in a knowledge of what works, what proved ineffectual, and what was downright poisonous. In the Pine Barrens, the Late Woodland Lenape are the first documented gatherers of plant parts to affect cures for specific ailments. For these indigenous people, it was as much spiritual as physical, for the Lenape believed that each plant had its own spirit, which took an active participation in curing illness. While some pioneering Europeans during the Contact Period prepared observation notes on what plants the Lenape used for medicinal purposes, the Europeans also brought their own herbal knowledge to the New World.

Dr. James Still

BORN IN 1812, the son of former slaves, James Still spent his formative years in and around Indian Mills, Burlington County. At the age of five, he witnessed a Dr. Fort administering vaccine to his siblings, which inspired his dream of becoming a medical doctor. Knowing the barriers in place for an African American becoming a physician in the mid-nineteenth century, he pursued an alternative career as a self-taught herbalist, using medicinal botanicals to create salves, tinctures, elixirs, poultices, and other delivery forms for his herbal concoctions. He derived some of these medicines from plants gathered on local farms and in Pine Belt woods, while others he purchased from suppliers in Philadelphia.

A very sober and industrious man, Still began acquiring land at an early age and at the time of his death in 1882, he was among the top five wealthiest men in Burlington County and the wealthiest African American in New Jersey. His autobiographical work, *Early Life and Recollections of Dr. James Still*, should be required reading for all school students.

Frontispiece from the autobiographical volume, *Early Recollections and Life of Dr. James Still*, published in 1877.

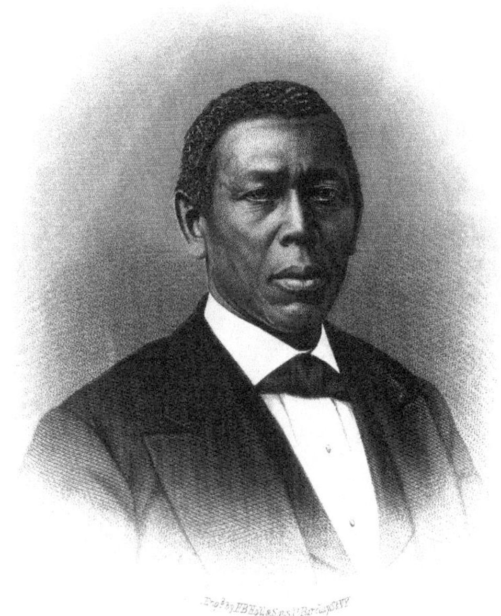

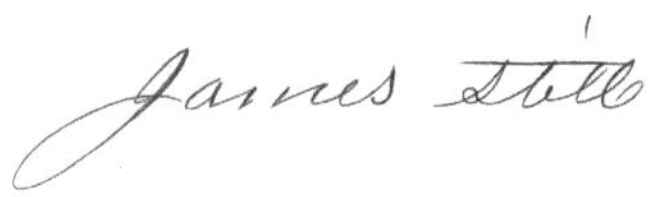

James Still

Residence of Dr. James Still, Medford Township, Burlington County, 1876.

This lithograph of James Still's office and home shows the affluent circumstances that he achieved later in life. From the *Combination Atlas Map of Burlington County, New Jersey* (1876). Courtesy of Archives & Special Collections, The Richard E. Bjork Library.

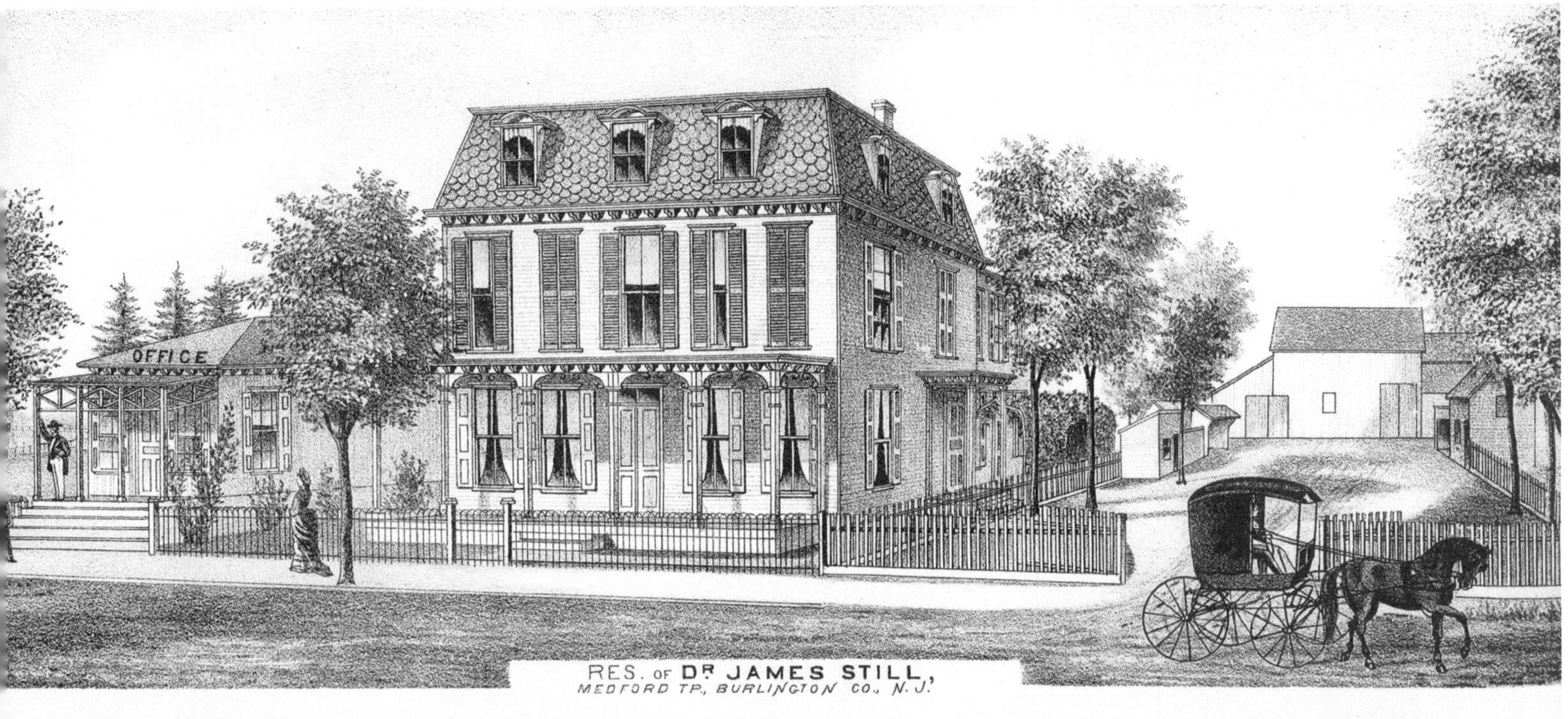

OFFICE

RES. OF DR JAMES STILL,
MEDFORD TP., BURLINGTON CO., N.J.

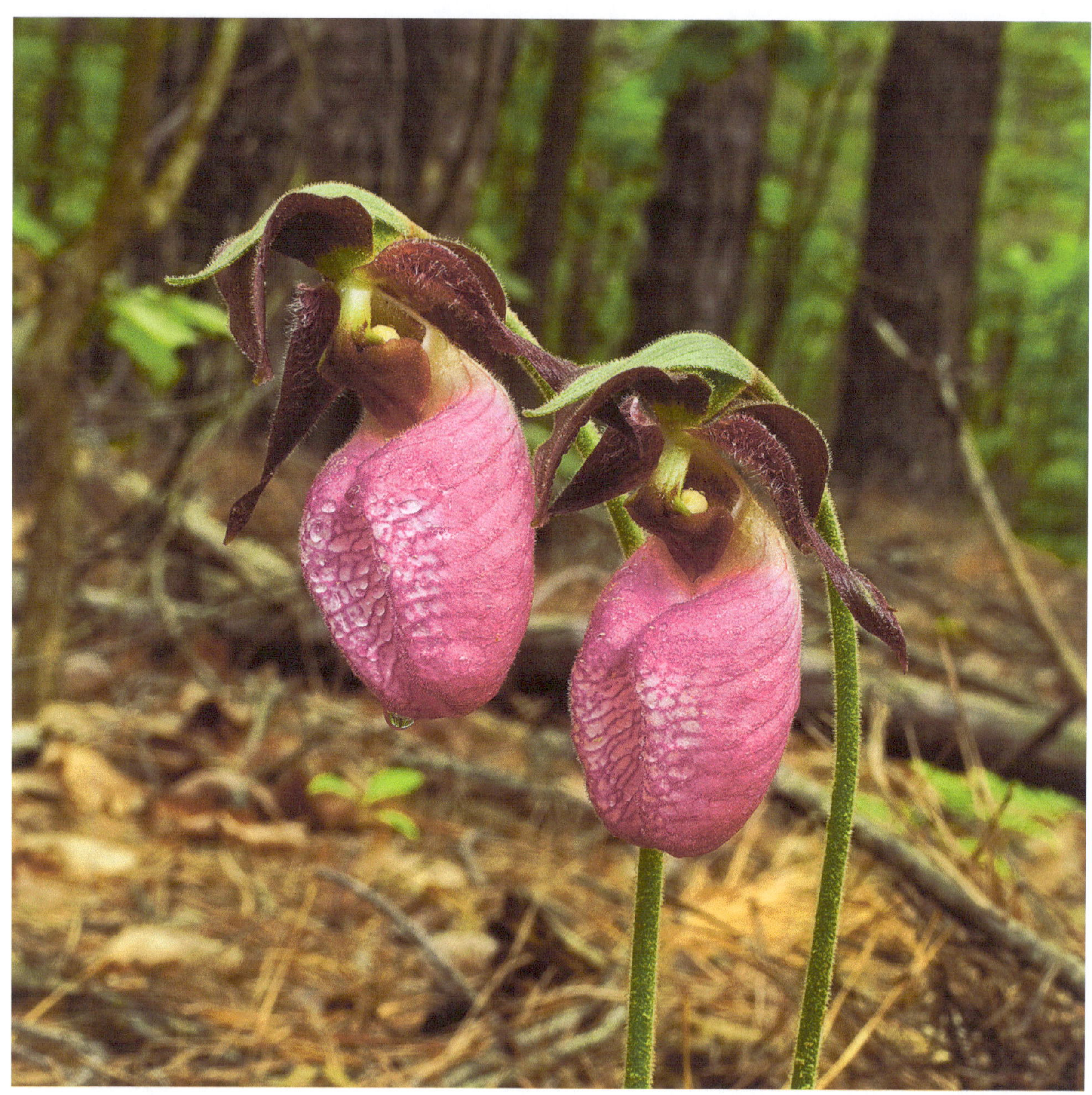

Lady Slippers, Albert Horner, 2014.
Cypripedium acaule

Botany in the Pines

FROM John and William Bartram to John Torrey, Jack McCormick, Howard Boyd, Ted Gordon, and many other notable botanists, the Pine Barrens hold a natural allure that few other spots in North America can offer. During the eighteenth century, John Bartram was the first to make regular forays to observe and gather specimens of the rare and unique flora found in the Pines. The early nineteenth-century discovery of the curly-grass fern at Quaker Bridge only served to enhance the Pines' reputation as a remarkable area that was anything but barren. The cedar swamps, bogs, blue holes, spungs, savannas, and pygmy pine forests all provide habitat for plants of exceptional beauty and rarity. Since the days of the Bartrams, botanists and naturalists have made innumerable pilgrimages to study the Pines and its plants. This interest has fostered the publication of many articles, books, and inventories of the plants found throughout the area.

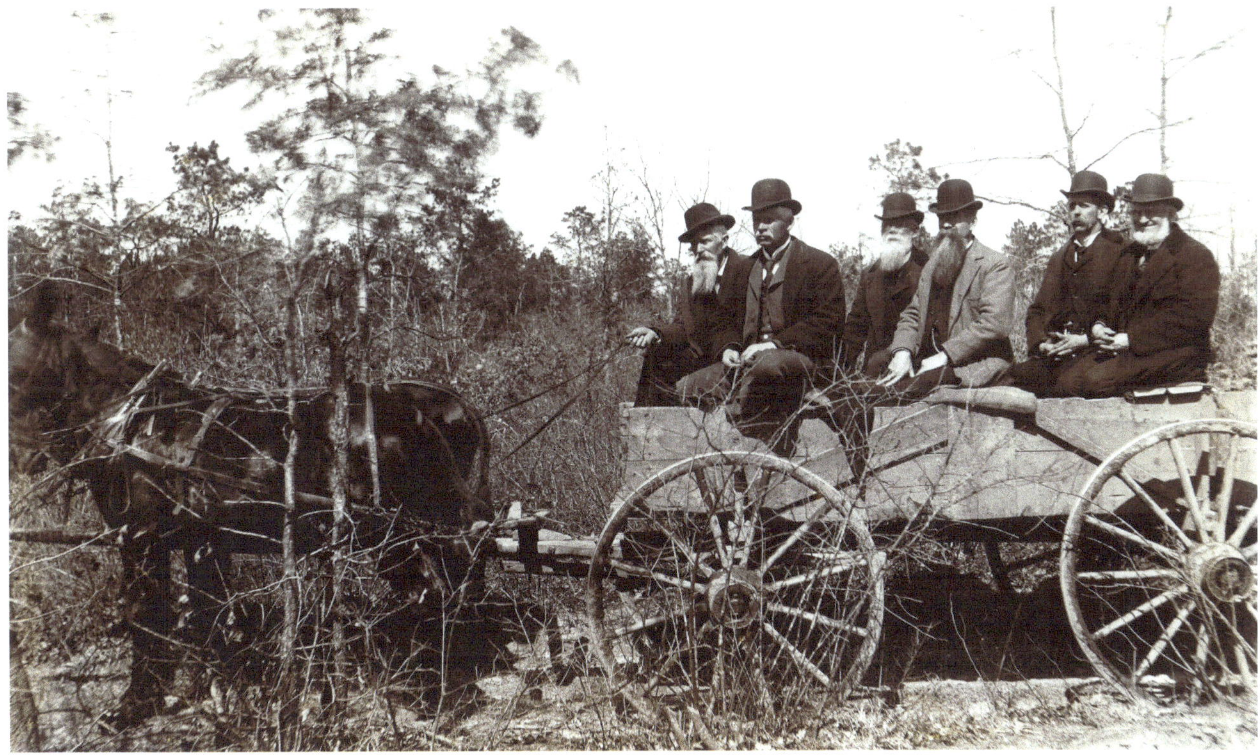

BOTANISTS VISIT THE PINES, c. 1895.

This photograph, from a collection of 10 unidentified images, chronicles a botany trip to the Pine Barrens. The trip probably occurred during the 1890s. Courtesy of the Paul W. Schopp Collection.

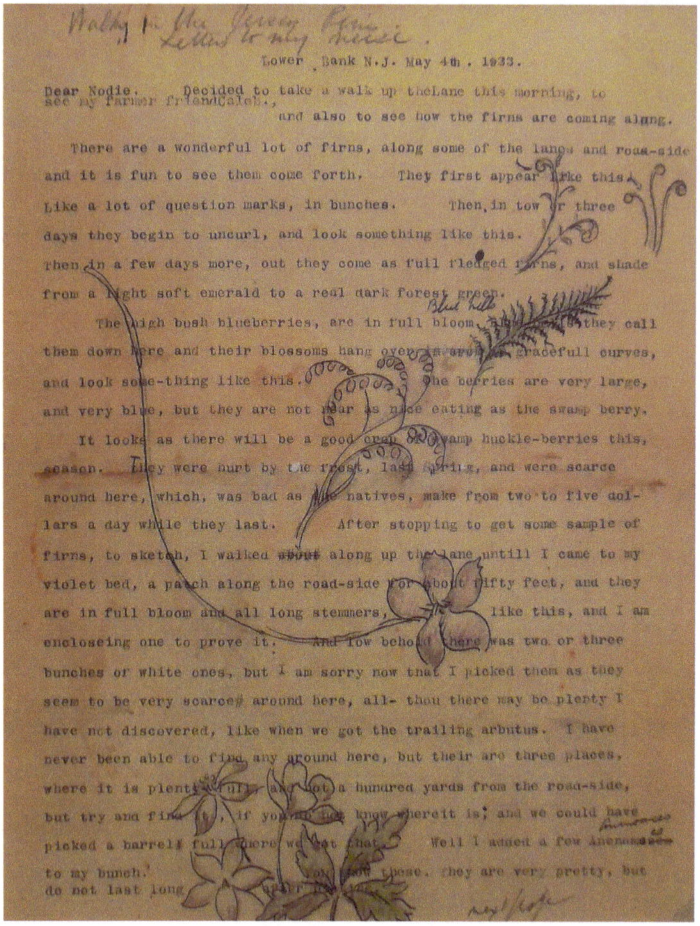

Lower Bank N.J. May 4th. 1933.

Dear Nodie. Decided to take a walk up theLane this morning, to see my farmer friendCaleb., and also to see how the firns are coming along.

There are a wonderful lot of firns, along some of the lanes and road-side and it is fun to see them come forth. They first appear like this. Like a lot of question marks, in bunches. Then, in tow or three days they begin to uncurl, and look something like this. Then in a few days more, out they come as full fledged firns, and shade from a light soft emerald to a real dark forest green.

The high bush blueberries, are in full bloom, [illegible] they call them down here and their blossoms hang over in [illegible] graceful curves, and look some-thing like this. The berries are very large, and very blue, but they are not near as nice eating as the swamp berry.

It looks as there will be a good crop of swamp huckle-berries this, season. They were hurt by the frost, last Spring, and were scarce around here, which, was bad as the natives, make from two to five dollars a day while they last. After stopping to get some sample of firns, to sketch, I walked along up the lane untill I came to my violet bed, a patch along the road-side for about fifty feet, and they are in full bloom and all long stemmers, like this, and I am encloseing one to prove it. And low behold there was two or three bunches of white ones, but I am sorry now that I picked them as they seem to be very scarce around here, all- thou there may be plenty I have not discovered, like when we got the trailing arbutus. I have never been able to find any around here, but their are three places, where it is plentiful, and not a hundred yards from the road-side, but try and find it, if you do not know whereit is; and we could have picked a barrel full there we got that. Well I added a few Anemones to my bunch. You know these. They are very pretty, but do not last long [illegible]

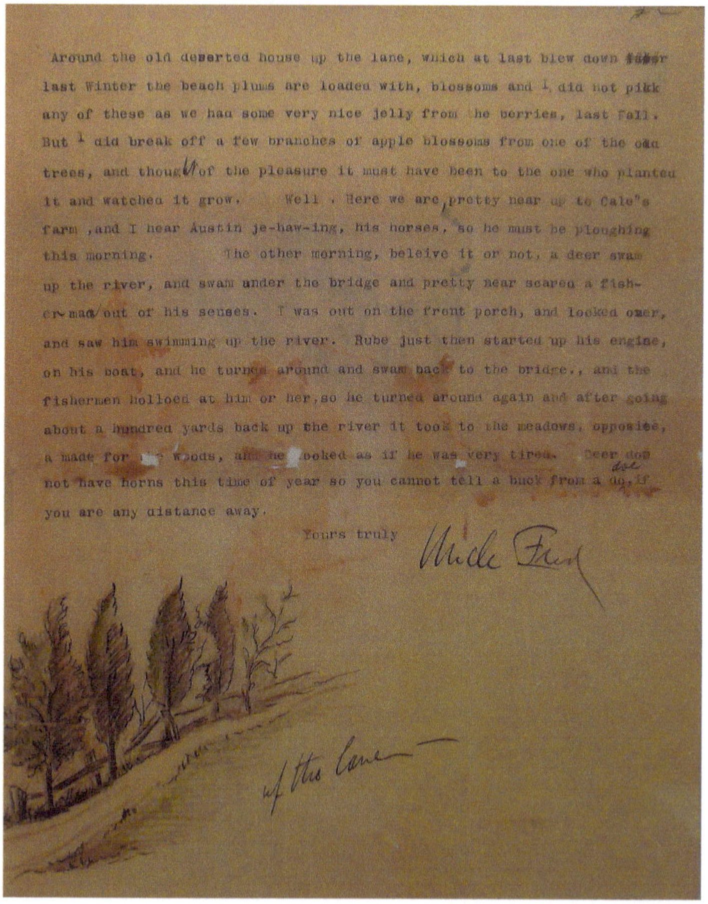

Around the old deserted house up the lane, which at last blew down last Winter the beach plums are loaded with, blossoms and I did not pikk any of these as we had some very nice jelly from the berries, last Fall. But I did break off a few branches of apple blossoms from one of the old trees, and thought of the pleasure it must have been to the one who planted it and watched it grow. Well. Here we are, pretty near up to Cale"s farm, and I hear Austin je-haw-ing, his horses, so he must be ploughing this morning. The other morning, beleive it or not, a deer swam up the river, and swam under the bridge and pretty near scared a fisher-man out of his senses. I was out on the front porch, and looked over, and saw him swimming up the river. Rube just then started up his engine, on his boat, and he turned around and swam back to the bridge., and the fishermen holloed at him or her, so he turned around again and after going about a hundred yards back up the river it took to the meadows, opposite, a made for the woods, and he looked as if he was very tired. Deer do not have horns this time of year so you cannot tell a buck from a doe, if you are any distance away.

Yours truly

Uncle Fred

Letter to Nodi, Fred Noyes Sr., 1933.

Fred Noyes Sr., father of the founder of the Noyes Museum, was a textile designer in Philadelphia in the early 1900s. After the stock market crash of 1929, his health declined and to escape the stress of the city he bought a summer cottage on the Mullica River in the town of Lower Bank, nestled within the Pine Barrens. There, he enjoyed walking through the Pines and noting the flora and fauna that he observed. On many occasions, as in the example here, he wrote letters to his niece, Nodi, describing the surroundings that he so admired. Glicee print, Courtesy of Judy Courter.

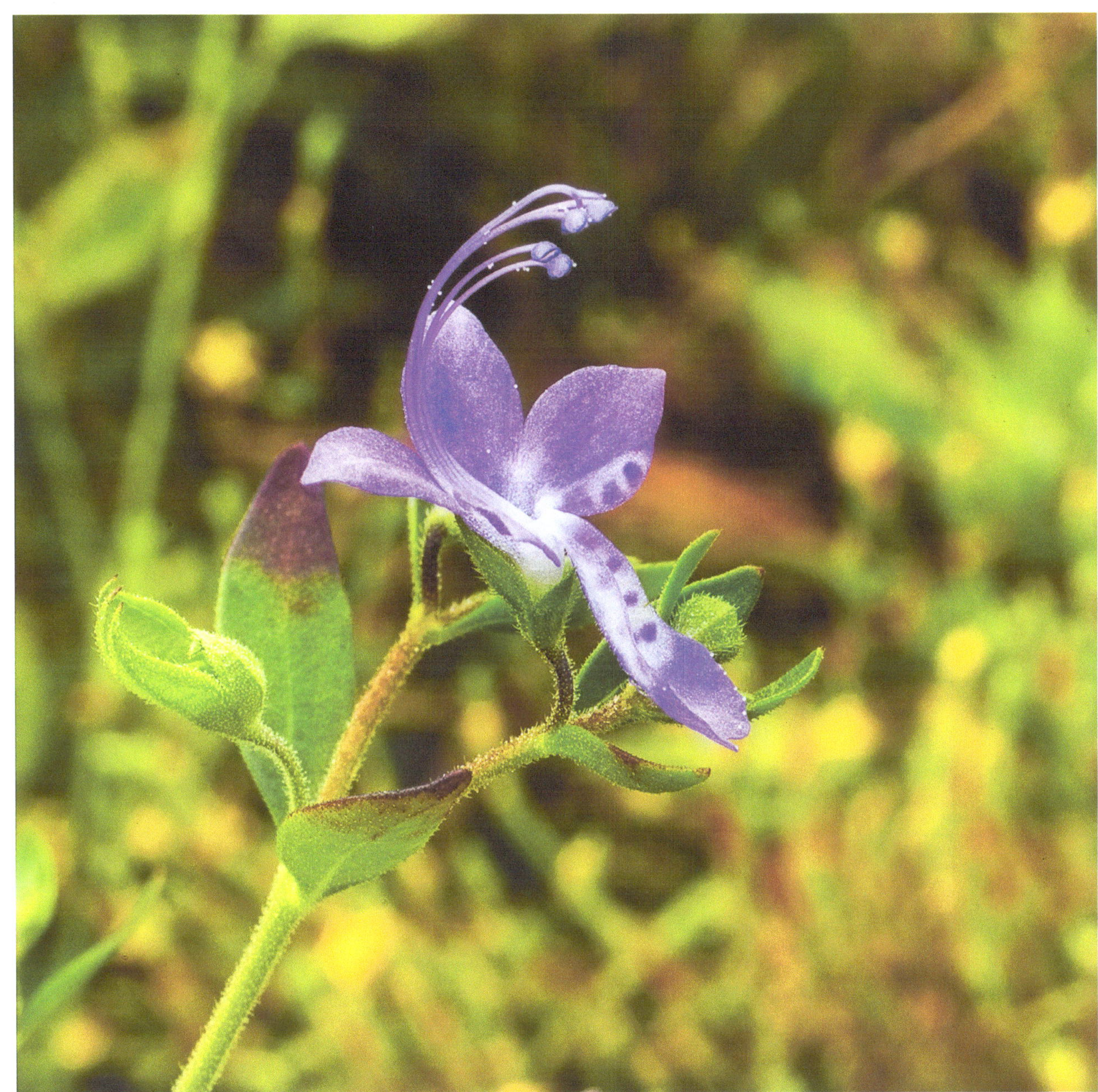

Blue Curl, Albert Horner, 2014.
Trichostema dichotomum

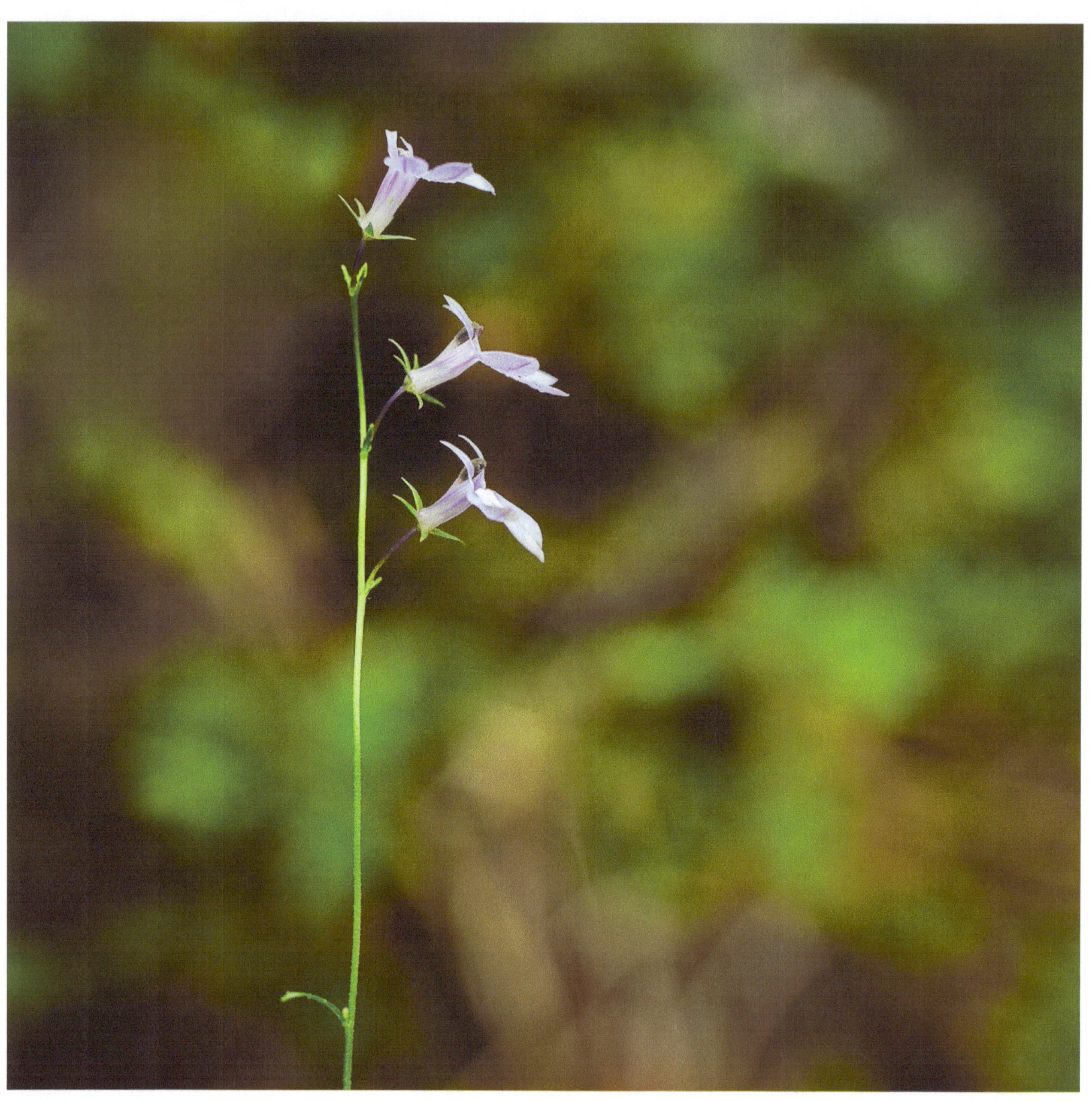

Nuttall's Lobelia, Albert Horner, 2014.
Lobelia nuttallii

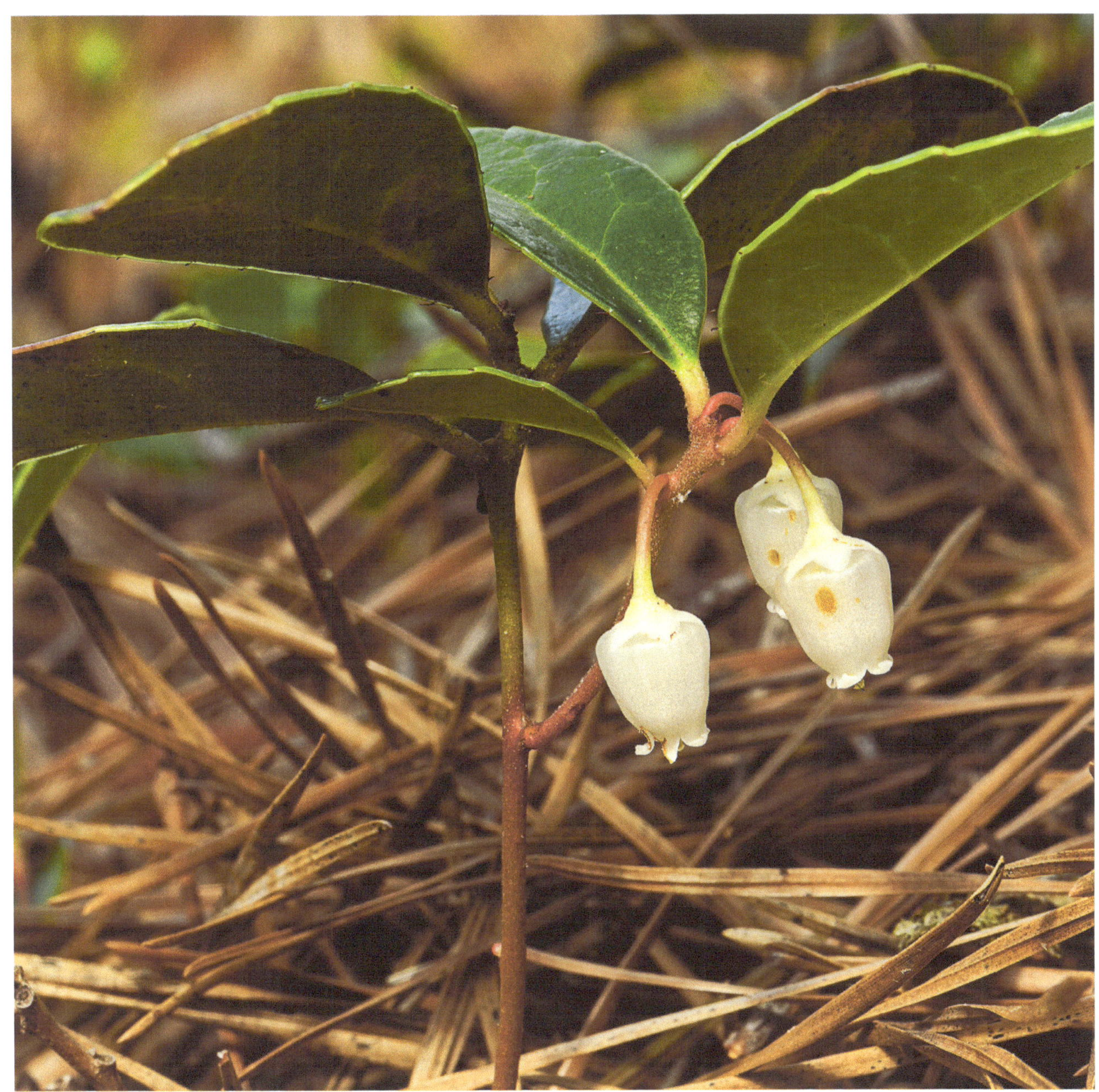

Teaberry, Albert Horner, 2014.
Gaultheria procumbens in early summer

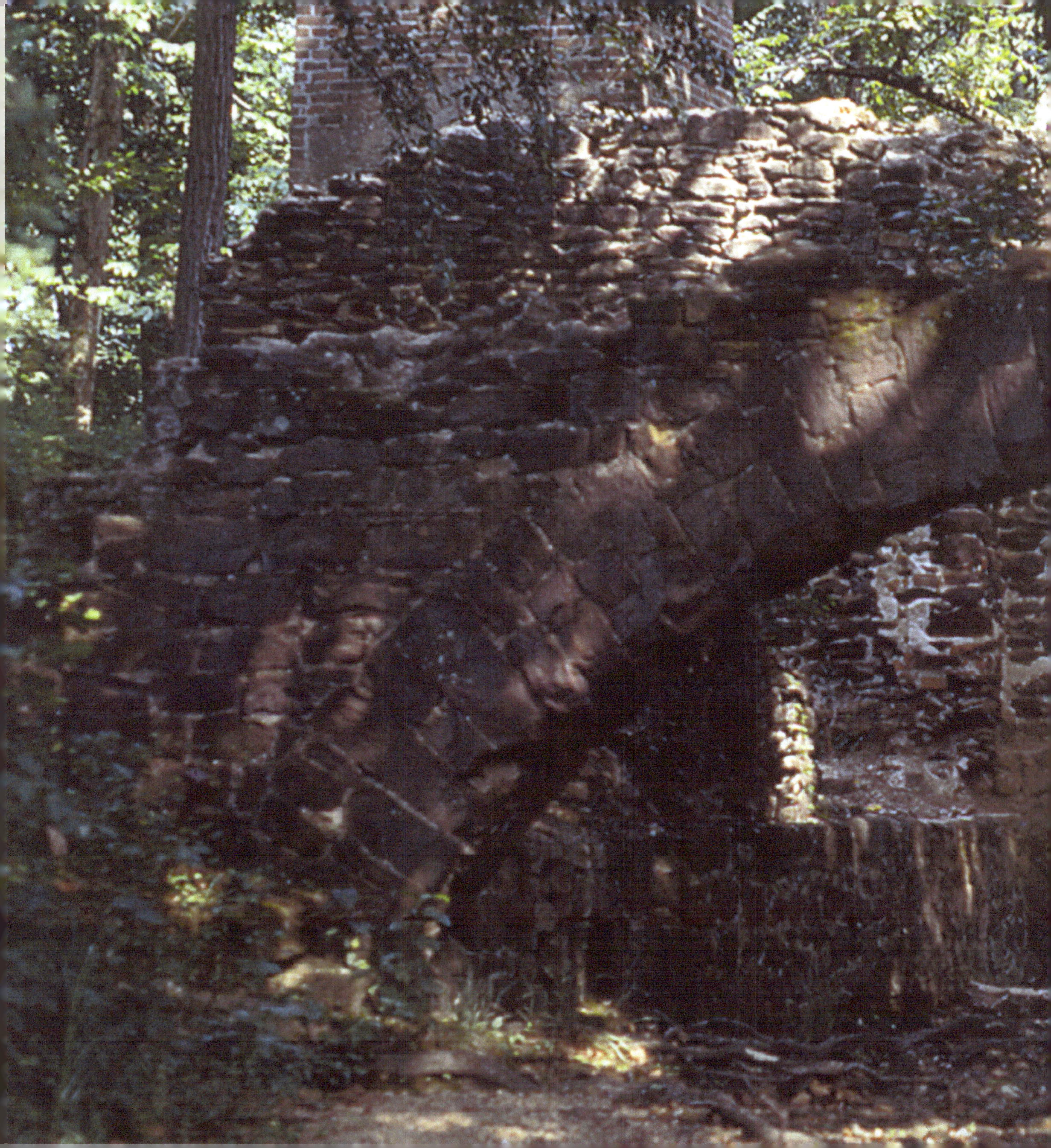

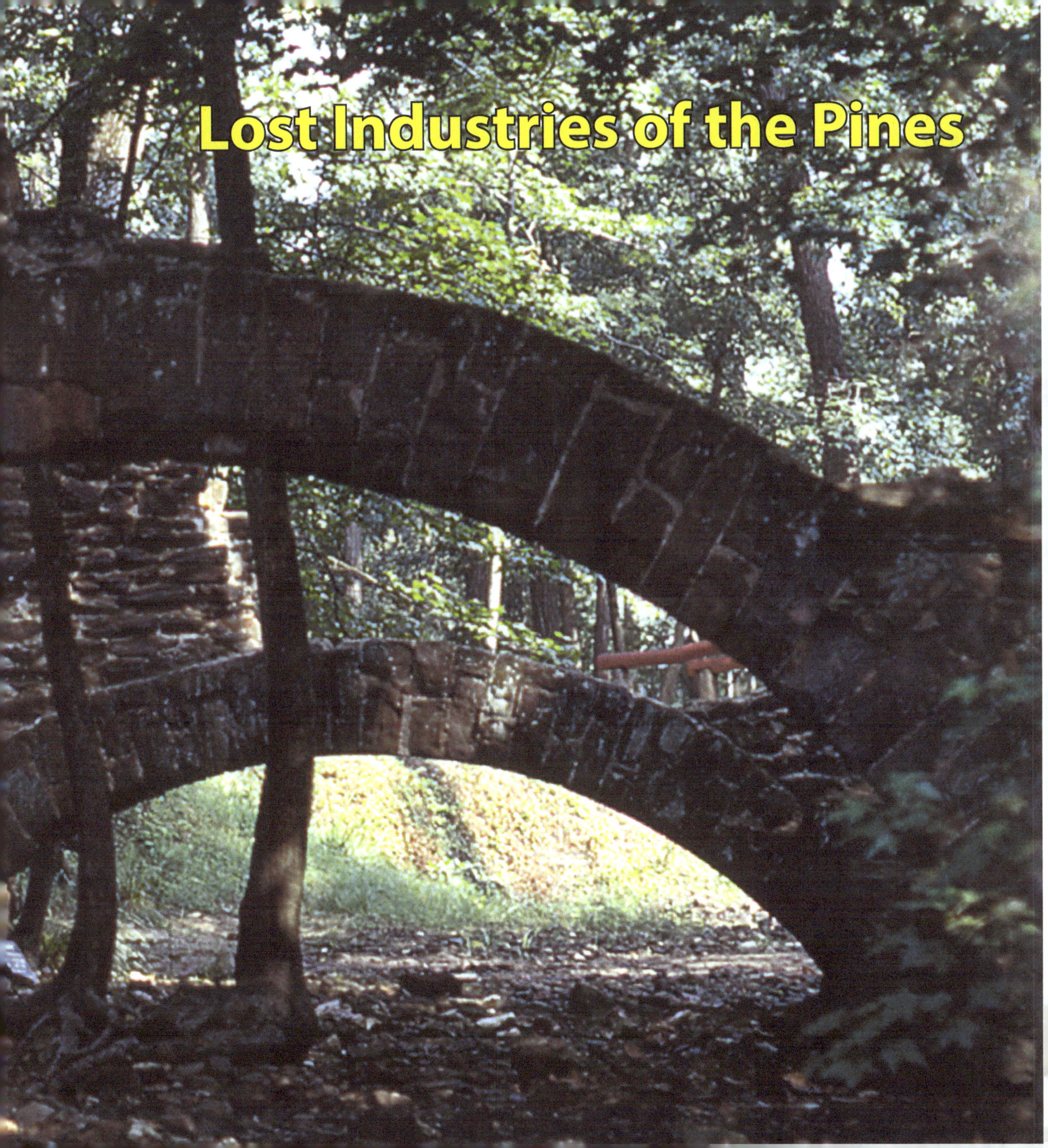
Lost Industries of the Pines

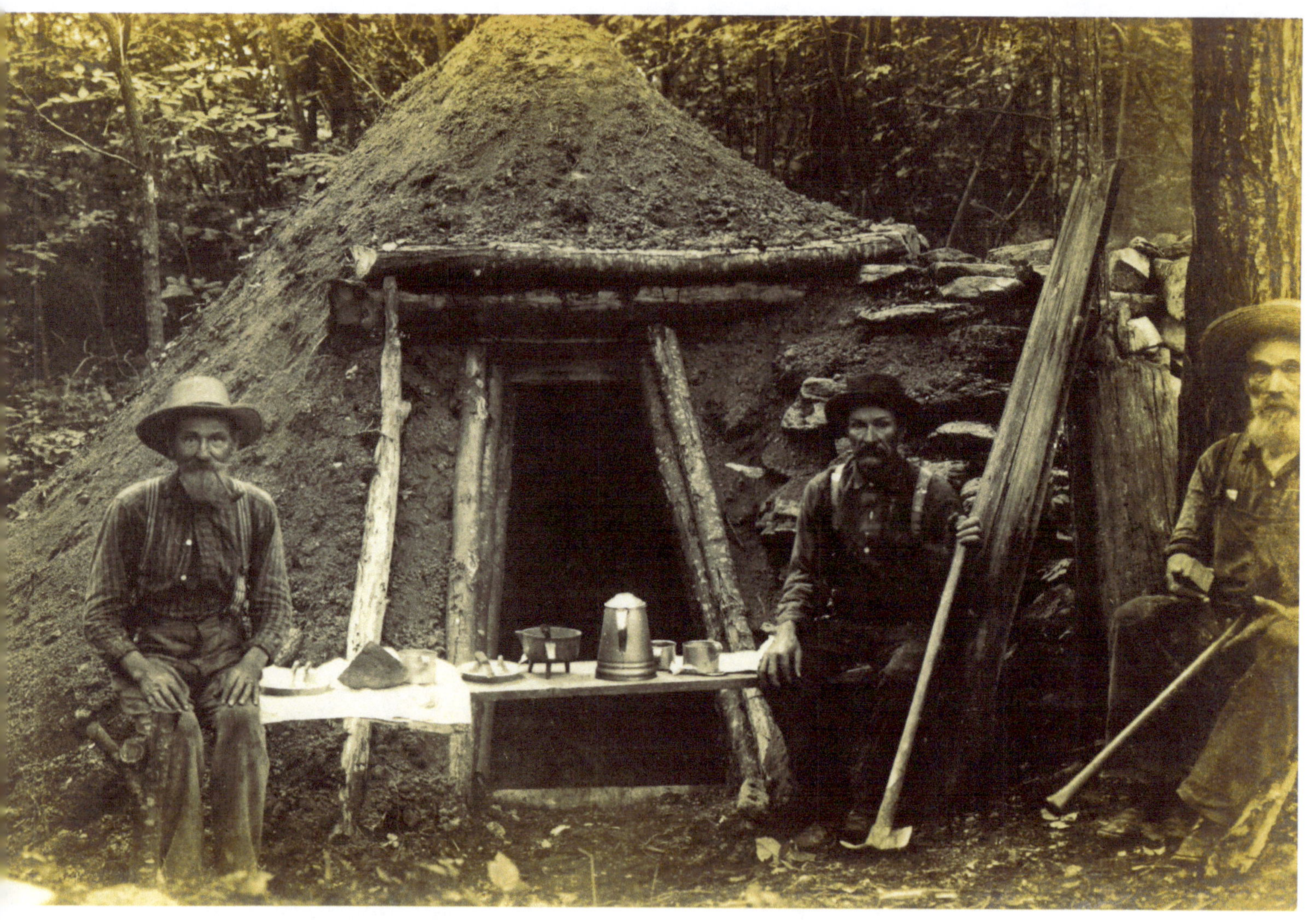

Woodsmen in Pilesgrove, Salem County, 1909.

Sitting in front of their dirt covered cabin, reasonable protection in all but fierce rains, three woodsmen named Horace, Wilbur, and Duke suggest the rigors, but also the civility of life in the woods. Notice the coffee pot with cooking and eating utensils. Duke, to the right, uses a whetstone to sharpen his ax – the day's work is ahead. Courtesy of the Paul W. Schopp Collection.

Ruins of Paper Mill, Weymouth, Atlantic County, 1974.

(Preceding Page) The millrace that once supplied water from the Great Egg Harbor River to power the paper mill at Weymouth. Note the brick chimney in the upper left. The complex still stands. Ted Gordon, photographer, August 1974.

In the Woods

VIRTUALLY ALL of the trees in the Pine Barrens today are no more than 70-100 years old with the exception of some cedars and an occasional large old oak tree. Harvesting forest products and frequent forest fires have repeatedly devastated the Pines.

Beginning in the seventeenth century, European settlers viewed the Barrens with great interest for the potential contained within its trees. Pine yielded distilled naval stores and firewood, while oak was cut for shipbuilding and house framing, and cedar for siding, shingles and boatbuilding. Pine and the oak were also used for charcoal production. Timber pilferage became a problem almost immediately upon the British settling the land, and in 1681 the Burlington Court appointed certain men as "Rangers" to prevent the unauthorized taking of trees. By mid-eighteenth century, it appears large swaths of the original-growth trees in the Pines were already cut, resulting in Lewis Evans describing the area on his 1749 map as "Sandy Barren Desarts."

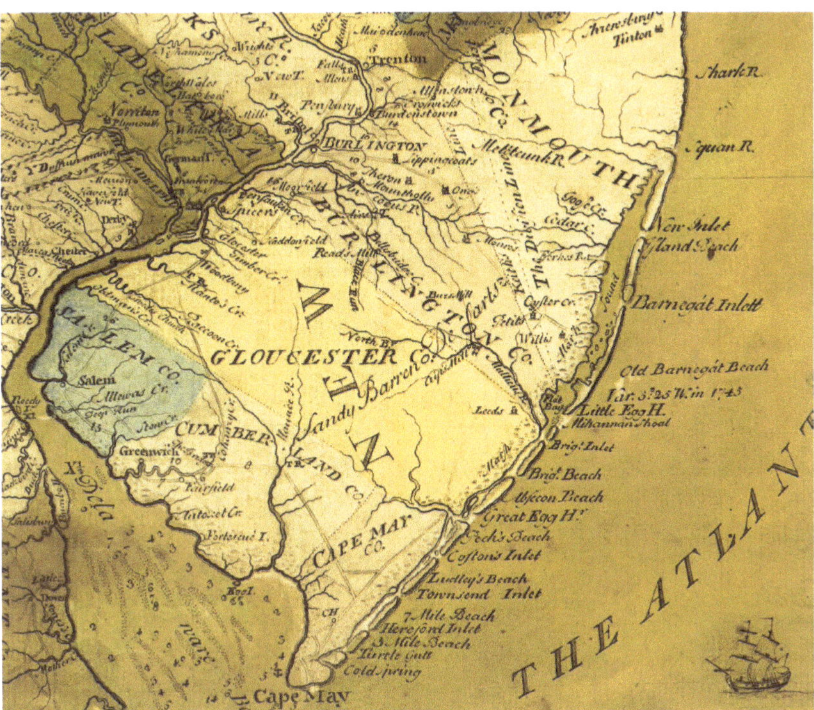

SANDY BARREN DESARTS, 1749.

Lewis Evans, surveyor and cartographer, emigrated from Wales to Colonial North America. He was a friend and associate of Benjamin Franklin, John Bartram, Governor Thomas Pownall, and other Philadelphia notables. This selection from *A map of Pensilvania, New-Jersey, New-York, and the Three Delaware Counties* shows the original counties of South Jersey. From the Geography and Map Division, Library of Congress.

A map of New Jersey dating from 1831 describes this same area as "Extensive Forest of Pine Trees," suggesting the regenerative growth of the Pines.

The demand for wood was relentless. Beginning in the second half of the eighteenth century, each iron furnace alone required 1000 acres of cut trees per year for charcoal production. The men who cut this wood were a hardy breed, arriving on site before dawn and working till dusk. Yet their life in the woods was not without camaraderie.

Cedar Mining

During the early nineteenth century, a specialized industry known as "cedar mining" began in Cape May County and later, and to a lesser extent, in Cumberland and Ocean counties. Using metal probes, miners identified trees at the bottom of cedar swamps. Either strong winds had toppled these trees or they snapped off and fell due to their own weight and size (they commonly reached three feet in diameter but could reach six feet or more). The durability and rot resistance of shingles made from these long-sunken trunks proved unequalled. Below are two nineteenth century sources that describe the process.

George Hamill Cook. *Geology of the County of Cape May, State of New Jersey.* Trenton, N.J.: Office of the True American, 1857.

The *cedar swamps* of the county are so extensive, and the deposits of peaty earth, or muck, which they have formed are so great, as to make an important feature in the geology of the county. The tree of which these swamps are composed, is the white cedar, the *Cupressus Thyoides* of the botanists. It is an evergreen, which thrives best in wet ground, and in favorable situations forms dense swamps. It is most commonly found on the head-waters of streams, and several of those in the county rise in such swamps. West Creek, East Creek, Dennis Creek, Great Cedar Swamp Creek, and many of their small branches, have cedar swamps through their whole lengths. There is no cedar on the streams south of those mentioned, except in a few spots of limited extent, where it has been planted. The area of these swamps has not been estimated, but there must be some thousands of acres. The largest is that which lies in the valleys of Dennis and Great Cedar Swamp creeks, and is continuous from the upper bridge on the former creek, to Dennisville on the latter. The timber which originally covered these swamps has now all been cut off, and there is no first growth to be found. Very few trees are known which are more than 100 years old, and most of the swamps are now cut off when the timber is of about sixty years growth. Formerly, trees of great age were found. Mr. Charles Ludlam counted 700 rings of annual growth in a tree which was alive when cut down. Dr. Beesley

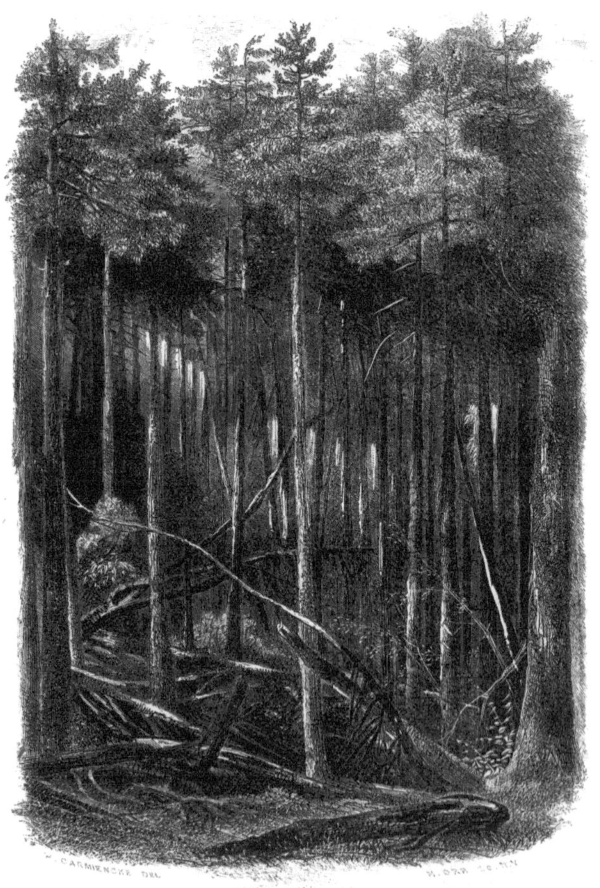

A CEDAR SWAMP, CAPE MAY CO.

counted 1080 in a stump; and Hon. J. Diverty found 1000 in a log dug up out of the swamp earth. The trees stand very thick upon the ground, and the first part of their growth is very rapid, but as they get larger they are more crowded, and their tops remain small. The annual growth is here very little; those of four, five, and six, and even seven feet, were found, but rarely. The accompanying cut was taken from a sketch of the swamp. It gives a correct general impression, though in the thrifty growth of trees these trunks are not half tall enough for their diameters.

The soil in which these trees grow is a black peaty earth, which, when dry, will burn. It is of various depths. Several soundings in the swamp near the Burnt Causeway, showed a depth of from two to eight feet; which was the deepest. Soundings in the Great Cedar Swamp near Long Bridge showed the gravel bottom to be from six to eight feet below the surface. Near Dennisville it has been found thirteen feet deep, with no mixture of mud or any foreign substance. It is very loose and porous, and always full of water. The trees which grow on it have their roots running through it in every direction near the surface, but not penetrating to the solid ground. Their evergreen leaves keep it continually shaded, and cool; and these conditions, with the constant presence of water, retard the decay of the twigs and leaves which fall every year: and thus there is a continual and rapid increase in the amount of this peaty soil, or muck. Mr. Charles Ludlam told me, that he recently found a log in the swamps which, from its cut ends, he was satisfied had lain there ever since the timber was last cut off, which was sixty years ago. It was about a foot in diameter, and the accumulation of matter on the surface since that time was enough to entirely bury it. Timber which is buried in the swamp undergoes scarcely any

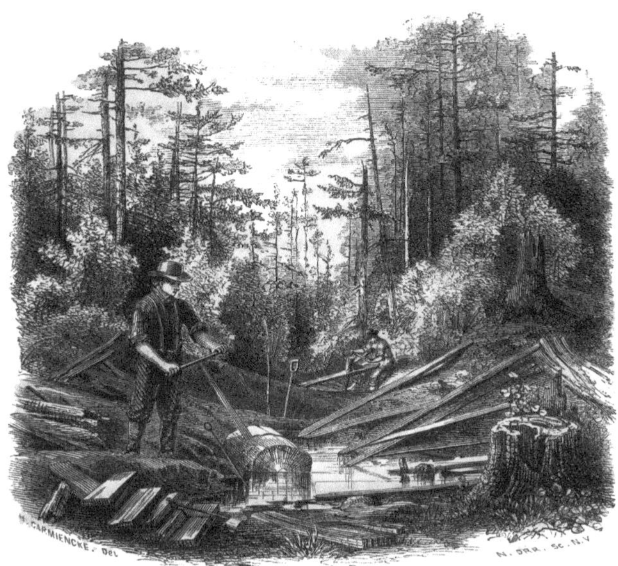

SAWING CEDAR-LOGS, AND MAKING SHINGLES.

change; trees which are found several feet under the surface, and which must have lain there for hundreds of years, are as sound as ever they were; and it would seem as if most of the timber which had grown in these swamps was still preserved in them. Trunks of trees are found buried at all depths beneath the surface, quite down to the gravel; and so thick, that in many places a number of trials will have to be made before a sounding-rod can be thrust down without striking against them. Tree after tree, from two hundred to one thousand years old, may be found lying crossed one under the other in every imaginable direction. Some of them are partly decayed, as if they had died and remained standing for a long time, and then been broken down. Others have been blown down, and their upturned roots are still to be seen. Some which have been blown down, have continued to grow for a long time afterwards, as is known by the heart being very much above the centre, and by the wood on the under side being hard and *boxy*.

These trunks are found lying in every direction, as if they had fallen at different times, as trees would in a forest now. The view of fallen timber which is here presented was sketched in the swamp of Mr. Henry Ludlam, near Dennisville. The living timber was cut off fifty years ago, and the swamp earth being exposed to the sun and air, had decayed from around the timber which was buried, and thus brought some of the uppermost sticks to view. It is not known how many others there may be under these, as there is still six feet of the swamp earth undecayed.

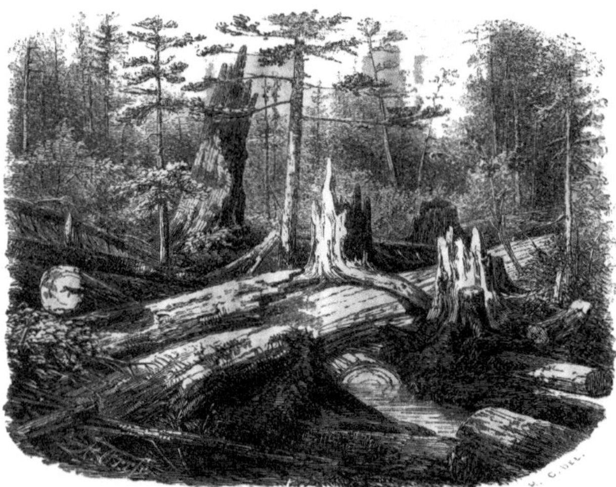

In this view, if we begin at the left hand, we notice the cut end of a small log, which lies across a second; this second has its broken and shivered end resting on a third and much larger log; and this third lies directly across a fourth, which lies with its cut end and partly in the water. By the side of this fourth log an old and decayed stump is shown, from beneath which a fifth log is seen projecting. The stump just mentioned must have grown since the fifth log fell, and yet its roots appear to run under the third log, as if it had grown before the falling of that; while just to the left of this stump, and partly behind the third log, is a second stump, the roots of which grow over the third log, thus showing that it had grown entirely since that has been lying in its present position. Both these stumps are those of trees from two hundred to four hundred years old; and we know not how long since the last one died. By looking at these permanent records of the age of the swamp, we soon come to reckon the time of its accumulation by hundreds, or even thousands of years. And yet this is only the last of a succession of such changes which have left their permanent mark upon this portion of the State; and all of them only carry us back through the last, and what has usually been considered the most insignificant, of all the periods of geological time. (*Pages* 57-65)

NOTICE.

PURSUANT to an order of the Orphans Court of the County of Cape May, made at December term A. D. 1847, the subscriber Administrator of John P. Willets deceased, will sell at public vendue on Saturday the 4th day of March A. D. 1848, the following described property to wit:

N. 1 Is a piece of marsh at the mouth of cedar Swamp Creek in the Upper Township in said County contan ing fourteen and a half acres.

No. 2 Is a right on Pecks Beach containing about forty acres be the same or less.

N. 3. Is a piece of Cedar swamp soil, in the Upper Township containing one fourth of an acre more or less.

No. 4. Is a Barn situated on the subscriber's Farm, in the Upper Township in said County.

Sale to commence at two o'clock P. M. of said day, at the dwelling house of the subscriber, where attendance will be given and conditions made known by

JACOB WILLETS.
Administrator &c.

Jan 20, wts

From the *Trenton State Gazette*, March 13, 1848.

Edward S. Wheeler, *Scheyichbi and the Strand or Early Days Along the Delaware.* Philadelphia, Pa., 1876.

The Recent formation of New Jersey, especially in the southern part of the State, is noted for extensive swamps and marshes. Those of the interior are heavily wooded, but none of them are much above tide level; the more elevated and solid are "timber swamps," and not only furnish good and desirable lumber, but might in many cases be improved by clearing and culture, and this make valuable farms. It seems remarkable more has not been done for the agricultural development of the interior of South Jersey, but the original settlers looked to the sea for their highway, and to a great degree for their harvest too; for which reason they made their homes along the upland of the shore.

Of late, through the enterprise of several parties, notably that of Charles K. Landis, of Vineland, the interior of the State has been better appreciated, and being extensively and judiciously advertised, has attracted many intelligent and industrious settlers, who have successfully planted many fine vineyards, orchards, and farms.

The cedar swamps, which are extensive on the banks of the rivers and around their sources, are overflowed, not stable land like the timber swamps; the White Cedar (the *Cupressus Thyoides* of the botanical nomenclature), which holds exclusive possession of them, flourishes only in submerged or saturated soils. In many places in South Jersey it grows in a peaty stratum, where there is neither clay, gravel, loam or mud, but only a compact mass of fibrous roots, and the débris of its own fallen growth. In such localities, as well as where more substantial components partly form a true soil, the white cedar grows densely, and in its young growth rapidly; afterwards it becomes crowded, and grows tall, but increases more slowly in diameter.

The vegetable remains which fall from the swamp trees into the wet mass are shaded from the sun by the evergreen foliage, and thus kept cool and saved from rapid decomposition. Settling gradually down, they become submerged and then buried, from which time their decay is almost imperceptible. In this way the surface of the swamp is gradually elevated; a layer of more than a foot thick has thus been formed in sixty years.

The original growth of cedars were sometimes seven feet or more in diameter, and immensely high; the average size of the full-grown trees, however, was but about two feet and six inches. There are none of these great trees left, and as the whole area of Cedar Swamp is cut over every second generation, or every sixty years, a living cedar tree a hundred years old is now a rare specimen; still, the natural term of the tree is a lifetime of successive centuries. Various parties have counted the annual rings in the logs and stumps of cedars, and various witnesses affirm the existence of from five hundred to over a thousand of them in a single specimen. Sir Charles Lyell, F.R.S., quoting a newspaper article of Dr. Beesley, of Dennsiville, says (*Second Visit to United States*, vol. I page 34) that "Dr. Beesley, of Dennis Creek counted 1080 rings of annual growth, between the centre and outside of a large stump six feet in diameter;" this grew atop of a *previously fallen tree*, which was half as old; thus fifteen centuries were registered in a couple of logs on the surface of a swamp, which has been sounded in places from eight to ten or even eleven or more feet deep, and is full of *fallen* logs to the very bottom.

The white cedar, though a very tall, slim tree, sends no roots down into the firm soil underneath the swamp, but spreads them laterally in the shallow, soft, black, peaty, wet earth which is its congenial place of growth. The timber standing in a natural ancient cedar swamp is but a fraction of the quantity which has fallen and become subterranean. The living timber thus buried is apparently indestructible, and has been *mined* from its place of deposit buoyant and sound, and used for the best quality of lumber, many hundreds and perhaps thousands of years after it had grown. This mining of timber has been carried on as a regular business in the swamps about Dennisville; between nine and ten thousand dollars' worth of shingles, at fifteen dollars a thousand, have been manufactured in a year from logs thus exhumed. The production of shingles did not consume all the timber taken, as a part of it was large, fine logs, more valuable for boards, into which it was sawn. More than forty thousand dollars' worth of cedar rails and lumber are produced by these cedar swamps every year, and an acre of good swamp, fifty years in growth, is worth from five hundred to a thousand dollars. The cedars are mined not alone in the growing swamps, but in meadows where only stumps and dead roots break the surface, and in places where a smooth turf entirely hides all traces of wood from surface observation, as well in a part of the tide marshes, which were once cedar swamps, but where the growth of timber has been stopped by the encroachments of salt water in consequence of the subsidence of the swamps along the shore. Of course many of the buried trees are unfit for use. Those which grew when the swamp was shallow and the roots of the trees touched the gravel bottom, are so *gnarly* as to be unfit for splitting. Some of the trees fell only from extreme age, deadness, and partial decay: these are worthless; some were prostrated and grew long after they fell: these are hard and boxy on one side, hence undesirable. The trees wanted by the miners are those not of the bottom layer, which were *broken down* by the wind or otherwise, and buried at the perfection of their growth.

The first tool of the miner is an iron sounding-rod; with this he probes the mud of the swamp, finding often that the logs lie so thickly across one another beneath the surface that it is only after repeated efforts that he can pass his rod among them. The miner judges of the value of the log he comes in contact with after examination with his probe, by signs known to an expert only; he feels out the size, shape, and position of it, and judges of the work required to secure it; he cuts down to the log through the peat with a sharp spade, and manages to get a chip from it; by *smelling* of this chip he can tell whether he is dealing with a *windfall* or a *breakdown*, the latter being most likely to be sound lumber. Removing the peat, mud, roots, and rubbish-timber as far as necessary, the miner then saws off the log at the ends, his saw working without injury, the soil being free from grit. The log may be thirty feet long, but is generally shorter. Having sawn the log off, the miner uses levers to loosen it from its place and to throw off superincumbent timber; this being done, the log floats upward with perfect buoyance; the under side being *most* buoyant, the log, as it floats free, always turns over. The logs for shingles are sawn into *bolts* or blocks, and *rived* and shaved into shingles on the ground. The ground is gone over again and again with success by the miners, as the logs, once disturbed, continually work toward the surface.

An inch of vegetable matter is deposited by the fall of foliage, twigs, etc., upon the surface of a cedar swamp in about five years, but as this fresh layer is itself buried, it partly decays and diminishes in bulk progressively very much by compression and other causes, so that no clue can be had from it as to the age of these remarkable swamps. Such a clue is found, however, in the buried cedars, which by annular rings tell, like a calendar, their own individual age, and by their relative positions demonstrate the successive generations of growth which must have taken place, before they could have appeared where they were left centuries since, superimposed and *grown*, one above another, in many layers.

The attempt to estimate the age chronicled by interwoven logs is confusing, but the certainty of thousands of years is evident, and even ten or twelve generations of such trees as Dr. Beesley examined may have grown and died since the oldest swamp began; and yet the age thus recorded is occupied by the most modern layer of a formation which is, in all and at the oldest, but the very latest evolvement of the most extremely short and insignificant of all the geologic periods.

If the record of ten thousand years can be preserved in mud and perishable wood, what is the chronology of the cycle in which obdurate gneiss and granite grows and disintegrates, crumbles and is recomposed of the old material, again and again, until the Azoic rocks develop into mineral wealth and fertile alluvium, tower into forests, bloom into flowers, ripen into golden harvests, nourish the beasts and birds, redden the blood of the animal world, and give strength and vigor to the body of man; the fitting tabernacle of the immortal soul? (*Pages* 111-15)

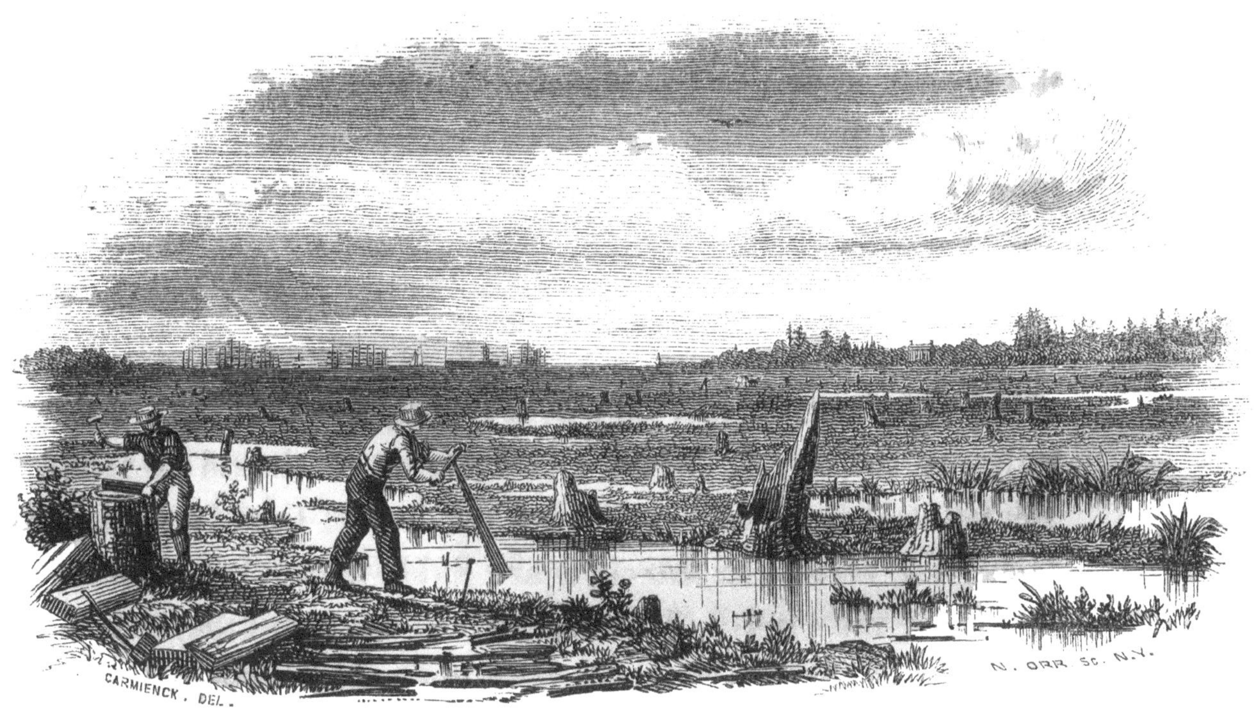

RAISING, OR MINING BURIED CEDAR TIMBER.

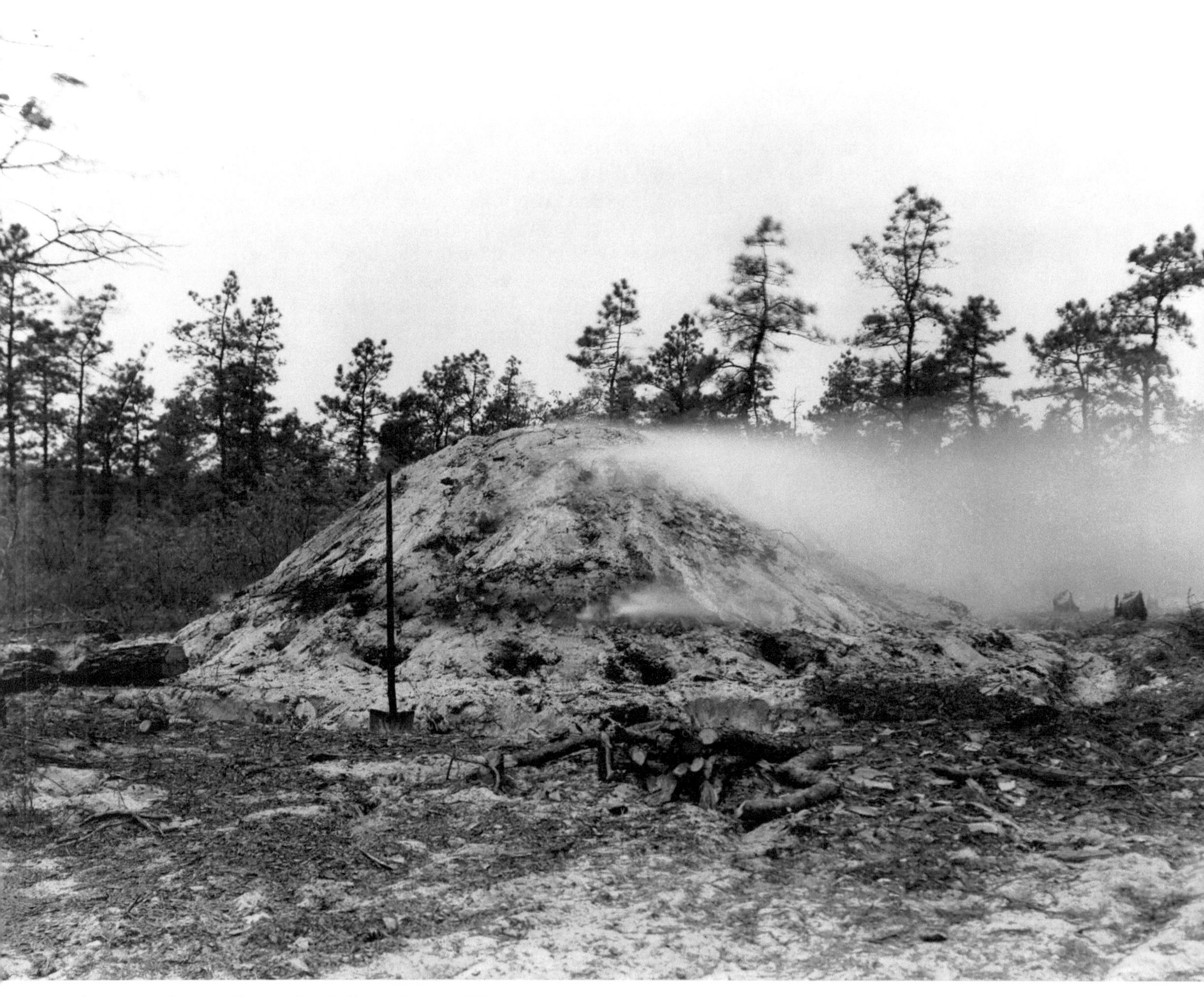

Smoldering Charcoal Pit, Lakehurst, Ocean County, 1936.

Colliers watched lit and smoldering charcoal pits on an hourly basis, 24 hours a day, for ten to fourteen days. Nathaniel R. Ewan, photographer, May 18, 1936; from the Prints and Photographs Division, Library of Congress.

Charcoaling

Charcoal was among the first products to be made in the Pine Barrens. Converting wood to charcoal was a laborious process, often dirty, and involved equal parts of skill and patience. Pine and oak, the primary species in the Pine Barrens forest, provided the necessary wood. Once it was cut to length, carters hauled the wood to a "coaling ground," where the setter stacked it in an intricate, time-tested pattern. It was covered with a layer of turf and then sand. Upon completion of the mound, fire was dropped into the center of the charcoal pit. Over the next ten to fourteen days the collier, a woodsman well learned in this trade, tended the slow, smoldering, oxygen-starved fire. The goal was to roast and burn off most oils and resins from within the wood, leaving behind lightweight chunks of almost pure carbon. This was the fuel for the iron furnaces and glass houses of the Pines, as well as for local blacksmiths and home heating throughout the Philadelphia area.

Often centrally located within the landholdings of an iron furnace, the coaling grounds were repeatedly used to make charcoal. They became well known, e.g. Atsion Coaling, and at night often served as gathering points for the men who worked in the area.

> As a general thing them old coal drawers knowed a good many stories. Nights, after dark, they'd build a fire on the pit hearth. Come out where he was watchin' coal – and the sand was warm. They'd lay down on this warm sand, and stay there maybe till twelve o'clock. And be some storyteller among them, tell these stories, sing songs. Charles H. Grant, 1942. (from Halpert's *Folk Tales*)

Some coaling grounds were less permanent, cut out of the forested area then being harvested for its wood. In these spots, colliers would erect simple shelters or carry in portable "cubbies," which served as shelter as they tended the charcoal pit, perhaps accompanied by a song and a jug of applejack from a nearby tavern.

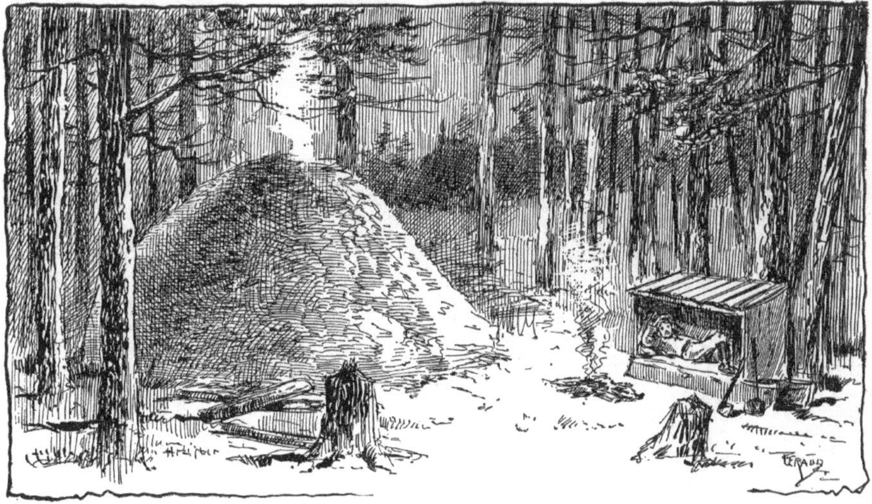

Collier with Cubby, c. 1889.

This illustration from *The New Jersey Coast and Pines* (1889) by Gustav Kobbé depicts a collier bedded down in his cubby close by the charcoal pit he was watching.

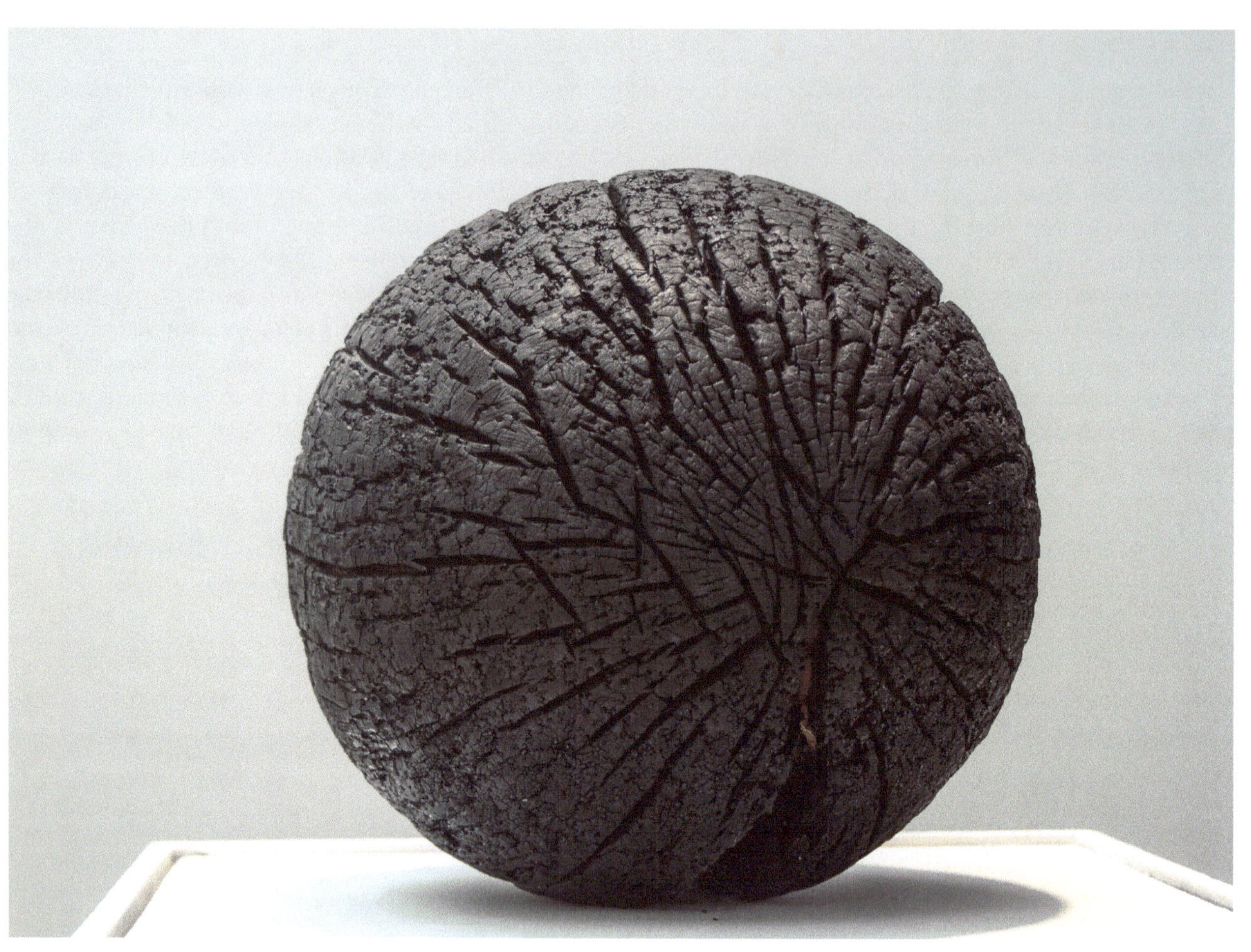

Scorched Earth, Rory Mahon, 1996.
Wood, carbon

Iron Furnaces

A natural resource found within the abundant low-lying bogs of the Pine Barrens spurred development of its first heavy industry. Bog iron is formed through a natural process in which iron-rich springs, acidic surface water, and bacteria form an impure ore, a hardened sludge. With men willing to dig this ore from its wetland beds and convey it to centrally located furnaces, often using ore boats, a key ingredient in iron smelting was readily available and quite literally growing within the Pines.

Smelting and purifying the ore also required fuel and lime. These items, too, were available in abundance. Charcoal fueled the furnaces and oyster shells from the Delaware Bay and coastal estuaries filled the need for lime, which chemically combined with impurities in the ore, allowing them to be removed as dross. While the ingredients for iron were available, gathering them in one place and applying the skill necessary to work a furnace and create quality iron was a laborious, time-consuming process.

Charles Read established the first ironworks in the Pine Barrens, beginning in the 1760s. His notable manufactories include Ætna Furnace (Medford Lakes); Taunton Furnace and Forge (Medford Township); Atsion Forge (Shamong Township); and Batsto Furnace (Washington Township). Speedwell dates to the 1780s as does New Mills Forge and David Wright's Forge. Another wave of ironworks was established in the 1790s, including Martha, Hanover, and Hampton furnaces and the forge known variously as West Creek, Westecunk, or Stafford. As the nineteenth century began, more than a dozen other forges and furnaces opened throughout and adjacent to the Pine Barrens. The last ironworks known to be established in the Pine Barrens was Mary Ann Forge (c. 1835).

By the 1840s, the supply of bog iron was nearly depleted – it simply did not form at a rate equivalent to its use – and the anthracite furnaces in the Lehigh Valley of Pennsylvania had almost completely eclipsed the production of South Jersey furnaces, so the Pine Barrens began to lose its ironworks. The Martha Furnace went cold about 1844 and the Batsto Furnace in 1848; many other furnaces and forges have similar closure dates. Some owners of these industrial sites attempted to reinvent their holdings. Weymouth changed over to paper production while Stephen Colwell repurposed the surrounding timberlands as a real estate venture; Batsto erected a glass house; the area around Martha became cranberry bogs; and the Gloucester Furnace lands spawned the Gloucester Farm and Town Association, which entity laid out Egg Harbor City.

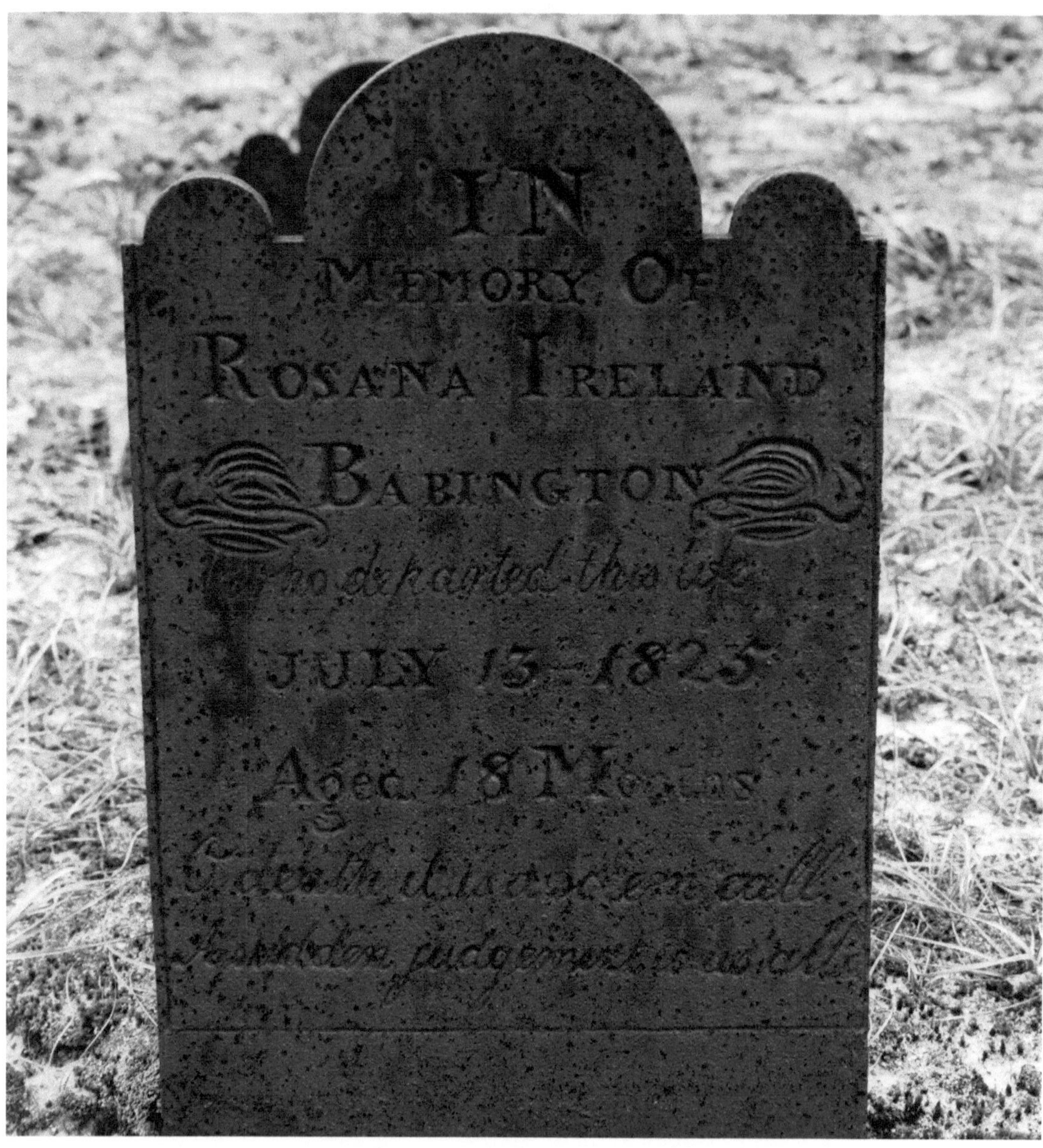

The Grave of Rosanna Ireland Babington, Weymouth Methodist Episcopal Burying Ground, Atlantic County, 1937.

This cast iron gravestone, now in the Batsto Village Museum, marked the grave of Rosanna Ireland Babington, who died aged eighteen months in 1825. The lines at the bottom quote the first two lines of an old hymn: "O death, it is a solemn call / A sudden judgement to us all." Nathaniel R. Ewan, photographer, March 20, 1937; from the Prints and Photographs Division, Library of Congress.

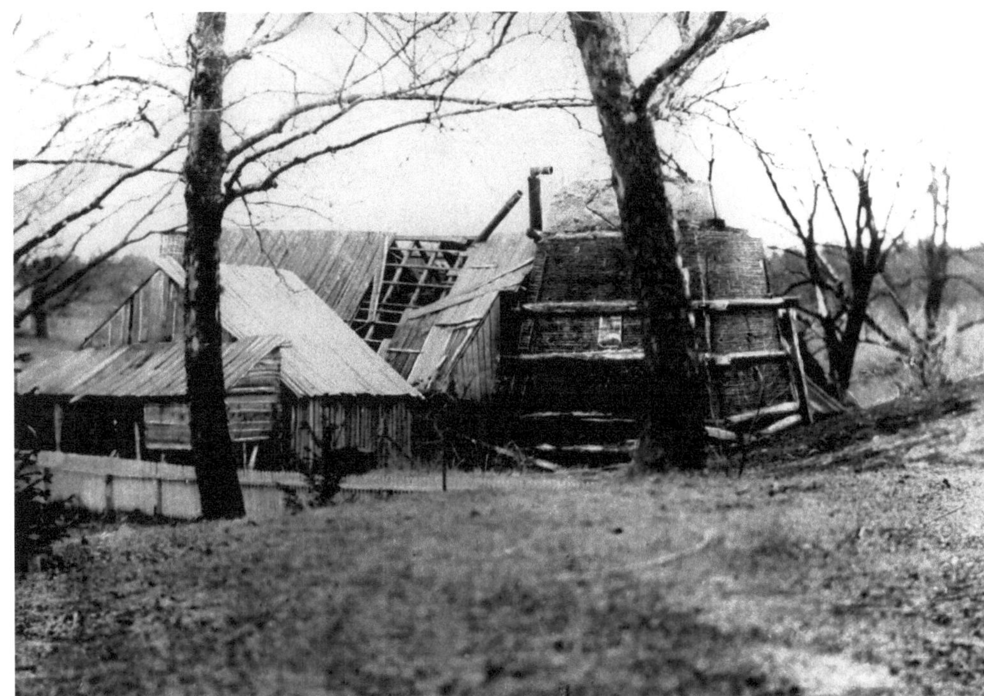

Pine Barrens Furnace Ruins, c. 1860.

Historians Charles S. Boyer and Nathaniel R. Ewan identified the ironworks in this photograph as Hanover Furnace, but, more recently, John E. Pearce opined that it is Speedwell Furnace. Regardless of the location, this is the earliest surviving image of a Pine Barrens' iron furnace. It reportedly dates to about 1860 and the original photograph was reputedly a Daguerreotype. The waterwheel and bellows are on the far left; the brick cupola or blast furnace is on the right; and the shed covering the casting floor is between the other two structures. Courtesy of the Paul W. Schopp Collection.

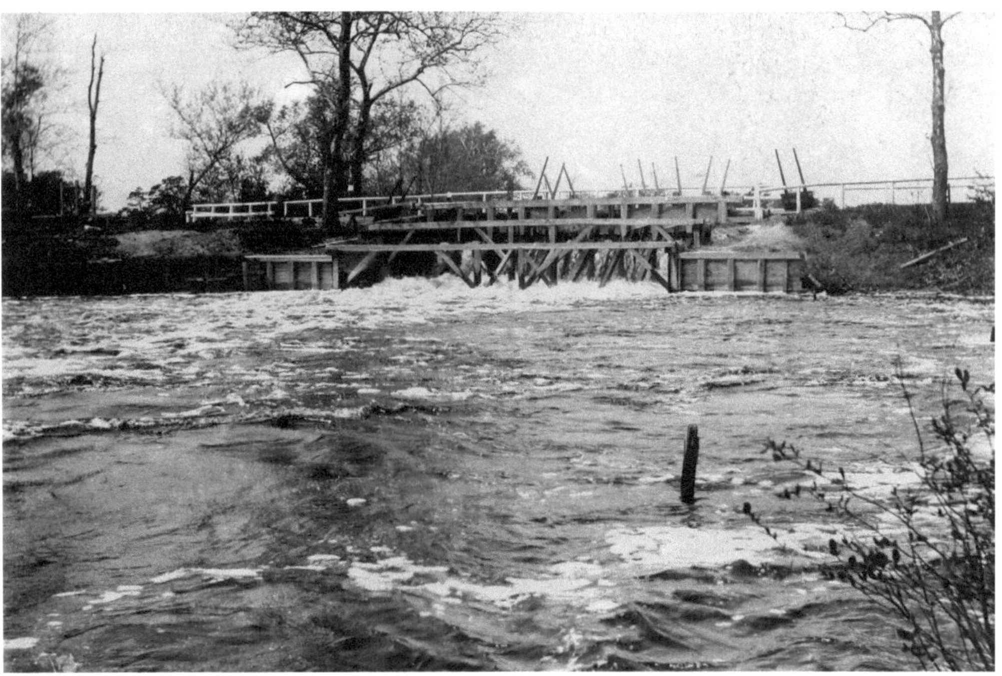

Batsto Dam, Batsto Village, Burlington County, c. 1906.

The control gates are all raised with four gates completely removed from their slides, suggesting an excess volume of water needed to be drained from Batsto Lake to prevent breaching. The water level in the lake was a direct determinant on the amount of horsepower generated for operating the bellows in the furnace and power for the grist and saw mills. Courtesy of the Paul W. Schopp Collection.

Life at Martha Furnace

MARTHA FURNACE, located on the Oswego branch of the Wading River, was a flourishing complex in 1834 that made about 750 tons of iron castings annually. It employed approximately sixty hands, who with their families, made "a population of near 400 souls." There was a gristmill and sawmill on site, along with a schoolhouse and 40 to 50 other outbuildings and dwellings. Apple and peach orchards provided fruit in season and presumably were key ingredients for the liquor served in off-site, but nearby, taverns (there were at least four within walking distance). The landholdings of the furnace totaled about 30,000 acres. It was a thriving industrial base in the heart of the Pines.

To the untrained eye, nothing can be seen of Martha today. The Pines have reclaimed virtually all of it. Budd Wilson completed an archaeological dig of Martha in 1968. His work, along with surviving documents, provides a good understanding of the physical appearance of the site. Luckily, a business diary kept by an unnamed employee between 1808 and 1815 provides insight into life at the furnace. A small number of diary entries are excerpted here.

From the Martha Furnace Diary

April 30, 1808. At 11 O'clock A.M. put the Furnace in Blast. Asa Lanning filled 1 turn. J. Hedger Banksman. John Cunning doing Gutterman's Duty.

November 1, 1808. Election at Bodines [Tavern]. John King sick. Keeping abed.

March 14, 1809. Philip Shaffer did nothing till after 9 o'clock but make a fire & talk over it. Jack Johnson worked at the House in afternoon. Teams arrived with corn.

May 9, 1809. Teams carting pigs to the Landing. Brought flour and pork back. Old Grey died. Teams hauled 32 Barrels Pork and 16 Barels Flour.

October 22, 1809. Good weather, moderately cool. All the men gone a deer hunting. S. Reeves drunk and wife dare not come to milk.

April 28, 1810. William King broke his arm. J. Moore Jr. went for Dr. Sawyer to set it. Jno. Luker carting logs. The rest of the Teams carting ore from down the River. Snowed this evening. Lannings children expelled from school for fighting.

October 4, 1810. Isabella Stuart made a general Muster. James Hughs after the midwife. Joseph Johnston working at James Nash chimney. J. McEntire at work.

January 16, 1811. Furnace went out of Blast. Rain part of Day. All in very high glee.

August 25, 1811. Peter Cox & John Craig had a clinch. Peter proving to be the strong[er] tore Craig's shirt. Craig swares he will have reparation.

December 10, 1811. Nicholas Venzant brot a boat load of shells. Eden Reed carted 1 Ld up.

December 30, 1811. Wood Choppers made a beginning this day. Craig returned after enjoying the pleasure of Matrimony and went to chopping.

February 18, 1812. Teams carting ore from Sassafras. Jane Hamilton conceived and brot forth a son. Mrs. Core put to bed. Women are all very fruitful, multiply & replenish.

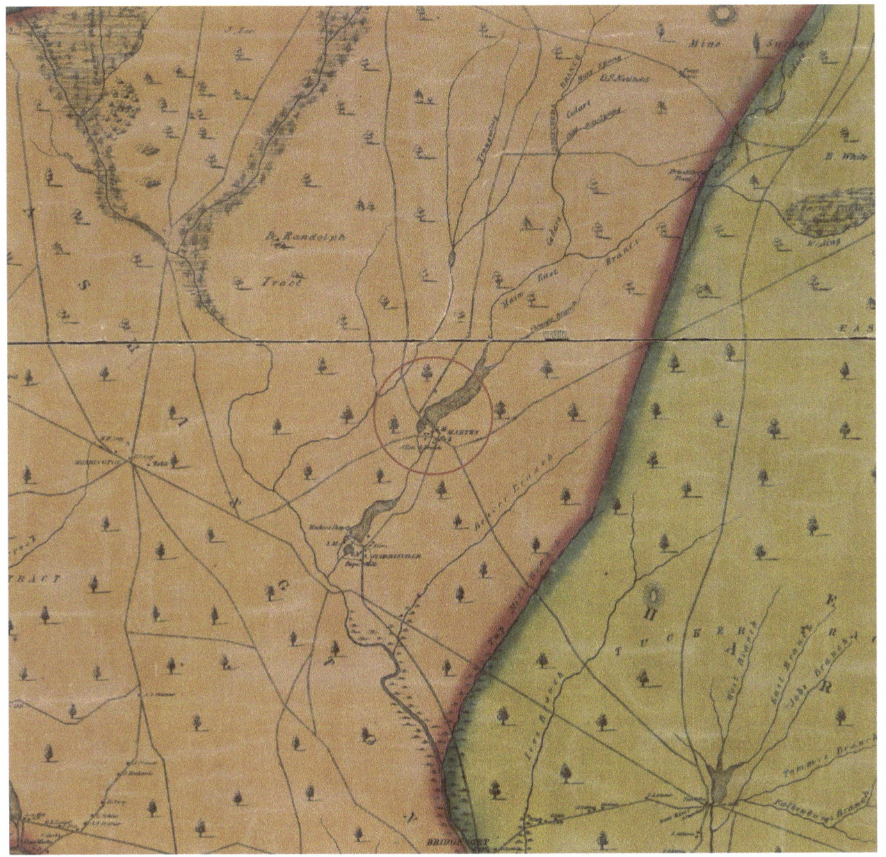

Area around Martha Furnace, on the Oswego branch of the Wading River, Washington Township, Burlington County, 1859.

Martha was about a mile and a half above Harrisville on the Oswego Branch of the Wading River. The Washington Hotel was less than a four-mile walk to the west and Bass River was five miles to the east. Selection from *New Map of Burlington County*, Wm. Parry, Geo. Sykes & F. W. Earl, 1859.

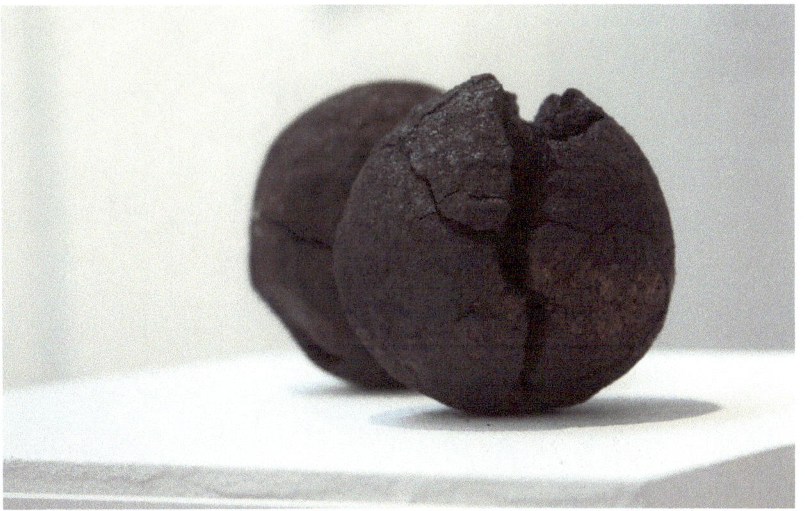

Cast-Iron Cannonballs

The iron furnaces in the Pine Barrens cast numerous iron products, ranging from stove plates to iron pots and pans. During the American War for Independence, Mount Holly, Taunton, and Batsto produced cannon balls of several sizes, along with other projectiles, for the American cause. The munitions production at Batsto excited the attention of the British Army and the Crown's forces made at least one attempt to attack Batsto and destroy the furnace and village. During the War of 1812, the Weymouth and Hanover ironworks also cast cannonballs and other munitions. These small cannonballs (4-pounders) were found in the Pines, although it is unclear which furnace manufactured them. Courtesy of John Mattel.

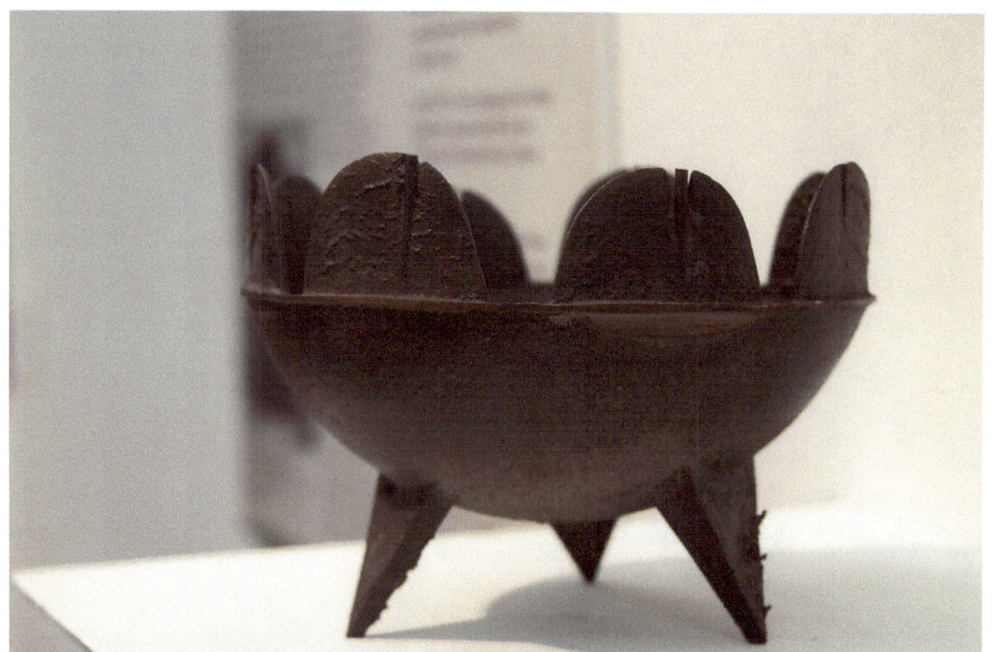

Ancient Vessel, Rory Mahon, 1980

Cast Iron

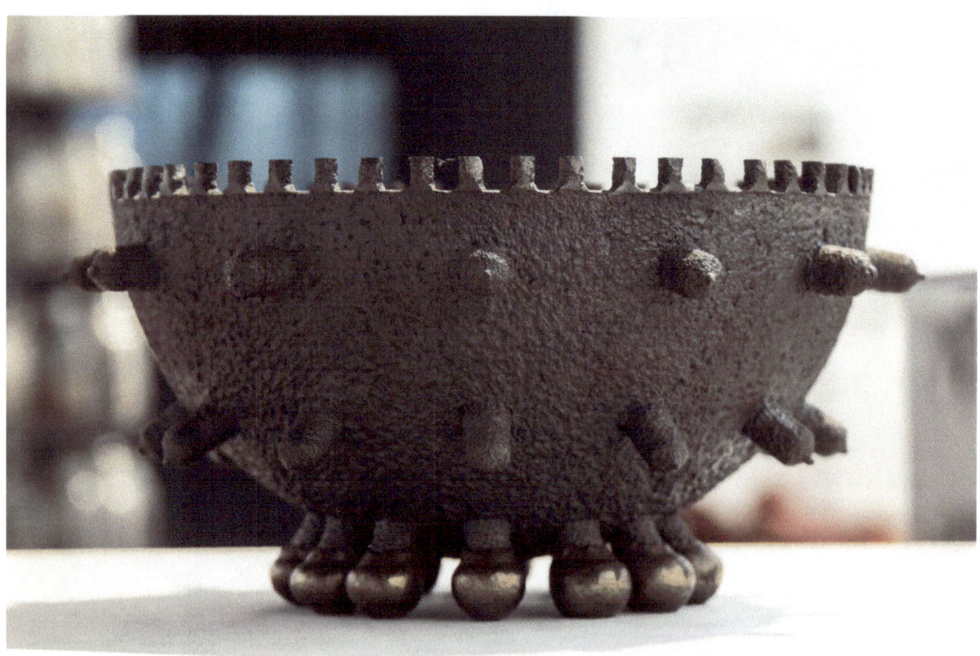

Iron Vessel with Bronze Feet, Rory Mahon, 1998

Cast iron, bronze

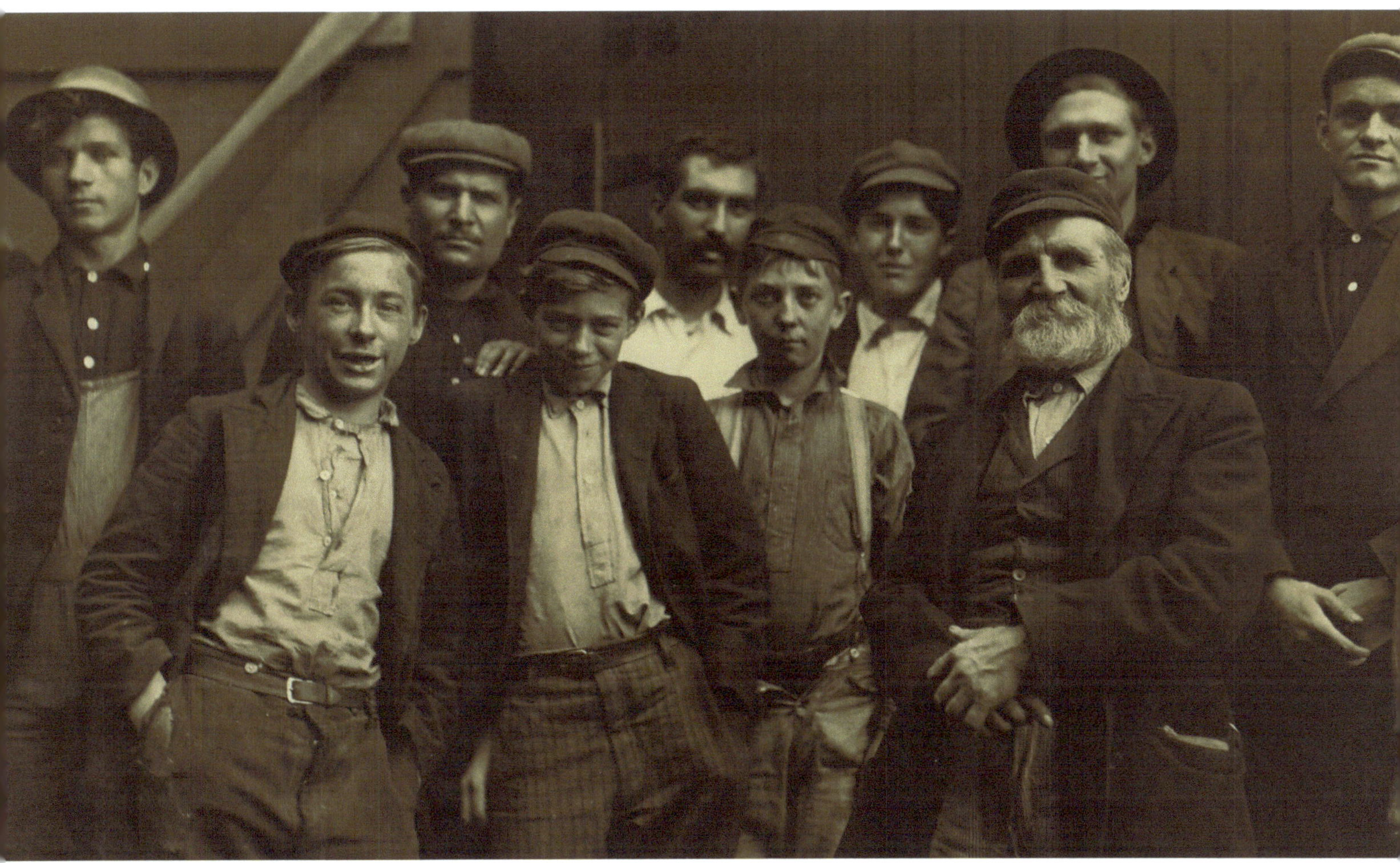

Glass in the Pines

DURING MOST of the nineteenth century, glass furnaces were a major source of income and employment within the Pines. The Clementon or Gloucester Glassworks was one of the first glass furnaces in the Pine Barrens, operating perhaps as early as 1804 and certainly by 1812. It was the fourth to begin operations in the state. Over the next century, other glass furnaces that opened in the Pines read like a who's who of ghost towns and small rural settlements: Lebanon, Jackson, Atco, Crowleytown, Bulltown, Hermann City, Nesco, Janvier, Minotola, Batsto, Winslow, Waterford, New Brooklyn, Estellville, Marshallville, Dennisville, Port Elizabeth, Fairton, Malaga, Medford, Tansboro, Greenbank, Clayton, and Kresson (Milford).

GLASS CARRYING-IN-BOYS, Cumberland Glass Works, Bridgeton, Cumberland County, 1909.

Glass factories hired large numbers of boys who worked long hours in cramped conditions. The job of the carrying-in boy was to take a finished piece of glass from the finisher, whether window, rolled glass or bottle, and carry it to the annealing oven for the final firing. Lewis Wickes Hine, photographer, November 1909; from the Prints and Photographs Division, Library of Congress.

Glass furnaces made a wide range of items: windows, hollow ware, glass buttons, milk bowls, bottles, flasks, and jars. To an extent, they also functioned as social centers. At the Atco Glass Manufacturing Company, Wednesday nights were known as "Girls' Night" because the second shift workers blew whimsies and novelties during their free time – also known as Tempo work – dear to the hearts of their girlfriends. At the Clementon Glass Works, popular entertainment included dances and sleigh parties that arrived to watch the glassmakers at work in the years after the War of 1812.

Among the last holdouts of the rural glasshouses was the Star Glass Works, which lasted until the early 1920s. Its heritage in Medford Village extended back some 90 years prior. As glass production faded from these remote locations, it became concentrated in more urban centers like Hammonton, Vineland, Millville, Salem, Bridgeton, Glassboro, Woodbury, Camden, and Egg Harbor City, ushering in an era of technological modernization. The glassworks were attracted to these cities in large measure due to the rail service available, the larger workforce, and/or the best deposits of glass sand.

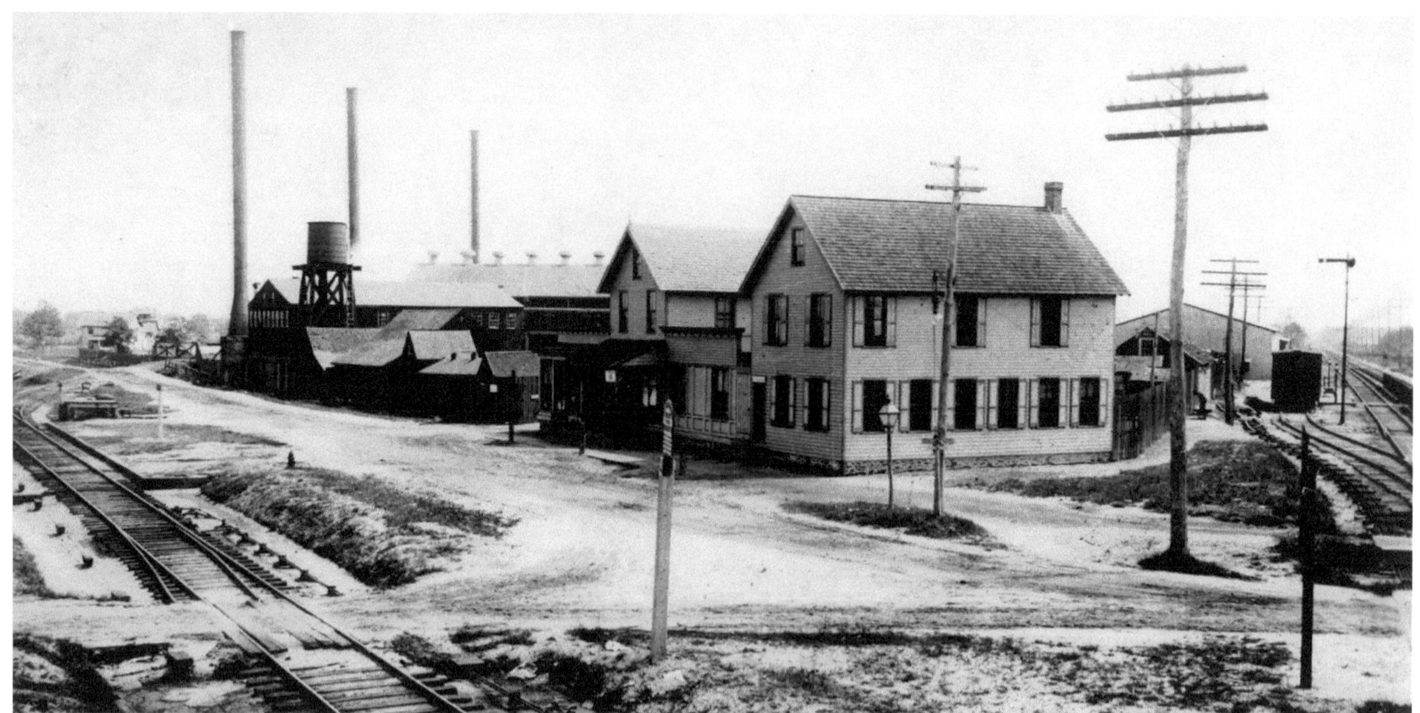

George Jonas Glassworks, Minotola, Atlantic County, c. 1908.

George Jonas began purchasing rural land in an unsettled section of the Pines. This area would become Minotola. By the mid-1890s, Jonas had established his glassworks for bottle production in town, but it was the site of labor strife almost from opening day. Fire struck the plant twice, with the second conflagration completely consuming the works. Within a 10-12-year period, Jonas had had enough with labor trouble and sold the works to another firm before Owens-Illinois acquired it. The last owner phased out the works in 1921. Courtesy of the Paul W. Schopp Collection.

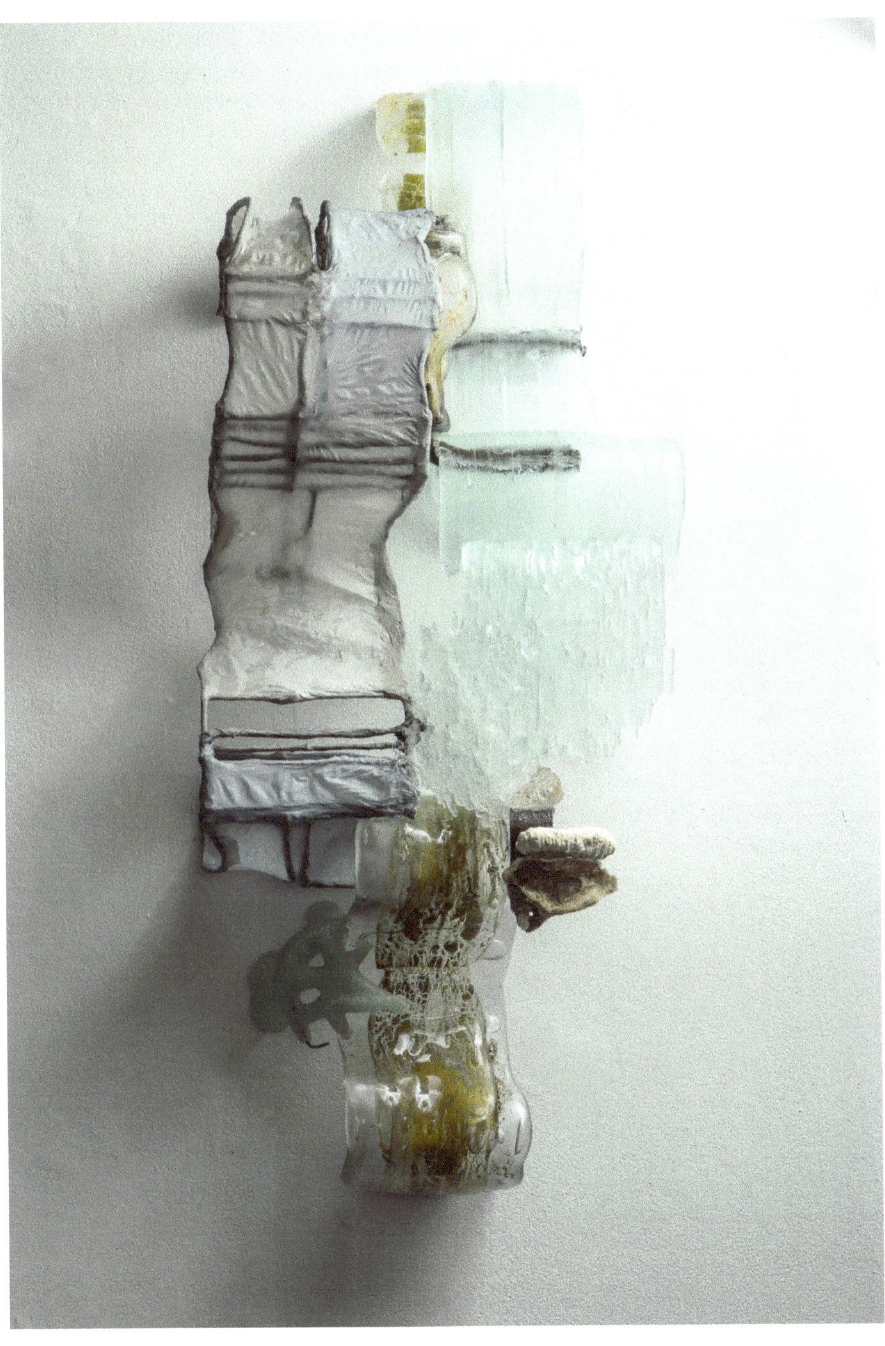

Like a River, Like a Road, Nancy Cohen, 2013.

Metal, glass, shell, handmade paper

Nancy Cohen's work resulted from months of intense study and observation of the biotic community (and its abiotic environment) that forms part of the complex ecosystem of the Mullica River and the Great Bay Estuary of New Jersey's Pine Barrens.

Through readings about the early history of the coastal wetlands she learned that from Colonial times through the late 1800s there was a paper-making industry in the Pine Barrens where local coastal grasses (specifically salt hay) were harvested and used. The glass industry made use of the local sands.

"In coming to know the Pine Barrens, I have begun to feel the ecosystem as a fragile presence in itself. As in our own lives, elements hang in the balance, each one is necessary, vulnerable, beautiful, and above all, interdependent. The waterways are in slow and constant evolution, much as we are."

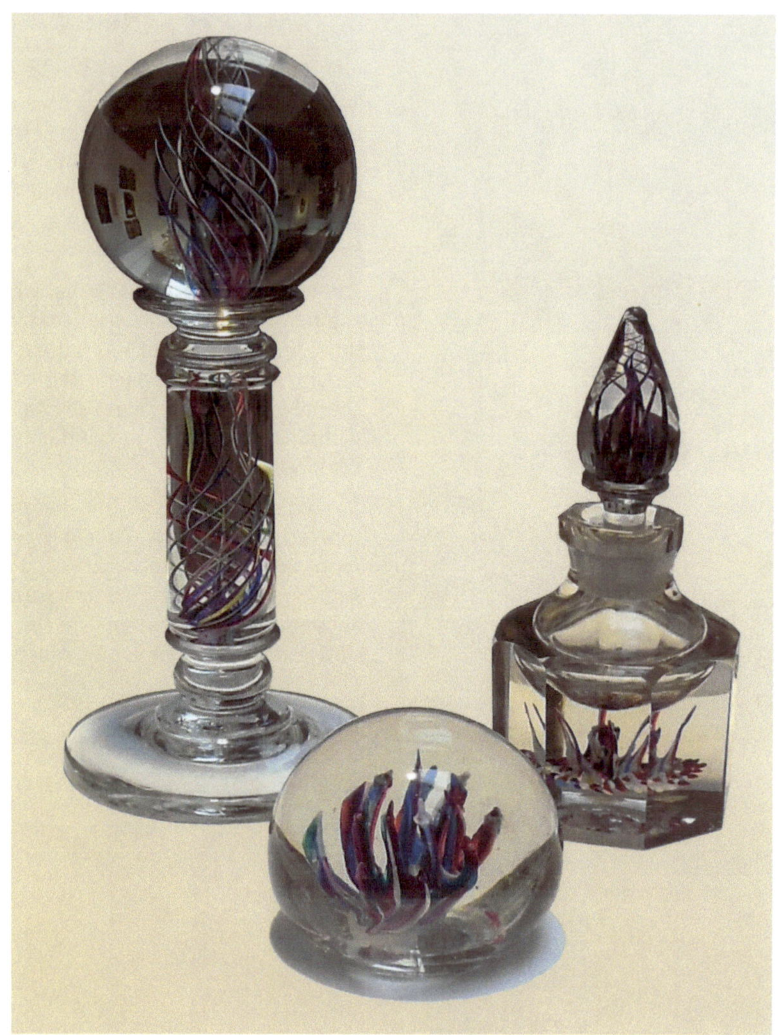

Devil's Fire

Old timers describe seeing "Devil's Fire" frequently in the Pines. Green lights, and sometimes white, seem to dance and move through the woods, leading those who follow to hidden treasure, or danger, or (most often) to a darker section of woods. This phenomenon, also called foxfire, will-o-the-wisp, or jack-o'-lantern, is a natural phenomenon, the result of swamp wood decaying and giving off an eerie glow produced by the fungi in the wood – bioluminescence.

Glass workers in South Jersey have been capturing this phenomena in glass since the 1860s when the first "Devil's Fire" paperweights were made at Whitall Tatum Glass Works in Millville. Glass blowers usually created the paperweights by introducing various colors within clear molten glass and then spiking the colors within with an ice pick. Courtesy of Museum of American Glass.

Preserve (jars), Diane Savona, 2015.

Mason jars and found objects.

The purpose of these jars was to preserve food. Here, they preserve history: not the actual artifacts, but the legends, the stories, and tangible interpretations of our story in the Pinelands.

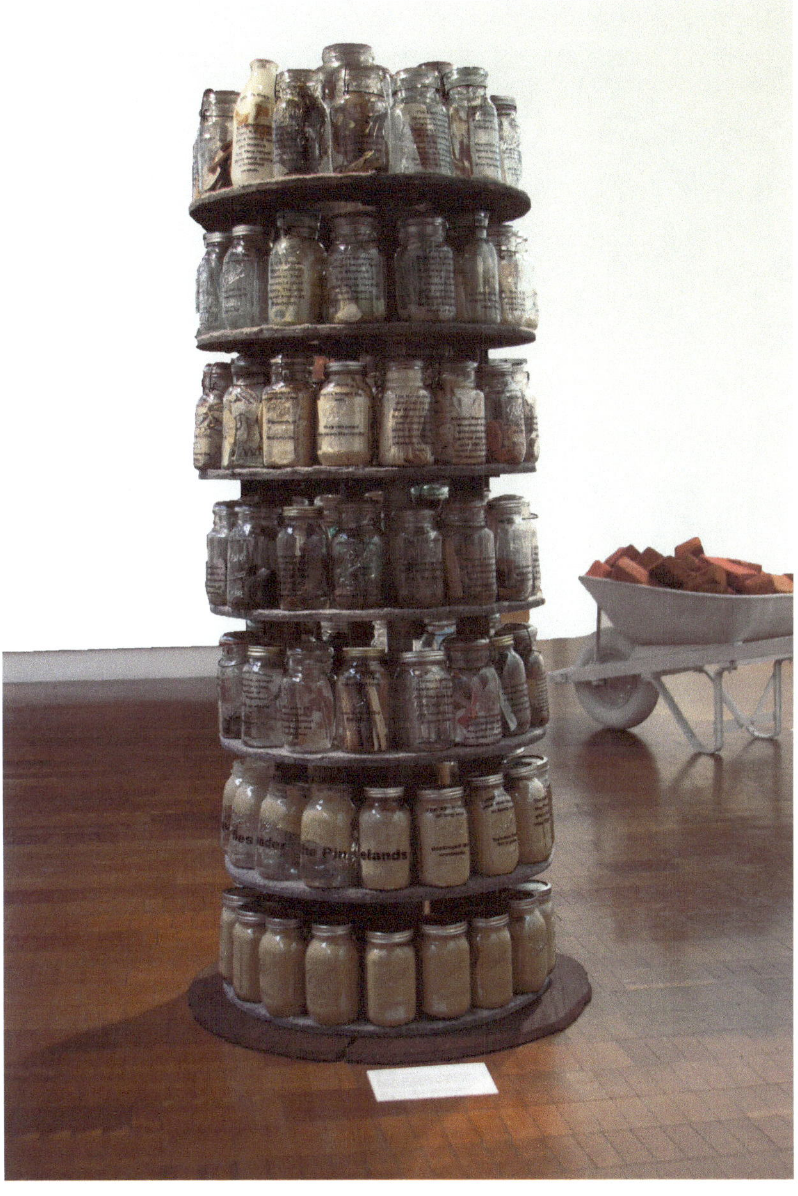

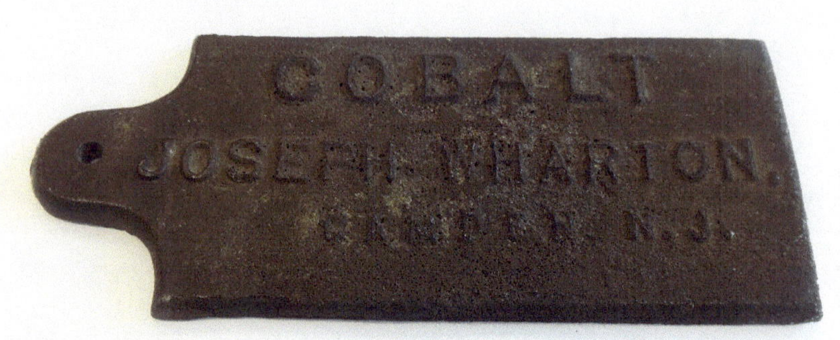

Cobalt Ingot, c. 1880.

Among Joseph Wharton's industrial enterprises, he owned the Wharton Nickel Refinery in Camden, New Jersey, located along the Cooper River. Nickel smelting included the production of cobalt as a byproduct. Glassmakers would throw ingots like this one into a molten batch to manufacture blue glass, often referred to as "cobalt blue" (below left). Courtesy of the Paul W. Schopp Collection.

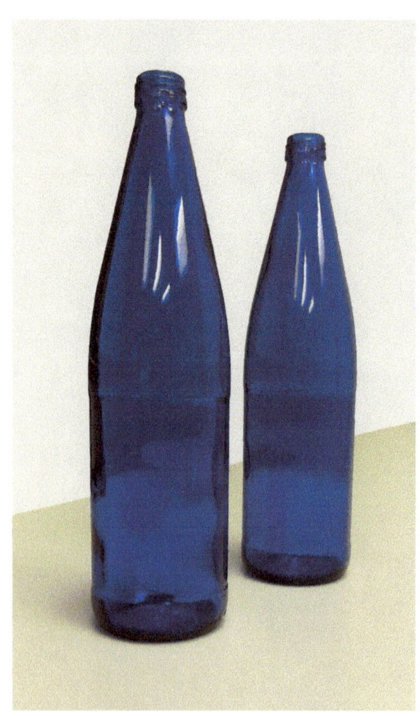

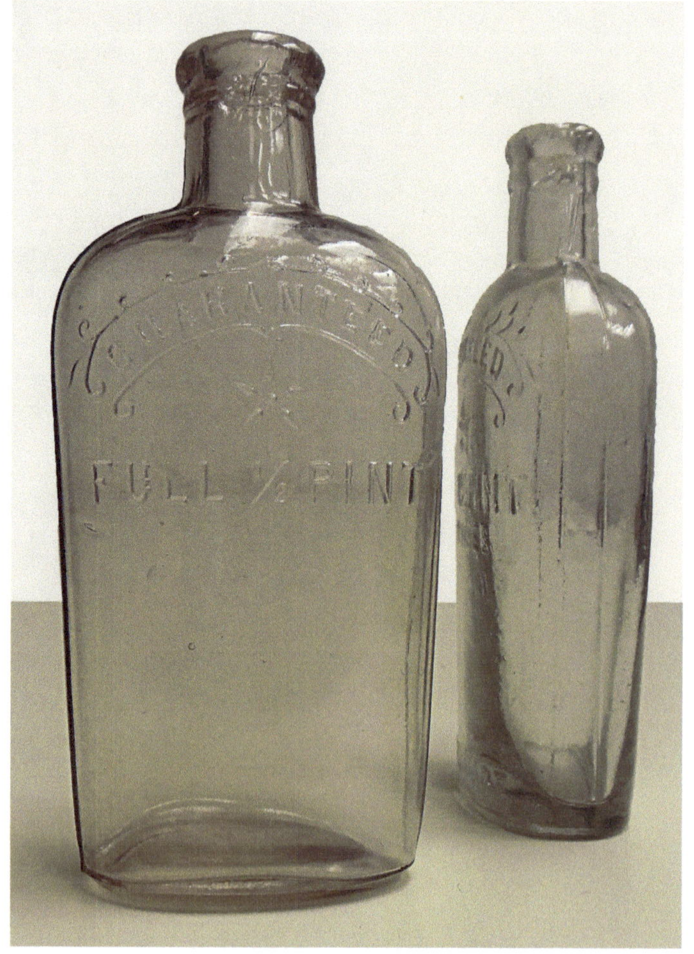

Star Glass Warranted ½ Pint Whisky Flasks, Early Twentieth Century.

The array of products blown at the Star Glassworks included warranted whisky flasks in a variety of styles and capacities. Courtesy of the Peter C. Hamilton Collection.

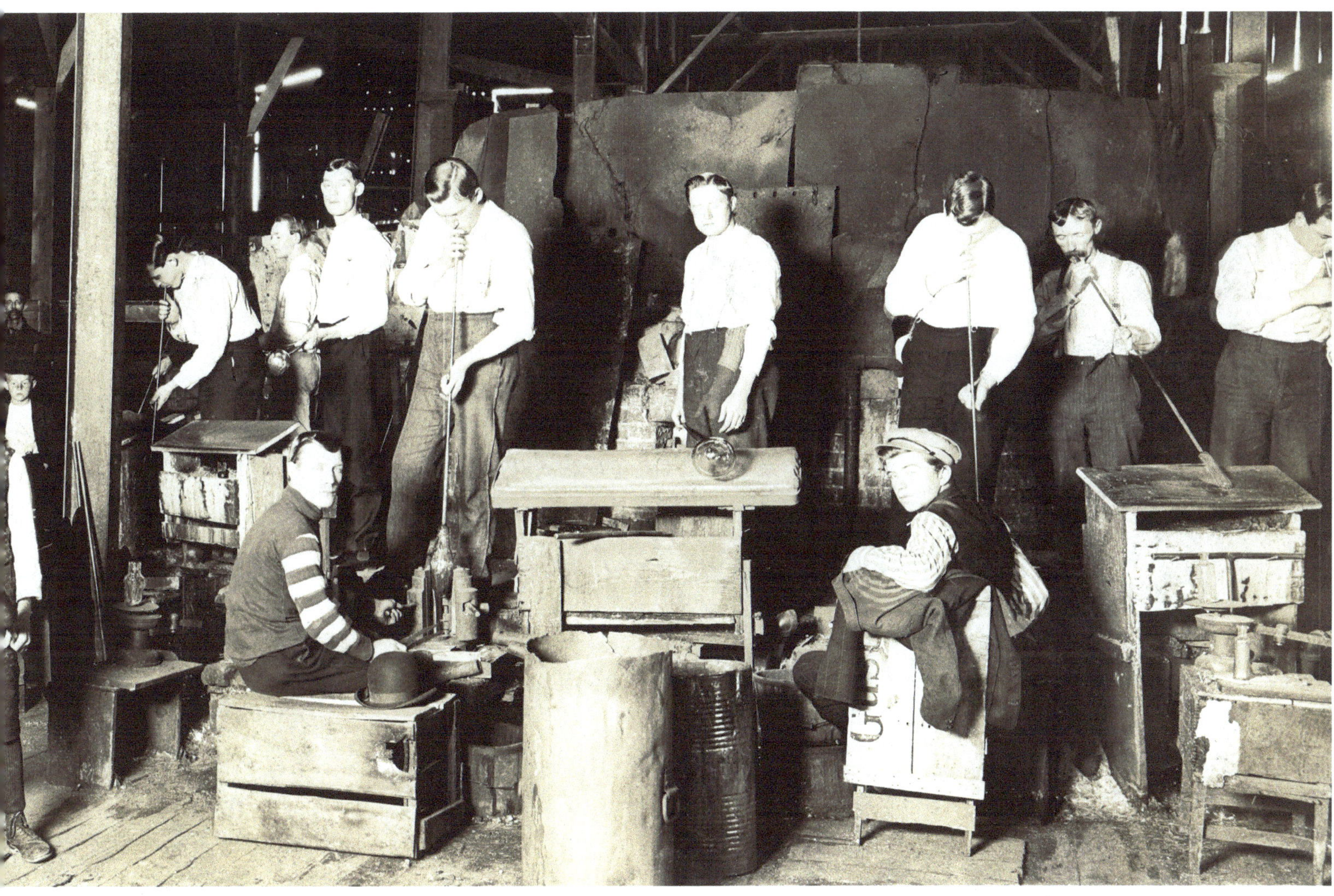

Gaffers, Star Glass, Medford, Burlington County, New Jersey, 1905.

Star Glass operated between 1894 and the early 1920s, one of a series of succeeding glass factories in Medford. At its peak it employed about 250 workers. Glassblowers were known as gaffers; these skilled laborers used a blow tube to inflate molten glass into a variety of useful forms. The men on the far right are marvering the gather (glob of molten glass) on a marble slab. The gaffer to the left of the center table is preparing to blow his gather into an iron mold as the mold-boy (with the stripped sleeves) is ready to close the mold. The glass furnace sits behind the gaffers. Courtesy of the Paul W. Schopp Collection.

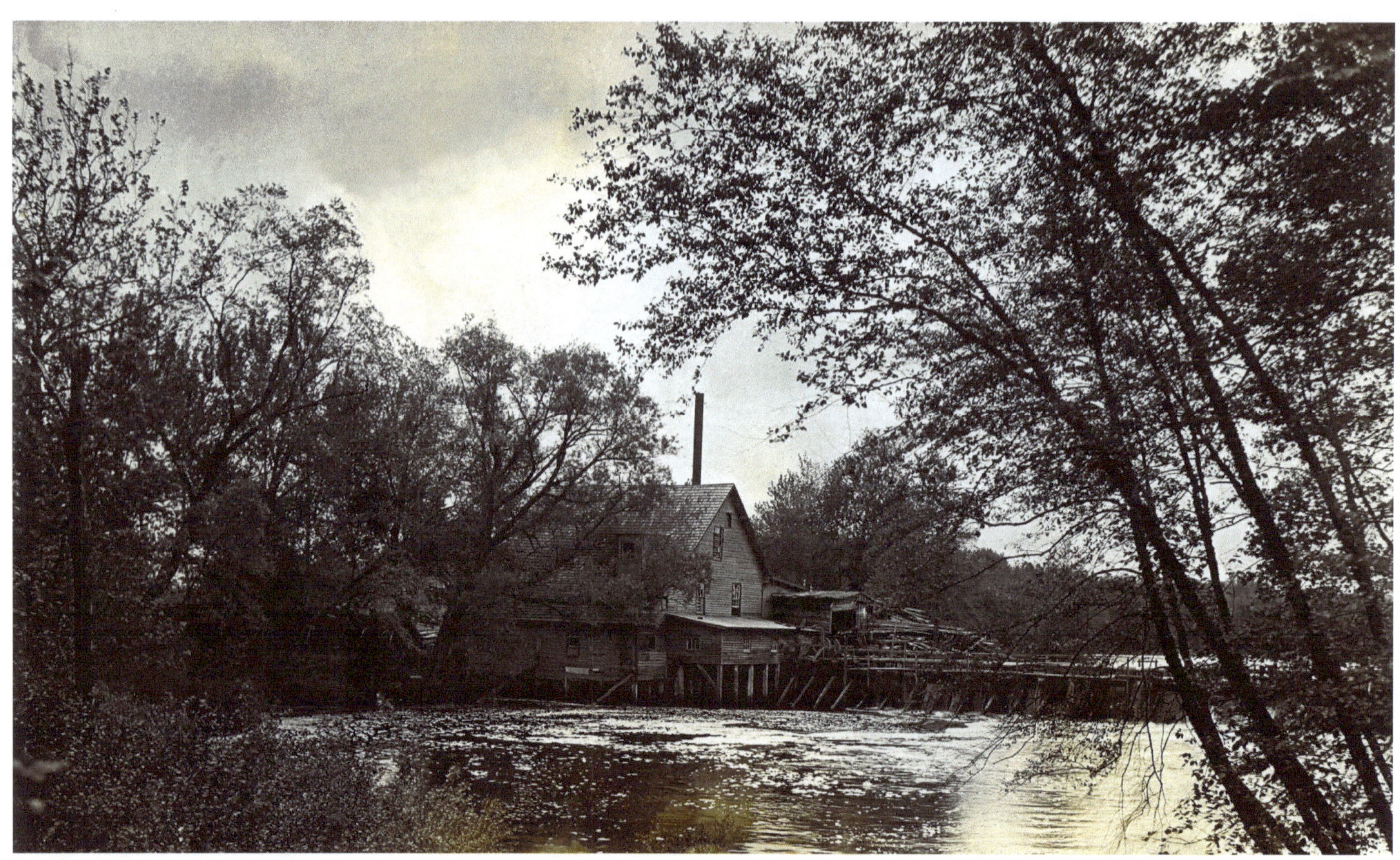

Oliphant's Grist and Saw Mill, Medford, Burlington County, c. 1906.

The first mill at this location dates to between 1690 and 1720. Members of the Oliphant family owned the grist and saw mill since 1763 and operated the complex until 1906, when a nephew, Joseph Hinchman, discontinued milling. It appears the mills have already ceased to function in this view. Courtesy of the Paul W. Schopp Collection.

Sawmills

Soon after Europeans arrived in what is now South Jersey they began to harness the creeks for powering grist, saw, and other types of mills. As these settlers moved into the Pine Barrens to exploit the natural resources there, beginning with the trees, they established sawmills for cutting the fallen timber into lumber and other wood products. Due to the relatively flat terrain, many of these sawmills operated with undershot wheels, with the flow of water turning the waterwheel from the bottom. Sawyers who constructed larger sand dams could operate their mills with either breast wheels, where the water hit the wheel just above center, or with overshot wheels, where the water dropped on the wheel from above. Undershot generated the least amount of power, while overshot provided the maximum. These sawmills all used up-and-down saws through the eighteenth and almost halfway into the nineteenth century before circular saws began to be accepted, although many mills retained the older technology. Pine Barren sawmills processed untold cedar, oak, and pine trees for a variety of products, including lumber, fence rails, cedar shingles, and clapboards. As steam and then internal combustion became accepted power sources, sawyers took portable sawmills into the Pines and continued to cut wood products. Timber harvesting continues today.

Pancoast Mill, Richland, Buena Vista Township, Atlantic County, c. 1906.

During the nineteenth century, Ambrose Pancoast built a dam and a water-powered sawmill about midway between Weymouth and Landisville on Deep Run, part of the Great Egg Harbor River system, around which a settlement known as Pancoastville developed. Water-powered mills remained an integral part of life within the Pines into the early twentieth century. Mills were often family-run businesses; three generations are depicted here. Courtesy of the Paul W. Schopp Collection.

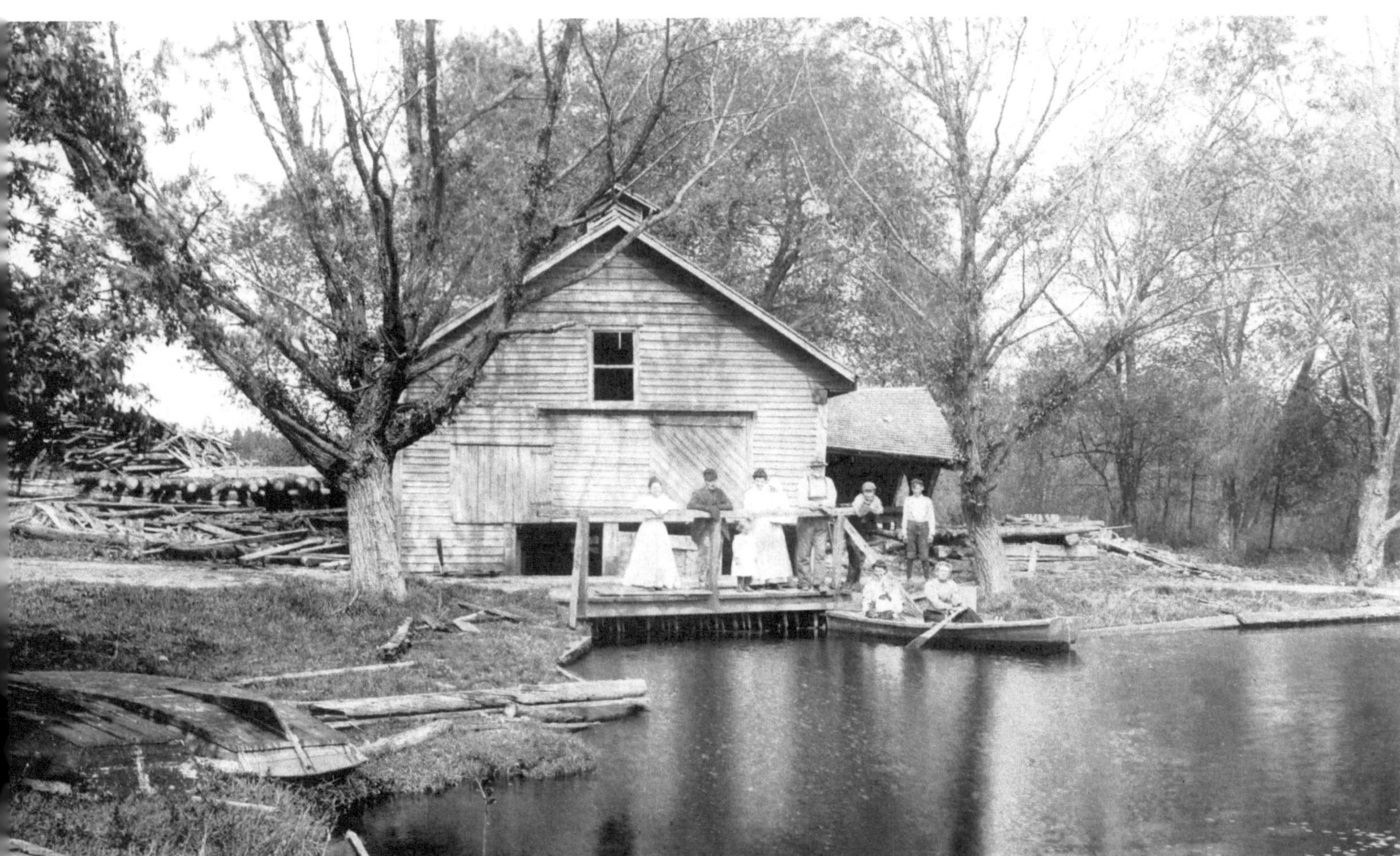

Gristmills

MILLS FOR GRINDING cereals were among the first mills Europeans established in the province of West New Jersey, since wheat and other cereal crops provided essential elements of the colonists' diet. Gristmills began to appear on the waterways of the Pine Barrens during the eighteenth century. The technology employed was simple: the grain would be ground into flour between a bed-stone that remained stationary and a runner stone over its face with just enough gap between the two stones to allow the grain to enter for grinding. Bolting chests allowed the miller to sift the ground grain into various grades and to minimize the minute pieces of grindstone mixed in with the flour. The miller retained 10 percent of the ground grain as his "toll" or fee for performing the work.

In 1795, Philadelphian Oliver Evans standardized mill and dam construction when he published his book, *The Young Mill-Wright & Miller's Guide*. For those unable to read, Evans' diagrams visually imparted much of the textual information. Gristmills could be found in many parts of the Pine Barrens, ranging from Medford and Vincentown to Port Republic and Oceanville. These mills initially provided ground grain to those farmers practicing subsistence agriculture, but as land and growing techniques improved, a portion of the cereal crops would be set aside for market, netting the farm a tidy profit. The local gristmill would often grind this grain and handle its shipment to market.

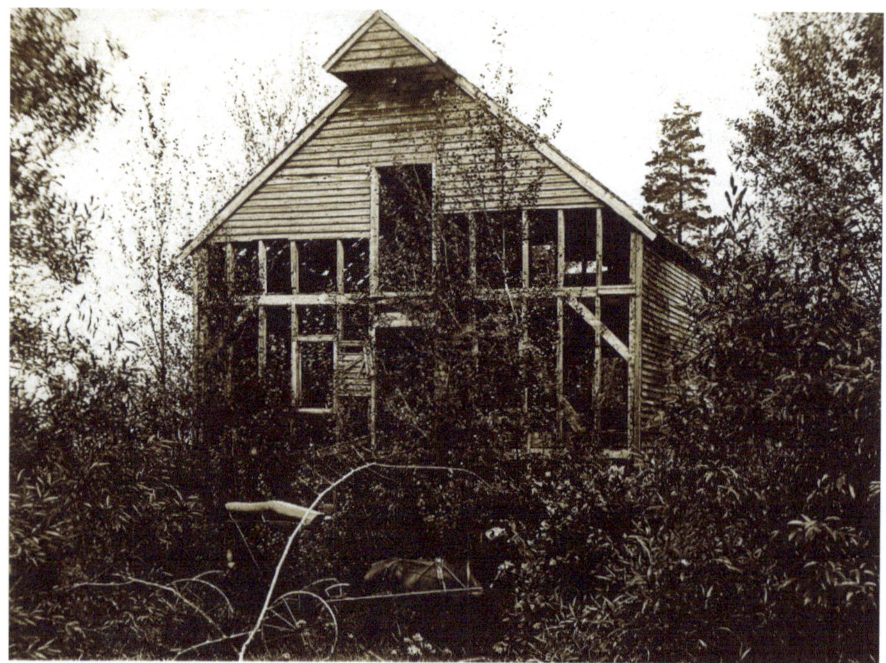

OCEANVILLE MILL, Oceanville, Atlantic County, c. 1906.

Sometime between 1812 and 1828, Daniel S. Shourds (b. 1777) constructed a dam on Tanners Brook and established a gristmill, powered by today's Lily Lake. By 1850, Daniel continued to work at the mill, although his son, Daniel, now owned it, valued at $3000. When this mill ceased operations is unknown, but it is clearly abandoned and decaying in this view. Courtesy of the Paul W. Schopp Collection.

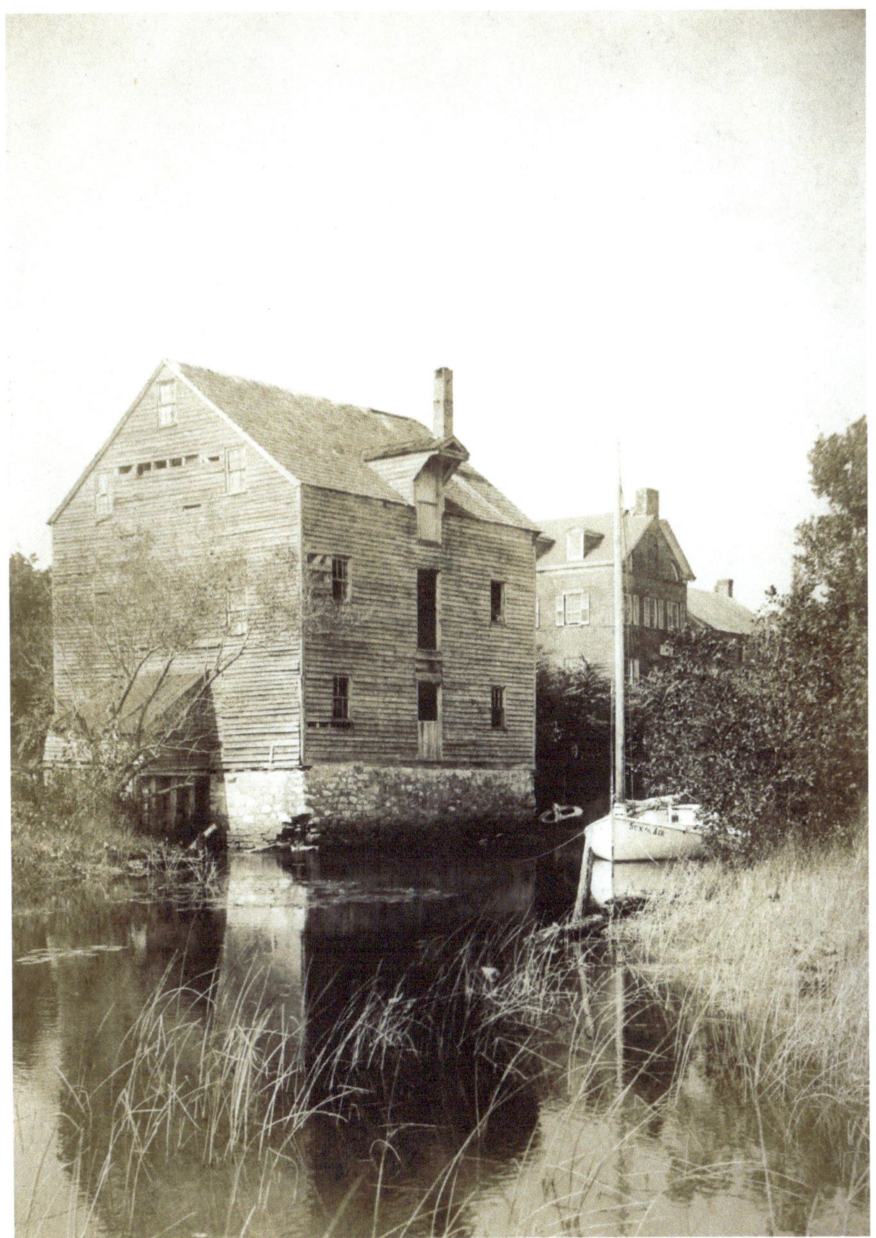

Port Republic Mill, Port Republic, Atlantic County, c. 1906.

In 1774, the New Jersey Colonial Assembly authorized Evi Smith, Hugh McCollum, and Richard Wescot to construct dams and mills along Nacote Creek. The partners proceeded to erect a dam and build a sawmill and the large gristmill shown in this view to the left. By 1838, David S. Blackman had acquired both mills. It is unclear how long the mill continued to grind grain, but it is obviously abandoned in this photograph. Courtesy of the Paul W. Schopp Collection.

Harrisville

Mill technology could be adapted for many different purposes. With a history that stretches from the eighteenth century across the nineteenth, milling operations at Harrisville began with a skit mill. The same mill seat served as a forge and slitting mill for Martha Furnace until fire destroyed it. John Hallock acquired the mill seat and established his castor and linseed oil mill in the heart of the Pines. Paper production at Harrisville began in the 1830s. In 1914, a fire destroyed the village and factory.

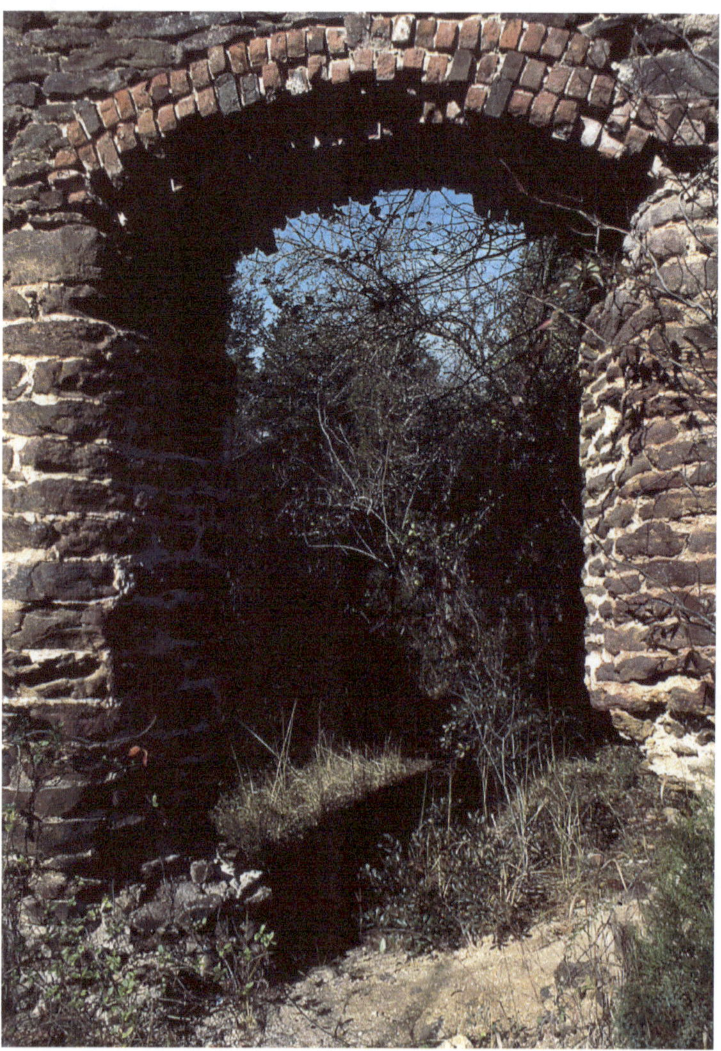

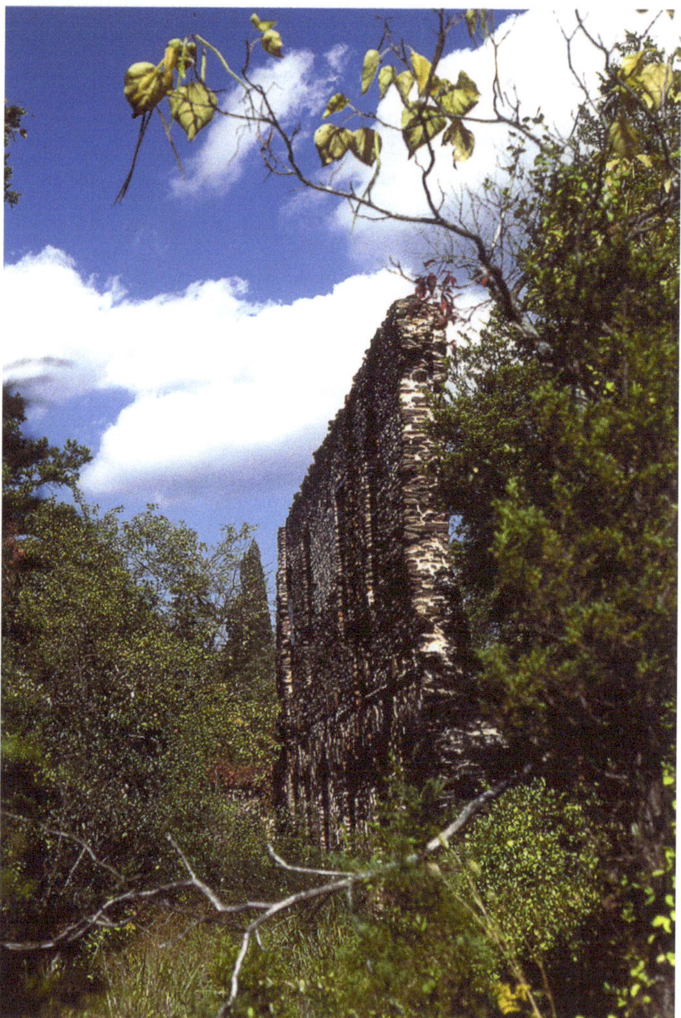

Ruins of Harrisville Paper Mill, Bass River Township, Burlington County, 1980s.

Ted Gordon, photographer, November 19, 1988 (left) and October, 1982.

Harrisville Paper Mill, Bass River Township, Burlington County, 1877.

Philadelphian Ernest Hexamer prepared this survey of the Harrisville Paper Mill in 1877 so fire insurance companies could assess risk. Note the complexity of this mill in the Pines. Courtesy of the Free Library of Philadelphia. Used by permission.

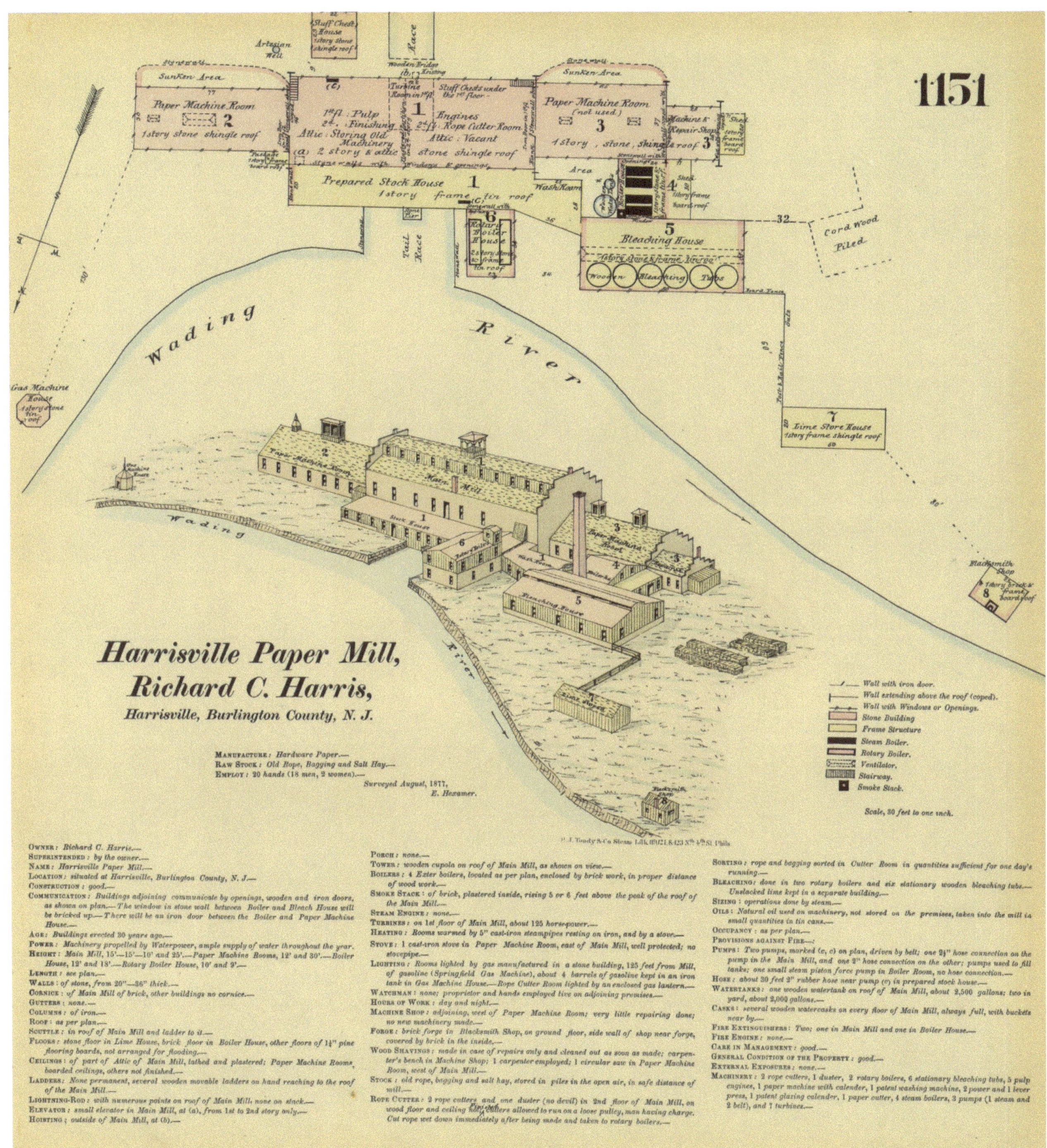

Harrisville Paper Mill, Richard C. Harris,

Harrisville, Burlington County, N. J.

Manufacture: *Hardware Paper.—*
Raw Stock: *Old Rope, Bagging and Salt Hay.—*
Employ: *20 hands (18 men, 2 women).—*

Surveyed August, 1877,
E. Hexamer.

Owner: *Richard C. Harris.—*
Superintended: *by the owner.—*
Name: *Harrisville Paper Mill.—*
Location: *situated at Harrisville, Burlington County, N. J.—*
Construction: *good.—*
Communication: *Buildings adjoining communicate by openings, wooden and iron doors, as shown on plan.—The window in stone wall between Boiler and Bleach House will be bricked up.—There will be an iron door between the Boiler and Paper Machine House.—*
Age: *Buildings erected 30 years ago.—*
Power: *Machinery propelled by Waterpower, ample supply of water throughout the year.*
Height: *Main Mill, 15'—15'—10' and 25'.—Paper Machine Rooms, 12' and 30'.—Boiler House, 12' and 18'.—Rotary Boiler House, 10' and 9'.—*
Length: *see plan.—*
Walls: *of stone, from 20"—36" thick.—*
Cornice: *of Main Mill of brick, other buildings no cornice.—*
Gutters: *none.—*
Columns: *of iron.—*
Roof: *as per plan.—*
Scuttle: *in roof of Main Mill and ladder to it.—*
Floors: *stone floor in Lime House, brick floor in Boiler House, other floors of 1¼" pine flooring boards, not arranged for flooding.—*
Ceilings: *of part of Attic of Main Mill, lathed and plastered; Paper Machine Rooms, boarded ceilings, others not finished.—*
Ladders: *None permanent, several wooden movable ladders on hand reaching to the roof of the Main Mill.—*
Lightning-Rod: *with numerous points on roof of Main Mill, none on stack.—*
Elevator: *small elevator in Main Mill, at (a), from 1st to 2nd story only.—*
Hoisting: *outside of Main Mill, at (b).—*

Porch: *none.—*
Tower: *wooden cupola on roof of Main Mill, as shown on view.—*
Boilers: *4 Exter boilers, located as per plan, enclosed by brick work, in proper distance of wood work.—*
Smoke Stack: *of brick, plastered inside, rising 5 or 6 feet above the peak of the roof of the Main Mill.—*
Steam Engine: *none.—*
Turbines: *on 1st floor of Main Mill, about 125 horse-power.—*
Heating: *Rooms warmed by 5" cast-iron steampipes resting on iron, and by a stove.—*
Stove: *1 cast-iron stove in Paper Machine Room, east of Main Mill, well protected; no stovepipe.—*
Lighting: *Rooms lighted by gas manufactured in a stone building, 125 feet from Mill, of gasoline (Springfield Gas Machine), about 4 barrels of gasoline kept in an iron tank in Gas Machine House.—Rope Cutter Room lighted by an enclosed gas lantern.—*
Watchman: *none; proprietor and hands employed live on adjoining premises.—*
Hours of Work: *day and night.—*
Machine Shop: *adjoining, west of Paper Machine Room; very little repairing done; no new machinery made.—*
Forge: *brick forge in Blacksmith Shop, on ground floor, side wall of shop near forge, covered by brick in the inside.—*
Wood Shavings: *made in case of repairs only and cleaned out as soon as made; carpenter's bench in Machine Shop; 1 carpenter employed; 1 circular saw in Paper Machine Room, west of Main Mill.—*
Stock: *old rope, bagging and salt hay, stored in piles in the open air, in safe distance of mill.—*
Rope Cutter: *2 rope cutters and one duster (no devil) in 2nd floor of Main Mill, on wood floor and ceiling not finished, cutters allowed to run on a loose pulley, man having charge. Cut rope wet down immediately after being made and taken to rotary boilers.—*

Sorting: *rope and bagging sorted in Cutter Room in quantities sufficient for one day's running.—*
Bleaching: *done in two rotary boilers and six stationary wooden bleaching tubs.—Unslacked lime kept in a separate building.—*
Sizing: *operations done by steam.—*
Oils: *Natural oil used on machinery, not stored on the premises, taken into the mill in small quantities in tin cans.—*
Occupancy: *as per plan.—*
Provisions against Fire—:
Pumps: *Two pumps, marked (c, c) on plan, driven by belt; one 2½" hose connection on the pump in the Main Mill, and one 2" hose connection on the other; pumps used to fill tanks; one small steam piston force pump in Boiler Room, no hose connection.—*
Hose: *about 30 feet 2" rubber hose near pump (c) in prepared stock house.—*
Watertanks: *one wooden watertank on roof of Main Mill, about 2,500 gallons; two in yard, about 2,000 gallons.—*
Casks: *several wooden watercasks on every floor of Main Mill, always full, with buckets near by.—*
Fire Extinguishers: *Two; one in Main Mill and one in Boiler House.—*
Fire Engine: *none.—*
Care in Management: *good.—*
General Condition of the Property: *good.—*
External Exposures: *none.—*
Machinery: *2 rope cutters, 1 duster, 2 rotary boilers, 6 stationary bleaching tubs, 5 pulp engines, 1 paper machine with calender, 1 patent washing machine, 2 power and 1 lever press, 1 patent glazing calender, 1 paper cutter, 4 steam boilers, 3 pumps (1 steam and 2 belt), and 7 turbines.—*

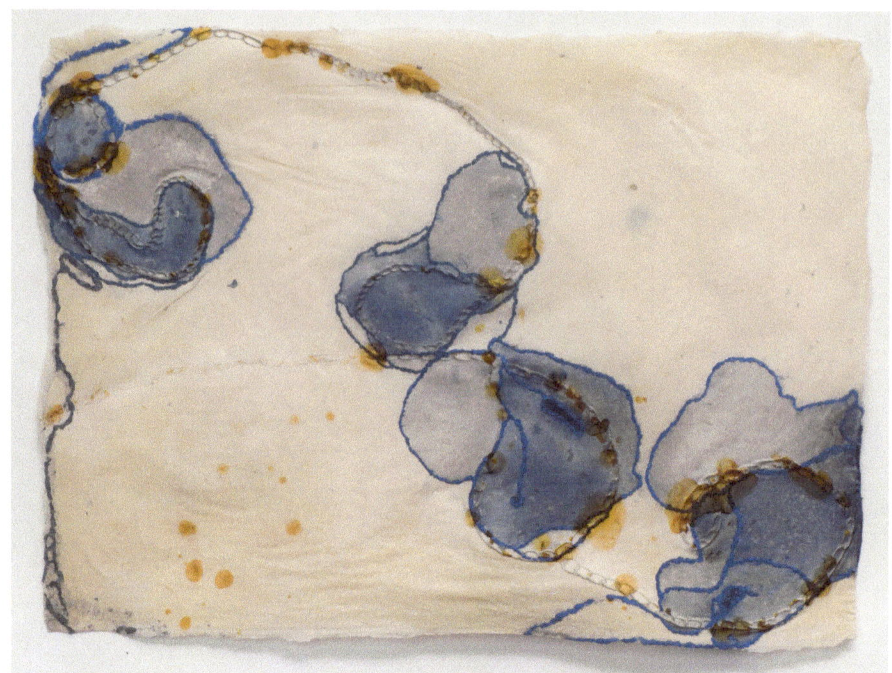

Elements of a Theory, Nancy Cohen, 2009.

Paper pulp, ink, rust and embedded wire on handmade paper

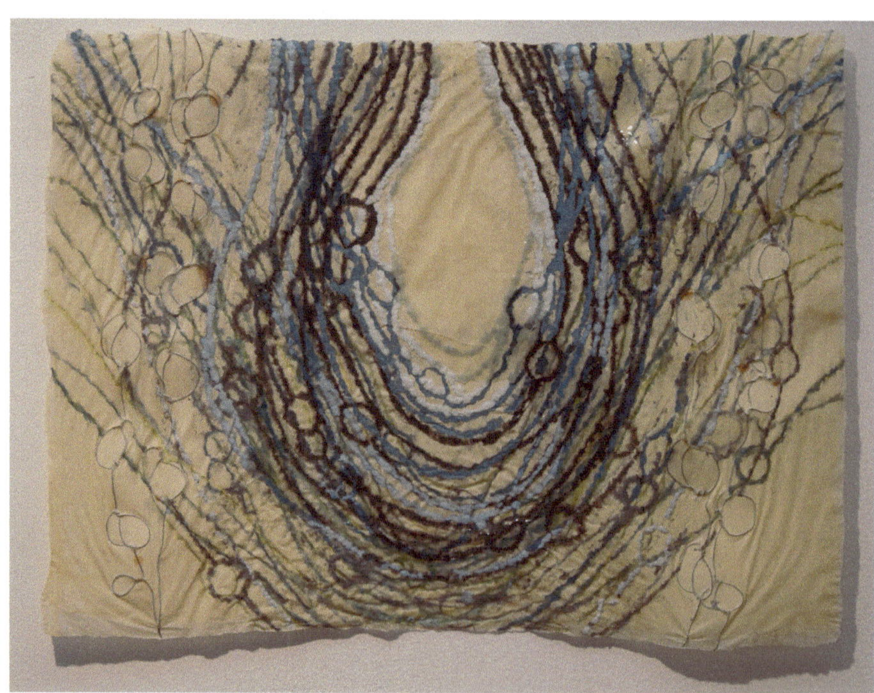

Undone, Nancy Cohen, 2011.

Paper pulp and rubber on handmade paper

Union Clay Works

Sometime between 1856 and 1858, an Irish immigrant named Lewis Neill moved to Union (now Lacey) Township, Ocean County, near the Burlington County line. Here, he established a brickyard and began excavating white clay from nearby pits at Old Half Way. While the clay did not prove satisfactory for producing brick on a large scale, Neill eventually changed over to using it in making pottery, which was successful, as well as furnace pots for glassworks. The 1860 federal census lists Neill as a "Fire Brick Maker" with real estate valued at $2000 and a personal estate of $200. Andrew Jackson McCall, a minister and cigar maker, lived nearby in Red Oak Grove and served as the brickyard manager. Although locally and historically known as the Union Clay Works, that title was never the corporate name for the works; Neill operated under the style of Lewis Neill and Company.

Neill's operations at the plant ended in 1865, when he sold the factory to the appropriately named Joseph Keasbey Brick, who converted the site to produce terra cotta pipe. When Brick died in 1867, his business partner, Edward D. White, assumed control, but operations at Union were spasmodic with intervals of idleness. The plant was not in operation in 1874 when New Jersey State Geologist George Hamill Cook, noted, "There is a considerable stock [of pipes] on hand and some in the kiln unburned." The presence of unfired pipe in the kiln strongly suggests that White abandoned the Union Clay Works sometime prior to 1874. No further information about the Union Clay Works appears until J.K. Brick's widow died in 1897. She left all of her real and personal estate, including the Union Clay Works, to the Brooklyn Memorial Hospital.

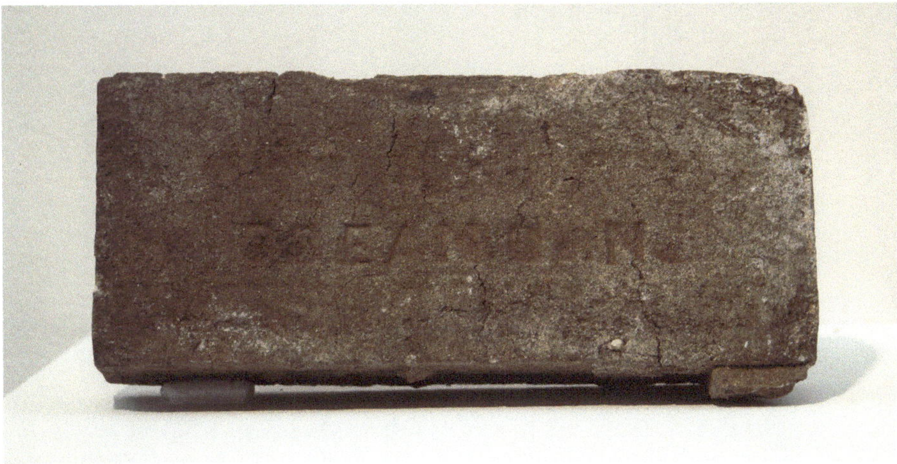

Brick from Union Clay Works, c. 1860.

Lewis Neill manufactured this brick during his tenure at Union Clay Works, which takes its name from the township of its location. The brick, indicative of the clay used in manufacturing it, carries the incised inscription, "Ocean Co., N.J." to signify the location of the brick's manufacture. The apparent mortar appendages and other markings on the brick suggest that it once was part of a wall or structure.

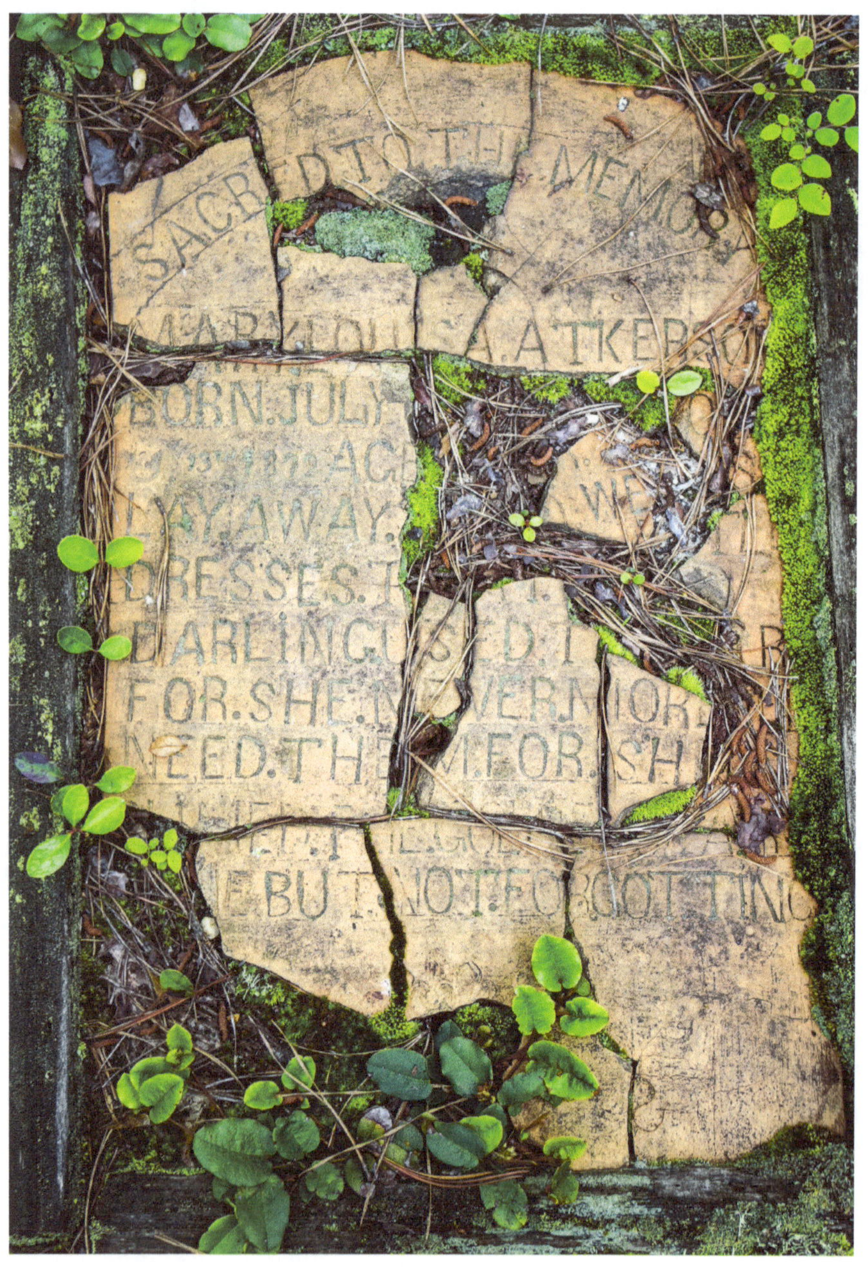

Sacred to the Memory of Mary Louisa Atkerson, 2003.

Ben Ruset, photographer, 2003.

Graves in Lonely Woods.

A strange graveyard that had about it the atmosphere of mystery and melancholy sadness was found a day or so ago in the heart of the New Jersey pines.

A traveler on his way from Brown's Mill to Manahawkin, impressed by the loneliness of the locality, left the roadside to walk a short distance in the virgin wilds. He had not gone far when he ran across five mounds in a row. As he drew nearer he saw the graves all marked by boards and one had a stone at the head roughly inscribed. It was evidently the most recent of the lot. The inscription told its pathetic tale as follows:

Sacred to the Memory of
Mary Louisa Atkerson.
Born July 19, 1872. Died Nov. 13, 1872.
Lay away those little dresses
Once our darling used to wear.
For she never more will need them;
She has climbed the golden stair.
Gone but not forgotten.

There was no inclosure about the graves; nothing but a few tall pines, the music of whose sighing branches was in perfect accord with the sad scene. A few bushes hid the graves. It would be only by accident that they could be found.

Inquiry was made for the Atkerson family. No one knew of them or had ever heard of them. They must have come, buried their dead and disappeared like birds of passage. The sad history of the graves and why they were made in such a lonely spot will probably never be known.—New York Times.

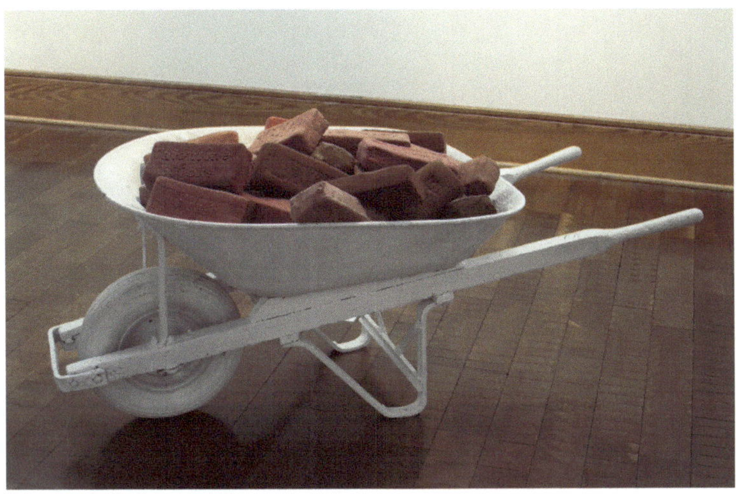

Maintain (bricks), Diane Savona, 2014.

Textile

Bricks have been manufactured in the Pine Barrens since the 1700s. Ruins of their manufacture – and pits left from the mining of clay – can still be found in the Pines. The bricks in this installation are embossed with names, places, dates and information related to the history of bricks in the Pine Barrens.

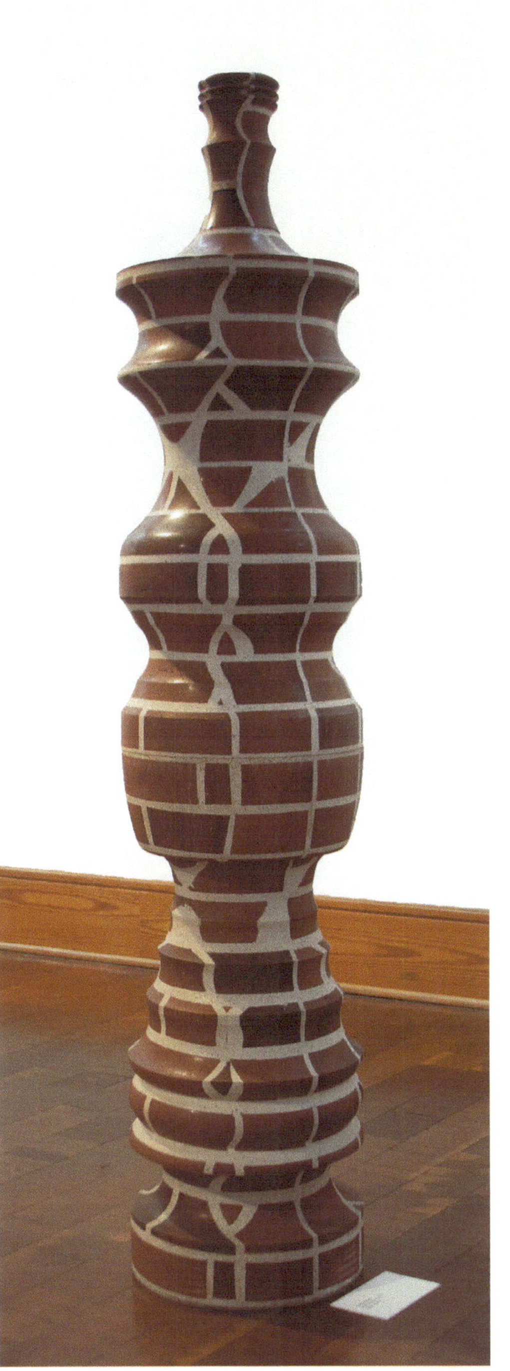

Brick Bollard, Rory Mahon, 2012.

Brick, mortar

"Graves in Lonely Woods," 1899.

(Left) Little more than 25 years after Mary Louisa Atkerson was interred, her grave and those nearby were nearly lost to the regrowth of the Pines: "It would be only by accident that they could be found." Her father likely worked at the Union Clay Works and created the terra cotta grave marker for his daughter using clay, tools, and the kilns at the factory. Other members of her family may be interred with her in this small burial ground, all potentially succumbing to the small pox epidemic that swept through Ocean County in the early 1870s. *Daily Herald* (Delphos, Ohio), from the *New York Times*, May 31, 1899.

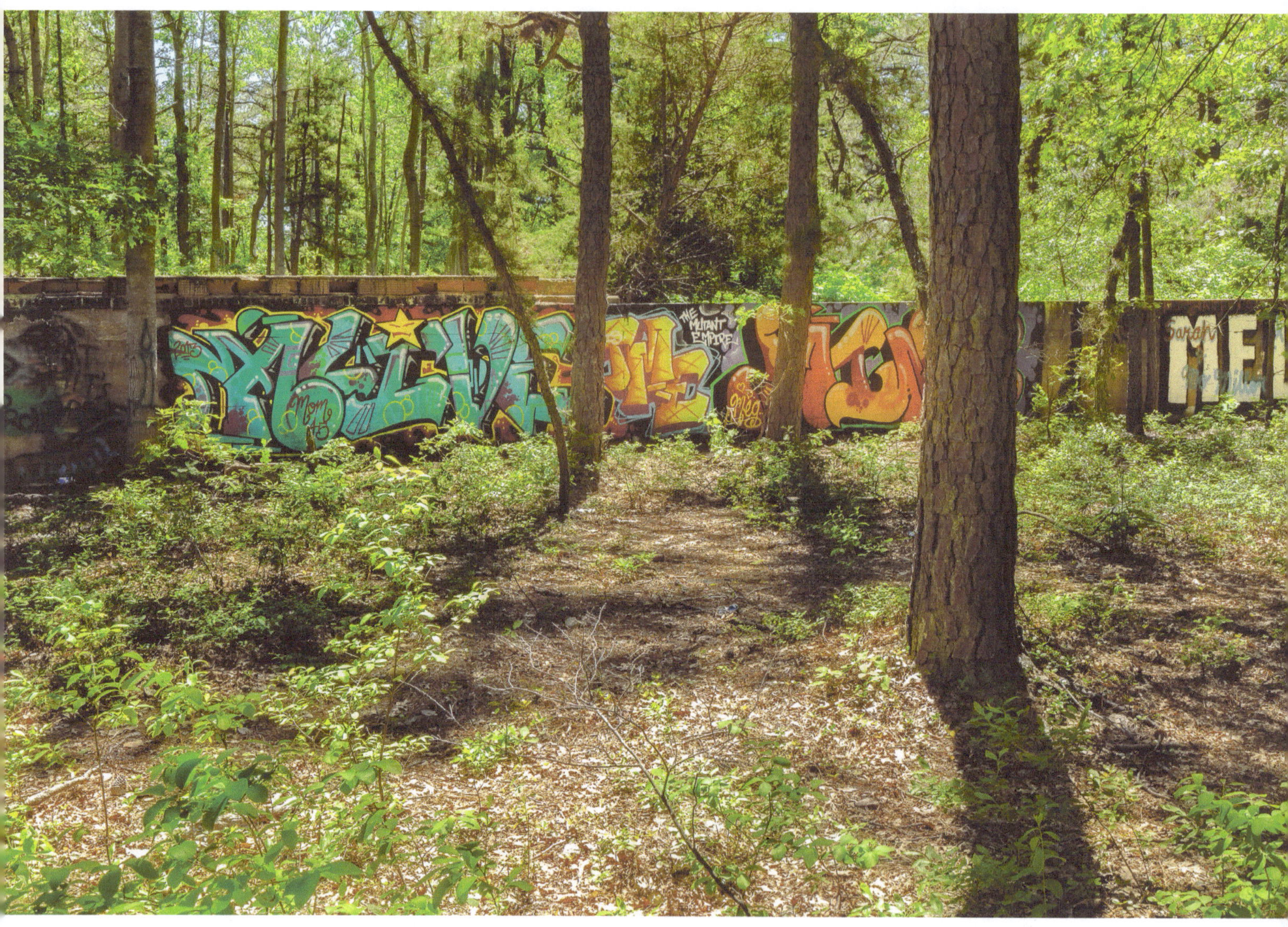

Brick Factory Wall, Albert Horner, 2015.

Photograph of the Brooksbrae Brick Company factory ruins, off Pasadena Road in Brendan Byrne State Forest.

Lost Industries, Lost Towns

Atsion, Batsto, Hanover, Harrisville, Hermann City, Martha, Speedwell, and Weymouth – whether naming iron furnaces, glass houses, brickyards, or paper mills in the Pines, each place supported small villages of workers and each, essentially, is gone. This list could be expanded four-fold at a minimum.

With the discovery of better sources of iron and coal in Pennsylvania, the iron industry in the Pines failed. Competition and technical improvements in manufacturing doomed most glass and paper manufactories. Catastrophic fires played a part as well in killing small Pinebelt communities. Some historic villages survive today – Whiting, Chatsworth, Tabernacle, Vincentown, Pemberton, New Egypt, and others – many once-vibrant communities survive only as names on old maps and as trivia for vocational and avocational historians.

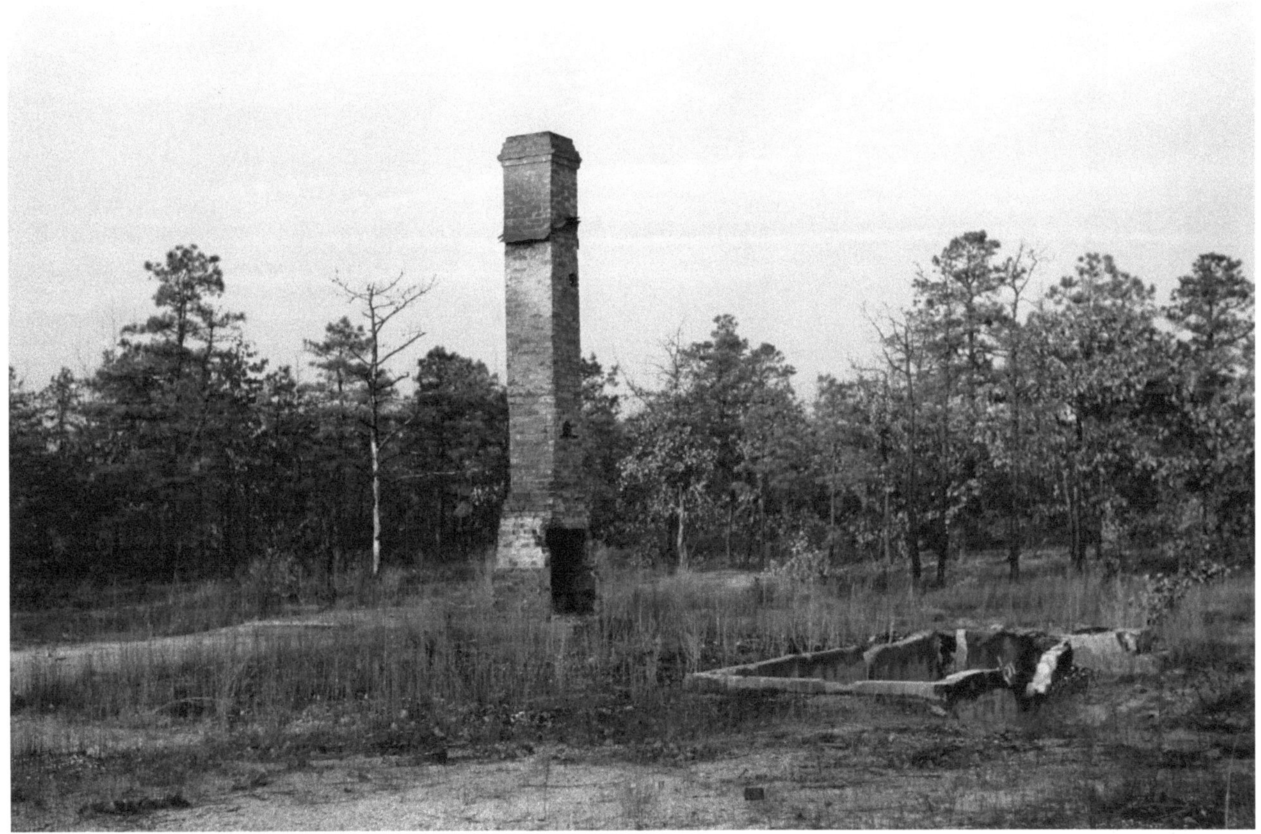

Remnant of the Past, Pine Barrens, n.p., 1938.

The remains of a once-substantial house (see the roof flashing near the top of the chimney) destroyed by fire in a cut-over area of the Pines. Russell Lee, photographer, January 1938; from the Prints and Photographs Division, Library of Congress.

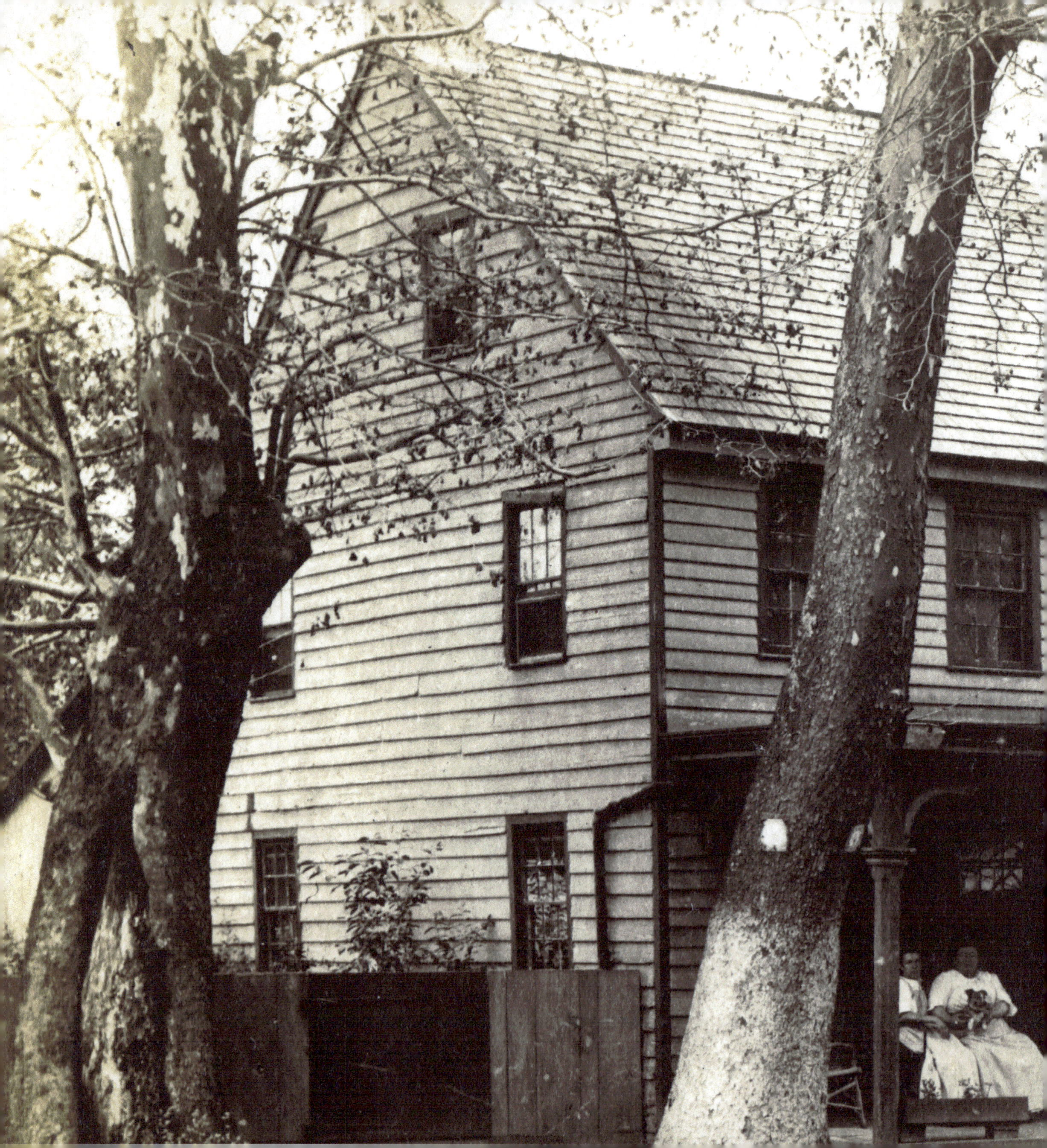

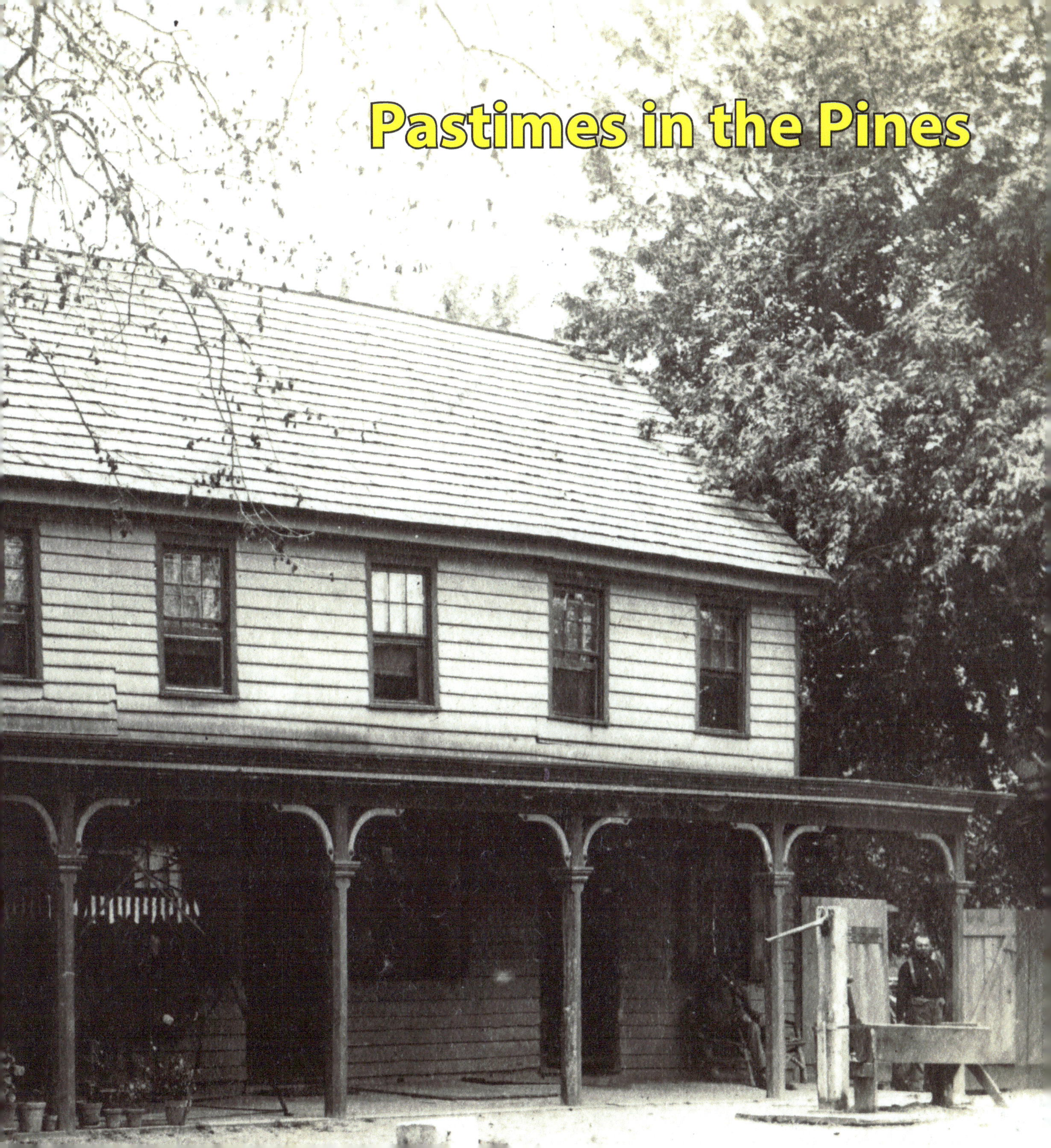

Pastimes in the Pines

Taverns in the Pines

TAVERNS AND HOTELS in and around the Pine Barrens provided much needed hospitality for travelers making their way along the sandy roads of the Barrens. These stopping places became prominent landmarks and centers of activity. To ensure a "safe" stay, local ordinances set prices for food, liquor, stabling, and horse feed. It was not unusual for lodgers to share rooms and even beds with fellow travelers.

The tavern also served as a gathering spot for local residents who ate, drank, sang, played fiddles, danced, and played games of amusement and chance. After a night of entertainment, travelers who had stayed overnight awoke to a breakfast of eggs, bread, coffee, and hashed meat. Taverns hosted many local meetings as well as elections. They were the one place that people gathered to gossip, tell tales, and meet strangers.

Jug Taverns

GUSTAV KOBBÉ's description of jug taverns below is perhaps overly stereotyped, but it attempts to convey the rustic flavor of taverns within the Pines. They certainly lacked the polish of town or city establishments.

> In the old days, when the furnaces were in operation, numerous taverns were scattered through the pines. They were called jug taverns, because their entire stock-in-trade usually consisted of a jug of apple-jack, out of which, however, the proprietor would pour any liquid refreshment called for, ranging from lemonade to brandy, and even mixed potables . . . The chief amusements in those days were huckleberry parties in summer and oyster suppers in winter. The latter were held in the taverns, and were preceded and followed by dancing. A fiddler enthroned in a chair, which had been elevated on to a table, scraped away at "Hi, Betty Martin," "Camptown Races," and the "Straight Four," dances which were perhaps varied by a "challenge jig" between two experts of the Pines. When the fiddler disappeared under the table, as he invariably did, the girls sang the airs and dancing continued all the same.
>
> From Gustav Kobbé's *The New Jersey Coast and Pines* (1889)

TANSBORO TAVERN, Tansboro, Camden County, 1906.

(Preceding Page) The village of Tansboro began when Cornelius Tice established a tannery with half a dozen tanning vats soon after the turn of the nineteenth century. Tice also constructed and operated the tavern in the nascent settlement, located directly across Berlin-Blue Anchor Road from the tannery. Subsequent tavern keepers included James Campbell, William Norcross, William Marshall and John Sharp, with enlargements to the tavern completed by at least two of these men. Soon after its construction and into the middle of the nineteenth century, many people frequented the tavern, but the coming of the railroad diminished the inn's importance. Nonetheless, it continued as a local gathering and entertainment spot into the twentieth century. Courtesy of the Paul W. Schopp Collection.

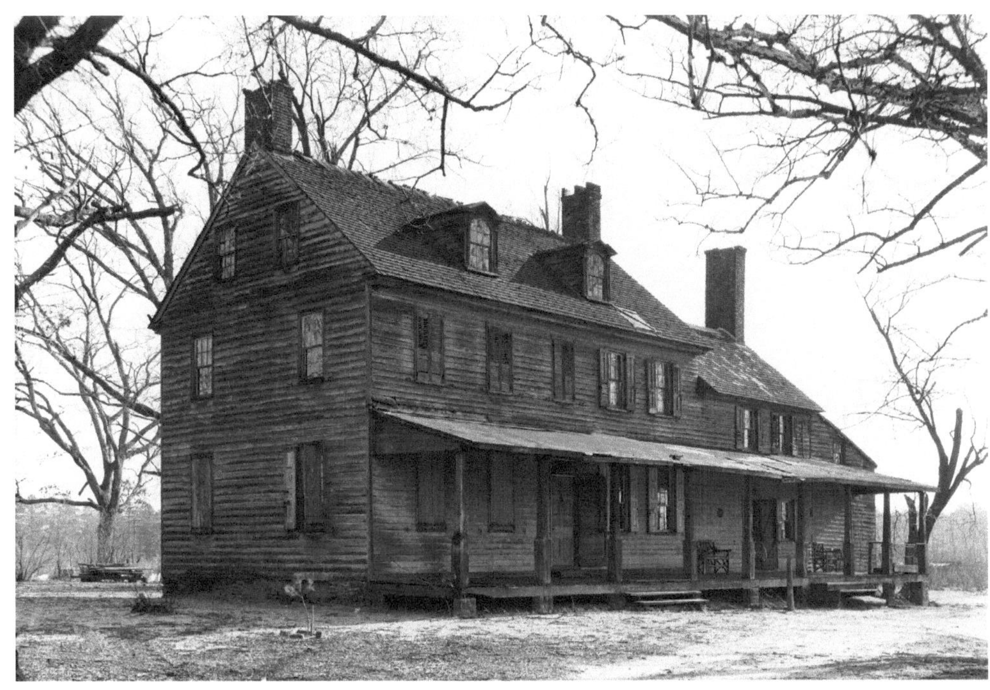

Spring Garden Inn, Ancora, Winslow Township, Camden County, 1939.

The Spring Garden Inn still survives on the Old White Horse Pike near Ancora. The inn dates from around 1826, but even in this later image, it sports an untreated cedar exterior. Nathaniel R. Ewan, photographer, February 9, 1939; from the Prints and Photographs Division, Library of Congress.

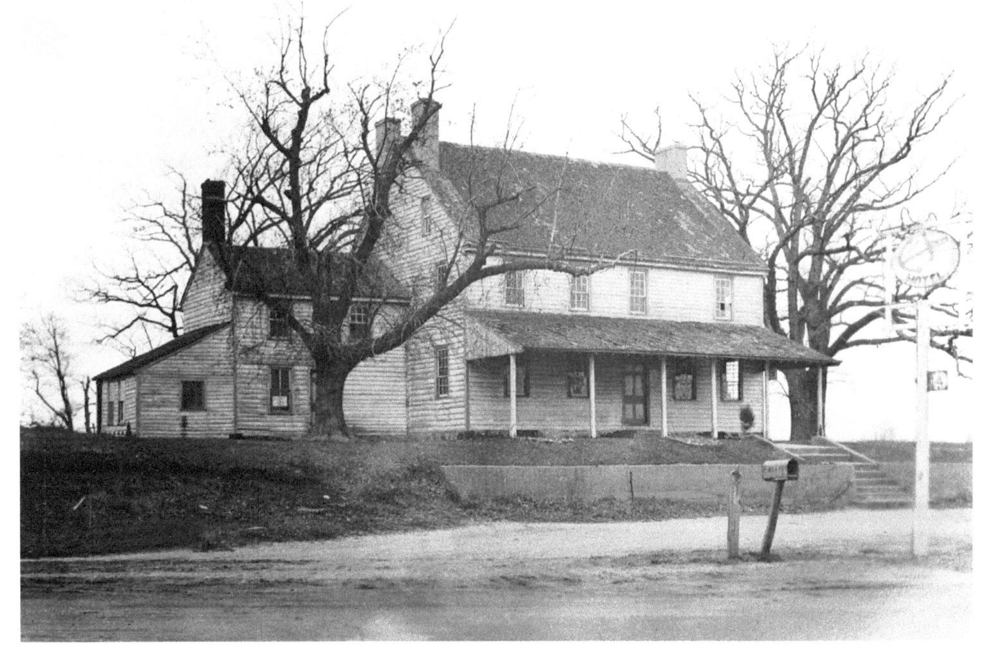

Blue Anchor Tavern, Folsom Road, Blue Anchor, Winslow Township, Camden County, 1936.

Gordon's *Gazetteer* (1834) describes Blue Anchor as a tavern and hamlet "in the heart of the pine forest." Established where an old Indian trail crossed the local cedar swamp, timber was a focus of the local economy. The first tavern was constructed of cedar logs. R. Merritt Lacey, photographer, October 14, 1936; from the Prints and Photographs Division, Library of Congress.

Dancing in the Pines

In 1781, the authorities reputedly captured the notorious Pine Barrens robber Joe Mulliner at the Indian Cabin Tavern near Batsto, having let his guard down while dancing with a pretty woman. Allowing inhibitions to fall in the Pines appears to have been something of a tradition. During the eighteenth century, itinerant fiddlers began traveling the sugar sand roads of the Pine Barrens, stopping at the various taverns secluded in the woods to entertain the patrons. As the fiddler played reels and other popular songs of the day, couples and strangers would spring to their feet and spontaneously begin dancing. Soon, Philadelphians of all ages learned of this opportunity to escape the oppressive moral strictures of life in the Quaker City. After crossing the Delaware River on a wherry to the landings in what would become Camden, or taking a packet boat to Burlington, those seeking to cast aside their normally straight-laced lifestyles undertook the arduous journey into the Pines to join with Jersey farm families and woodsmen to kick up their heels.

This popular dance craze led to the passage of the New Jersey Immorality Act on March 16, 1798, which strictly forbade the presentation of "interludes or plays, dancing, singing, fiddling, or other muse for the sake of merriment . . . on the Christian Sabbath, or first day of the week called Sunday." This law had very little effect on those taverns hidden away in the Pines, as evidenced by a seven-page tract printed in 1801, reporting on a Tuckerton resident named Edward Andrews, who became a convinced Quaker and gave up a life of debauchery. The tract specifically reported that before his conversion Andrews had been resident "in the Jersey, near the sea-shore, among a wild sort of people. Indians and others – vain and loose in their conversation; fond of frolicking, music, and dancing; among these he acted the part of the fiddler."

On June 22, 1809, a young Philadelphian named Sarah Thomson departed the city by ferry and stage for Tuckerton in the company of other family members and strangers. Nine in all boarded the stage: the rear luggage pocket "was stuffed full of bags, banboxes, bags without number, and one poor old man about 80 years of age." The stage stopped in Haddonfield and then Evesham (Marlton) for a meal, spent the night at the tavern at Quaker Bridge, and arrived in Tuckerton in time for dinner on June 23rd. Two days later, Sarah attended her first of several dances. On June 27th, she recorded, "Introduced to some fine girls in the evening, had a dance, enjoyed myself very much." On July 4th, after commemorating the day, Sarah "Had a dance in the evening. Eliza looked beautiful and danced till 12 o'clock. Had plenty of cherry pie." On August 10th, Sarah

> Went after a fiddler but the man's wife would not let him come. All really mad, had a great notion to go and tie the woman up and fetch the husband off. Concluded to dance by our own music. Started for home at nine, kept it up a dancing until 11 o'clock.

Moving forward through the nineteenth century, the dancing craze exponentially grew, requiring the construction of open-air pavilions to accommodate the hordes of people who arrived to shake off their normal everyday sensibilities. The Greenwood Boarding House had such a dance floor. In late July 1845, Edmund Morris, the editor of *The Burlington Gazette*, had the opportunity to see first-hand the crowds that arrived at Greenwood, and at nearby Brown's Mills, to take every advantage of the amusements offered at these two recreational facilities, including dancing.

“Big Saturday” in the Pines

We have been wondering for the last four weeks, what in the world could be the meaning of some six to a dozen large four horse stages, crowded with passengers, driving daily through our streets from the wharf into the interior of the country. Besides the passengers aforesaid, we remarked great quantities of mammoth travelling trunks, guns, dogs, &c. together with an absurd collection of band-boxes, the latter generally in proportion to the number of female passengers. Multitudes of these things were piled on the stage top, where also, the driver was frequently perched, having been driven to a seat above, by the press of passengers below. On enquiring as to where this multitude of people could be going, some persons mentioned “Greenwood,” others said “Brown’s Mills”; but as neither of these places is marked down even on the latest edition of the map of New Jersey, we rested content with a very slender amount of information on the subject. A fortunate circumstance, however, has completely illuminated us as to the mysterious movements of these people.

On Saturday last, while seated at our desk, having just commenced an editorial article which we feel certain would have electrified our readers, but which they may very shortly look for, three good friends drove up to our office door, and invited us to make a fourth passenger in their projected trip to these identical places of Greenwood and Brown’s Mills. The thing was irresistible – we dropped the pen – and taking a seat with two aldermen and one judge, left behind us for a whole day, the plagues of proof sheets and of editorials.

After a ride of some two hours through the rich and highly cultivated country which lies back of Burlington, we drove up to the hotel door in Pemberton. This was nearly ten o’clock – yet already the whole world of New Jersey seemed moving. Carriage after carriage drove by, turning off at the road by the County House on their way to Greenwood and the Mills, and loaded with sprucely dressed beaux, with girls in white dresses, pink ribbons and green veils, who seemed not only to laugh, but to grow fat amid the clouds of dust which ever and anon rose up on either side of the road. These vehicles were of all descriptions, from the light trotting-sulkey down to the canvass covered farm wagon, the former carrying the fashionable buck of the township, the latter jammed with the man having a wife and thirteen children, all on their patient way to spend the day at Greenwood and the Mills. These symptoms of a great gathering were abundantly realised as we plunged into the tall pine forest which surrounded the Greenwood boarding house. Here we alighted, and securing our horses in the woods, began our observations on a succession of scenes which were entirely new to us.

Greenwood is a large shingle palace, standing solitary and alone, just in the edge of the Pines, about twenty miles from Burlington, at the termination of the Kinkora railroad. This road was built by a company for the purpose of bringing into market the vast quantities of pine timber which had long been comparatively valueless, owing to its distance from market. It commences on the Delaware below Bordentown, and stretches up into a body of magnificent timber, whose tall trunks rise up without a single limb to the height of thirty and forty feet. Much of this has been cut off and taken to market over the railroad, but thousands of acres yet remain untouched. The railroad, however, from causes we are not acquainted with, has proved a disastrous speculation, inasmuch as the benign agency of the sheriff has recently been called in to decide the question of ownership. The Greenwood House was built when speculation was busy in predicting the future increase of the place. Now, speculation being dead and buried, it is devoted to the entertainment of summer boarders from the large cities, who flock in crowds to breathe the healthful and hunger-breeding air of the Pines. A good table is kept by the proprietor, and numerous waiters are every thing, in the way of attention, that could be desired. Greenwood has now about sixty boarders, assembled from all parts of the adjoining states, who pass their time pleasantly enough, in conversation, eating, sleeping, bathing in a branch of the Rancocas near at hand, and – walking in the sand.

Leaving the house, you walk a hundred yards into the woods, where the peculiar tastes of Jerseymen are strikingly displayed. Here were two ten pin alleys, crowded with players and lookers on. Between them stood a long, roughly built shell of pine boards, used for dancing. The sound of the fiddle, and the shuffling of many feet, indicated that dancing had already begun; and such was the energy of the Jersey girls, that we were in continual alarm for the safety of their bustles. For aught we know they may be dancing at this very moment. In the woods surrounding these houses, we counted nearly sixty carriages! After dinner there was a general moving off to Brown's Mills, some three miles further, the road being clear white sand, winding over stumps and bushes, and presenting on either side, traces of the recent destructive fires which have traversed over these regions, coming within a quarter of a mile of Greenwood itself. But if Greenwood presented a lively scene, Brown's Mills exceeded it in every way. Here five times the number of visitors were assembled. The woods were fairly jammed with wagons of all kinds, probably two or three hundred being scattered about wherever there was an opening to tie the horses. Stalls, or perambulating pie carts, were stationed about in various quarters, at which poor oysters and worse gin were in incessant demand. At least ten to fifteen hundred visitors were on the ground, exclusive of the regular boarders at the two houses at the Mills. Here also were two ten pin alleys and two dancing houses – all built of the roughest boards in the roughest manner possible, and all crowded with players and dancers, the latter having barely room to exercise their legs among the shins of the admiring crowd which pressed around them on every side. Even the windows of these dancing rooms were packed with gaily dressed girls, looking on with absorbing interest on the scene, and drinking in with high relish, the strains of music which proceeded from the well worn fiddle strings of the great stimulator of the dance. The dancing was carried on with true republican independence. Some of the gentlemen danced in boots and hats, some without coats, and many of the girls with bonnets and veils.

The idea occurred to us (about dinner time), how was this enormous assemblage of people to be fed. So taking a turn in the rear of the kitchen, we noticed the most extensive gastronomic preparations. One group of four women were engaged exclusively in splitting a pile of chickens down the back, previous to bedevilling them. As the Romans counted the number of their enemies slain in battle, by the bushels of rings they gathered from their fingers, so did we estimate the quantity of dead poultry; for in one single pile we saw a bushel of gizzards. But ample preparations had been made: for it seems that this practice of assembling at these places has long been fashionable among Jerseymen, and the company was therefore expected. In July, after the harvest is fairly in, the farmers meet by common understanding, every Saturday in that month, to spend the day in the Pines. As the month advances, so the congregation increases, and the last Saturday is known as the "big Saturday." After that the company thins off. It happened, therefore, that we were witnesses of the orgies of the "big Saturday." Almost every part of the state was represented. There were whole families from Salem; trains of wagons from Monmouth; delegates from Trenton; bright faces from Camden; and the number of Burlington folks which we met at every turn, kept us in a state of continual surprise. Altogether, it was such a scene as we never before witnessed.

Browns Mill's has long be celebrated as a summer retreat. There are now about one hundred boarders at the two houses. They constitute a highly respectable community; and though drawn from several distant States, yet the society enjoyed among them is singularly agreeable, in which intelligence, refined manners, and a disposition to be sociable and pleasant with each other, mingled with the charms of female society, renders this solitary dwelling place in the Pines a most delightful summer resort. The air of the Pines – the water – the absence from the perplexities of business – the perfect relaxation of the mind – added to the good fare and polite attention of the hosts – are found to be highly beneficial to the inmates. They of course have no connection with the swarms of "big Saturday" visitors; but on these great occasions quietly yield the ground for them, and from the loop holes of their retreat look on with amazement at the scenes presented by this great assemblage.

As night approached, we left on our homeward journey: but we understand the evening scene is much more lively than that during the day. Fires are then lighted up on platforms raised some ten feet from the ground, in various places through the woods, and dancing rages with a perfect furor. So great is this passion for dancing, that as we stopped at Wrightstown on our way home, we found the same amusement carried on at both the public houses there. In one of them, there was dancing in three rooms at the same time, all to the sound of one fiddle; now and then a girl was carried out, exhausted by the heat and exertion, but a fresh hand supplied her place, and the sport went on without interruption. In addition to this, a fight sprung up in the bar-room, but was speedily suppressed. Finally the night was pitch dark and rainy. Several wagons were upset in the road, the drivers being unable to discern the track: and from what we saw of these upsets, we are quite sure that some of the girls do not believe a harvest home in the Pines is what it has been cracked up to be.

Our own opinion is, that a deplorable school of morals is opened by these annual gatherings. As multitudes of young men and girls participate in them, we can readily understand how fatal they must be to the temperance, sobriety, and chastity, of some who go into them, even with the best intentions.

Edmund Morris, *The Burlington Gazette*, August 1, 1845.

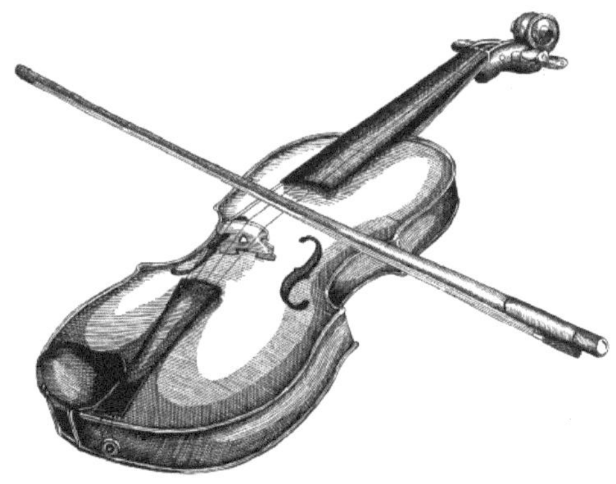

The Musical Tradition

The origins of music in the Pines, like the origins of dancing and storytelling, are untraceable. Early settlers, chiefly from the British Isles, brought their musical traditions to the area, and passed them from one generation to the next. In the late 1930s, Frelen C. Bozarth of Hainesport, Burlington County, an accomplished singer, reminisced about gatherings during his youth in the 1870s. After dinner his father would entertain family and neighbors with his repertoire of folk songs; young Frelen would sit off to the side and learn. The social aspects of music and song so evident in religious settings remained strong within secular family and community life.

Albert Music Hall

Joe and George Albert carried the musical tradition of the Pines into the second half of the twentieth century by hosting weekly gatherings at their hunting cabin, Home Place, in rural Ocean County. These gatherings grew over time from a few friends passing the time picking songs to larger community events that gained the attention of local media. When George Albert died in 1973, the music stopped at Home Place. But within months in 1974 a big bare room at the Waretown Auction Building was rented and dubbed Albert Hall, and the Pinelands Cultural Society formed to keep the Piney music tradition unbroken. Today's hall dates to 1996 as a stand-alone building with a smaller building to its side known as the Pickin' Shed. In the Shed, after the evening's performances are through, pro and amateur sit side by side playing their instruments. Musicians enjoy themselves, passing the time but also the tradition.

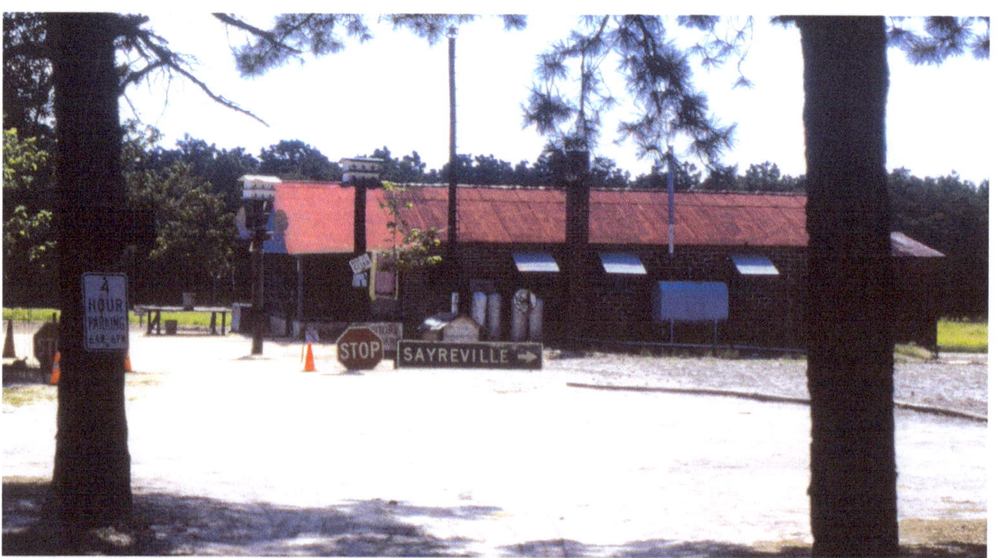

Home Place, Ocean County, 1978.

Home Place, the hunting cabin of Joe and George Albert, as it looked a few years after the music stopped. Photographer, Ted Gordon, August 18, 1978.

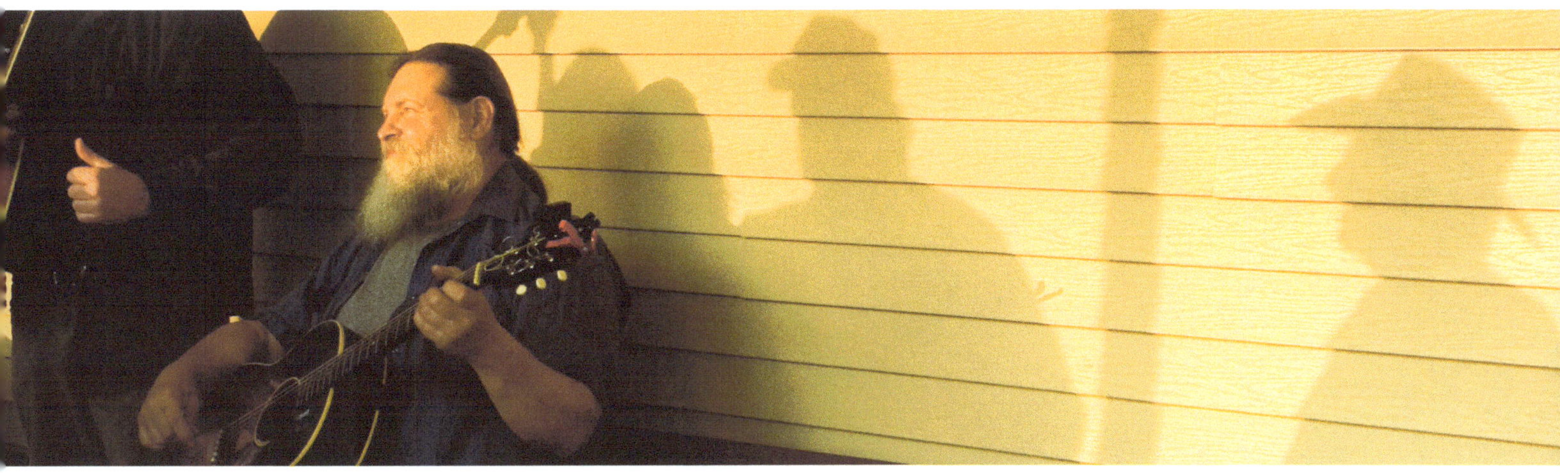

Porch Music, Janet Greco, 2007.

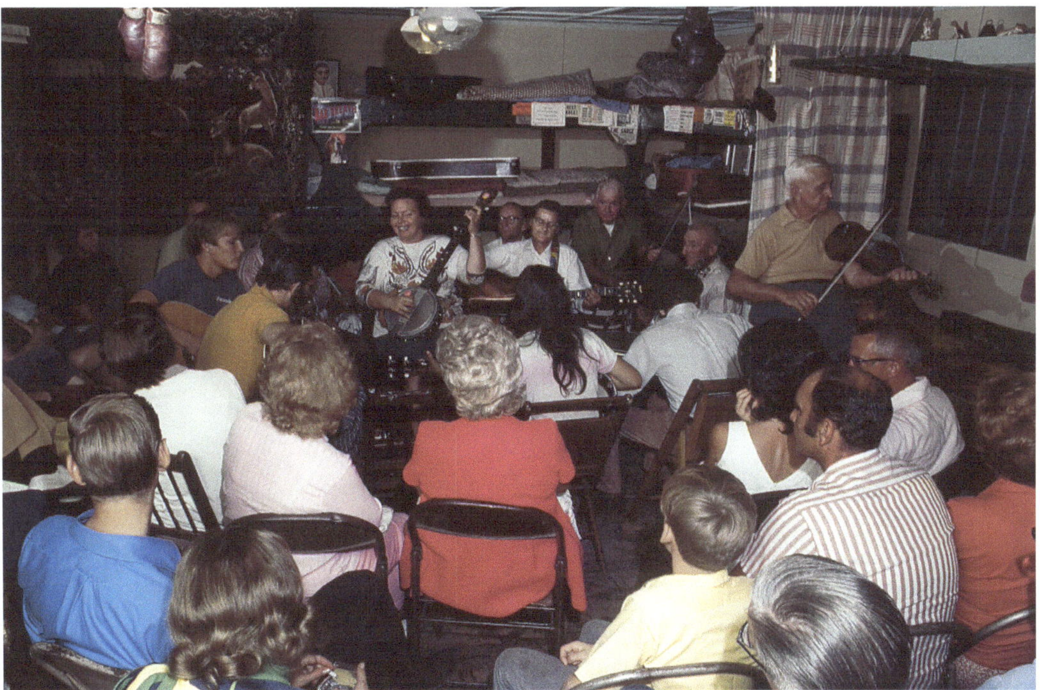

The Pineconers at Home Place, Ocean County, 1972.

The Pineconers playing at Home Place: Janice Sherwood on banjo, Gladys Eayre on rhythm guitar, Joe Albert on washtub (or gut bucket) base, Sammy Hunt on banjo, and George Albert on fiddle. Photographer, Ted Gordon, September, 1972.

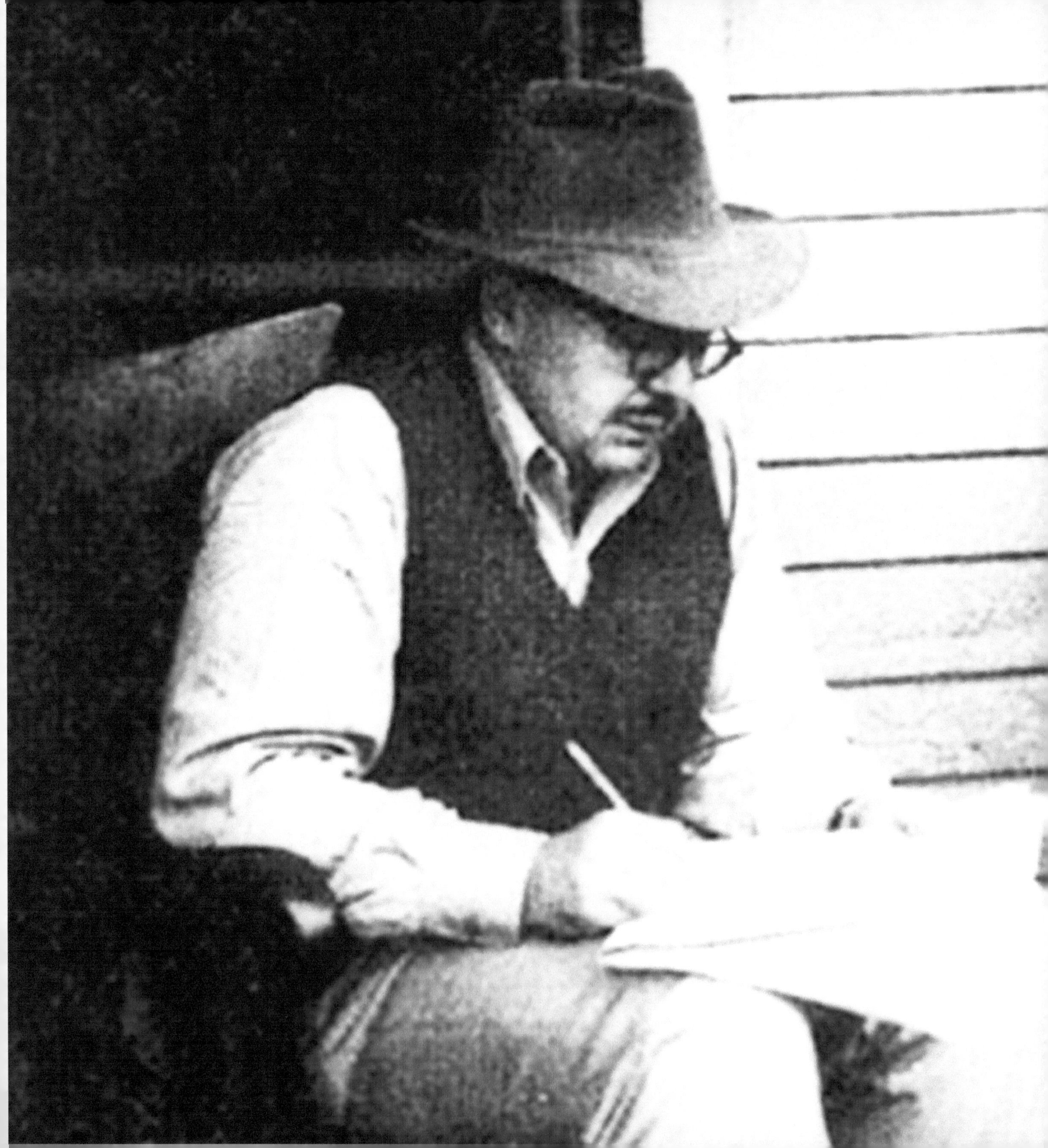

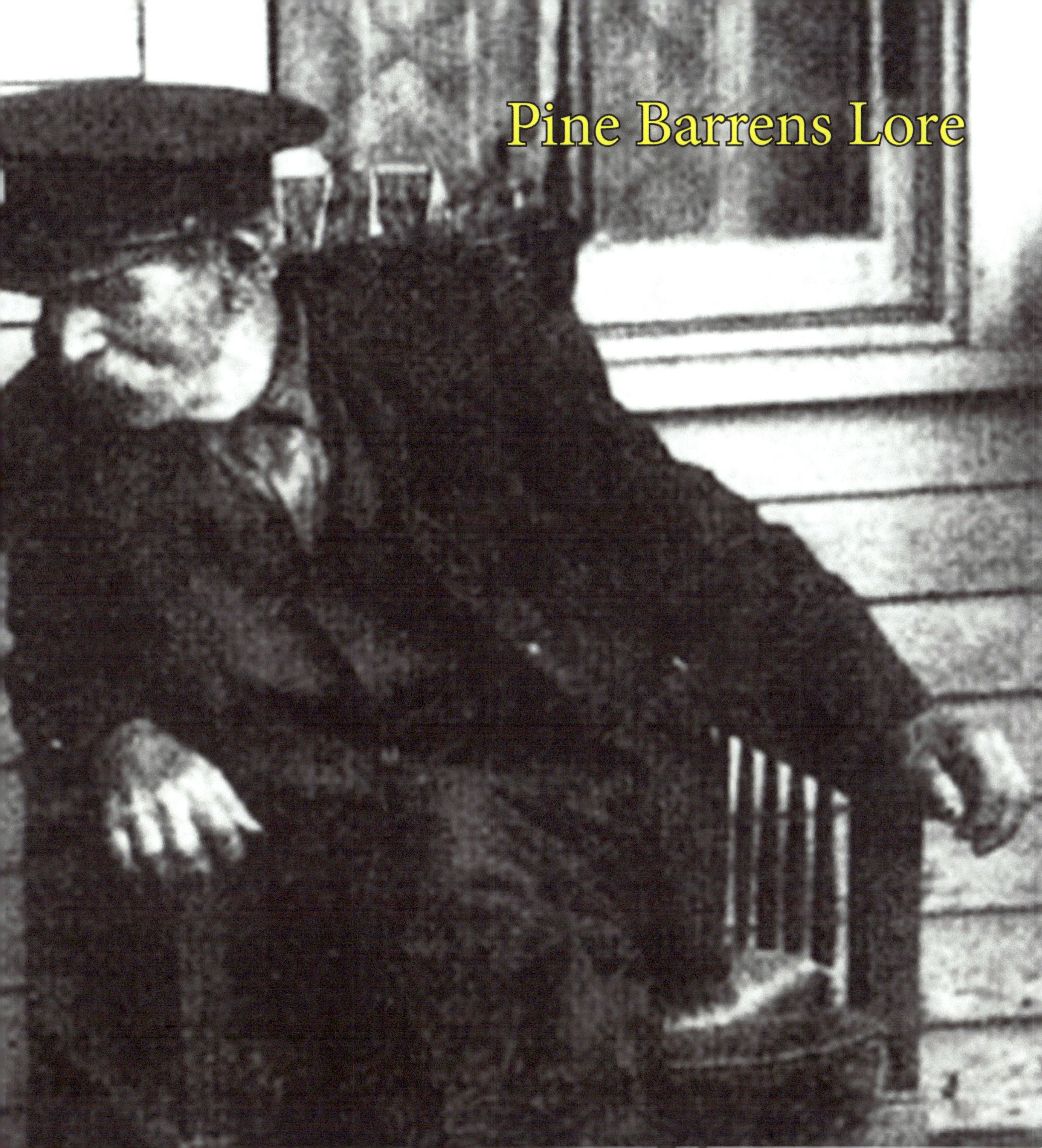
Pine Barrens Lore

Storytelling in the Pines

FROM AT LEAST the middle of the nineteenth century till the outbreak of the First World War, storytelling was a principal form of entertainment in the Pines. Children grew up listening to jokes, riddles, and tales told by parents, neighbors, and itinerant storytellers. One old-time resident, remembering these days, reported that in winter, "Pretty near every night would be story night or riddle night." Dancing and music might round out an evening, but it was the tale telling that became a pastime for many and an amusement to all.

A wide variety of stories were told in the Pines – tall tales, comic tales, and tales of the supernatural – and though nearly all had a semblance of factual truth, the tall and comic tales were understood to be "entertainment," not serious history. Stories of the supernatural, however, were more readily accepted and provide insight into common beliefs and superstitions of the time.

Some tales coalesced around figures in the community. Everyone seemed to have known Sammy Giberson the fiddler. Less people, but a distinct group, knew of Peggy Clevenger the witch. These were real people around whom supernatural stories developed. Other tales were ascribed to less readily identifiable people. Jerry Munyhun the wizard and the Leeds Devil were given names, but there is little proof that either existed except in the folklore of the Pines.

Collecting the Stories

STORIES were told at family gatherings, when visiting neighbors, at local taverns, hotels, and stores. They helped to pass the time at work. Woodcutters swapped stories during long, strenuous days in the woods. Colliers, keeping an eye on their smoldering charcoal pit, told stories late into the night. When a well-known storyteller came through an area, people gathered to listen. Competitions would break out to see who knew the most stories or the best. In some cases, men used storytelling to court women, weaving comical stories to win favor. But stories were chiefly told because the people enjoyed listening to them.

From the late 1930s through the early 1950s, folklorist Herbert Halpert collected the stories of the Pines from older residents. These stories, preserved in his transcriptions and recordings, remain one of the great treasures of the Pines. Here are brief samplings from the story cycles of Sammy Giberson, Peggy Clevenger and Jerry Munyhun, drawn with permission from Halpert's delightful *Folk Tales, Tall Tales, Trickster Tales and Legends of the Supernatural from the Pinelands of New Jersey* (2010).[1]

---

[1] The tales of Sammy Giberson, Peggy Clevenger (and generic witches), and Jerry Munyhun were recorded by Herbert Halpert in the Pines. So were Charles H. Grant's observations about the Bards of the Pines on the following page. All are used with the generous permissions of Halpert's literary executor, Nicholas Halpert, and The Edwin Mellen Press.

HERBERT HALPERT WITH INFORMANT, C. 1946.

(Preceding page) Anthropologist and folklorist Herbert Halpert (1911 – 2000) collected both folk songs and folk tales. During his productive career he worked in the Pine Barrens, but also in Pennsylvania, New York, Mississippi, West Virginia, Kentucky, Indiana, and Newfoundland.

The Bards of the Pines

"As a general thing there'd be someone there, a kind of worthless character – wouldn't be good for anything else just tell these stories. He'd get 'em off – some I s'pose he'd heared in his travels. These fellers just traveled around, didn't do much else. That's the way they lived. They'd come some'eres on a visit – they knowed everybody in the Pines – and stay in one place one night, next night go to some other little town – coalin', whoever'd put 'em up. In them days wasn't no such thing as a newspaper down in the Pines, and them fellers they carried the news from one place to another. Glad to see 'em, find out what was goin' on. They just made a business of it – get their livin' out of it. They'd tell stories; tell what was goin' on in other towns. Sometimes they'd stay one day, sometimes two or three. Hardly ever stayed in one place more than one night 'fraid of wearin' out their welcome."

Charles H. Grant, Hornerstown, Monmouth County, 1942

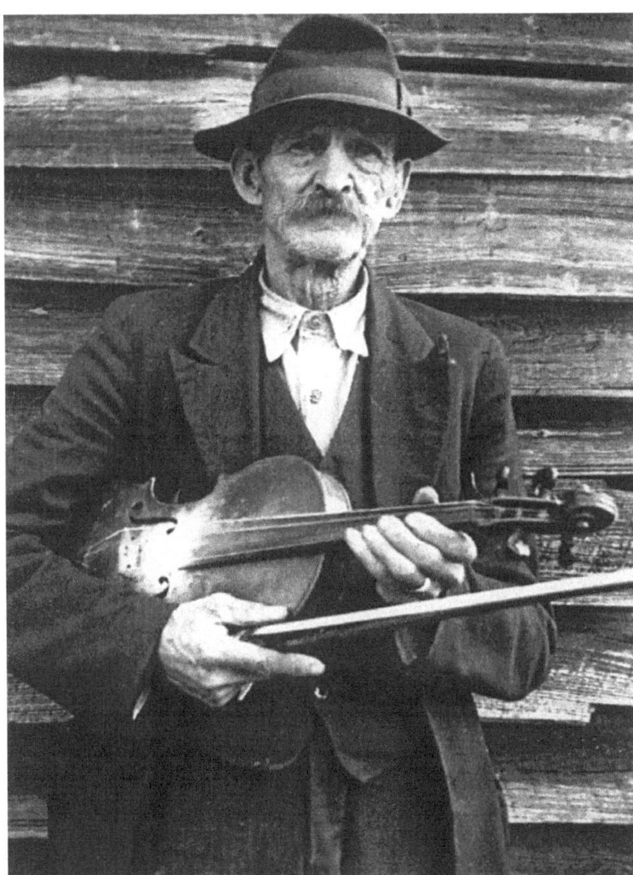

Elven Sweet, Magnolia, Burlington County, 1939.

Elven Sweet (1872 -1951) was a long-time resident of the Pines and prominent fiddler. As a boy he first heard these tales from his father. A favorite time for storytelling was at night after the day's work was done. This image is reproduced from a photo in Herbert Halpert's *Folk Tales*, The Edwin Mellen Press, 2010. Used by permission.

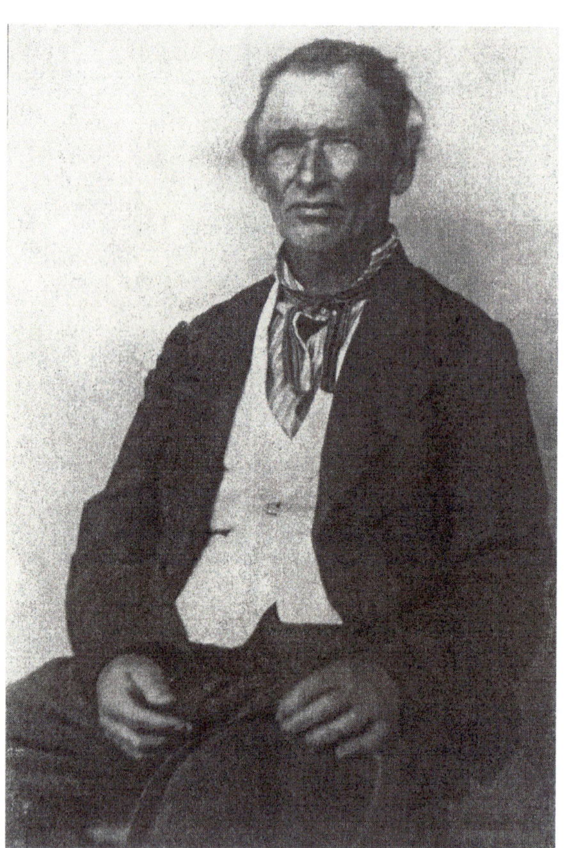

Sammy Buck Giberson, n.d.

"Old Sammy B. Giberson – they called him Old Sammy Buck for short . . . He didn't do nothin' else just travel from one hotel to the other and play his violin for them in hotels" (Charles H. Grant). This image is reproduced from an undated photo in Herbert Halpert's *Folk Tales*, The Edwin Mellen Press, 2010. Used by permission.

Sammy Giberson: Great Fiddle Player, Great Dancer

Sammy Giberson (1808 – 1884), famous throughout the Pines during the nineteenth century, was skilled enough as musician and dancer to make a living entertaining in the Pines. People traveled for miles to hear Sammy play the fiddle and watch him dance. His exploits became the focus of many tales retold by residents well into the twentieth century.

In 1946 Charles H. Grant described Sammy, whom he had met several times in his youth:

> He was about five foot six inches tall, weighed about 140 pounds, with a straight and well-built posture. He was a nicely dressed and distinguished looking man who made a common suit of clothes look fantastic. He played the fiddle with extraordinary skill, jig dancing at the same time. He would often play the fiddle behind his back as he danced. He was a good-humored man who had a smile for everyone and whom everyone liked.

The charismatic Sammy liked to tell stories about his travels and exploits. Those stories, and his well-attested skill at fiddle playing and dancing, gave birth to one of the great story cycles of the Pines.

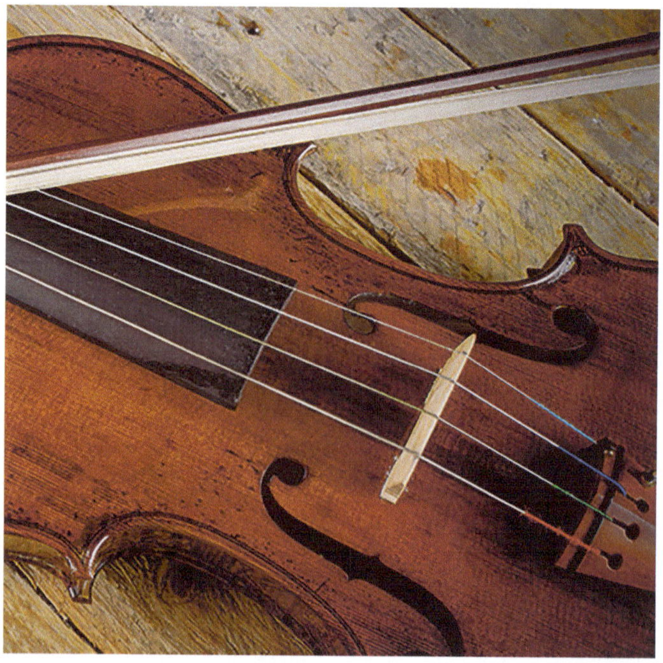

Tales of Sammy Giberson

"He was up to Philadelphia, and this feller took him in the theatre to dance, jig dance against this woman. She'd take a step, you know, and he'd take the same step that she did. And she took all she knew, and then Sammy went her one better. And she hit him 'longside the head and hopped off the stage. – He was good.

They offered him all kinds of money to stay there – play the violin and dance. He says, 'I'll go home and ask my folks about it. If they're willing, I'll come back.' But he didn't have to ask them anything. He was his own boss. He wouldn't leave the Pines – not to stay."

Frank H. Reynolds, Whiting, Ocean County, July 31, 1946

"Old Sammy Giberson he was playin' to a dance, and after he got done, he said he could beat the Devil. So – on his road home, he come to a bridge – he had to cross a bridge. And the Old Man appeared to him right on the bridge – that's the Devil hisself. 'I understand,' he said, 'you can beat the Devil playin' the fiddle.' 'Well,' Old Sammy says, 'that's what I said and that's what I meant.' So they went at it and, by God, old Sammy played every piece the Devil did, and the Devil played every one that he did, except one, and old Sammy heard the tune comin' through the air, and that's where he beat him. The Devil couldn't play it and old Sammy could. That's it, that's all of it."

Elven Sweet, Magnolia, Burlington County, June 23, 1940

"Sam Giberson he was a man that ketched the Air Tune. He heared it a-playin' in the air over his head – and he went right in the house and took his fiddle down and played the same tune.

And before you could ever get him to play that, you had to get him 'bout half drunk. And talk about a tune – it would bring the tears in your eyes."

Samuel Sprague, Cedar Run, Ocean County, June 25, 1941

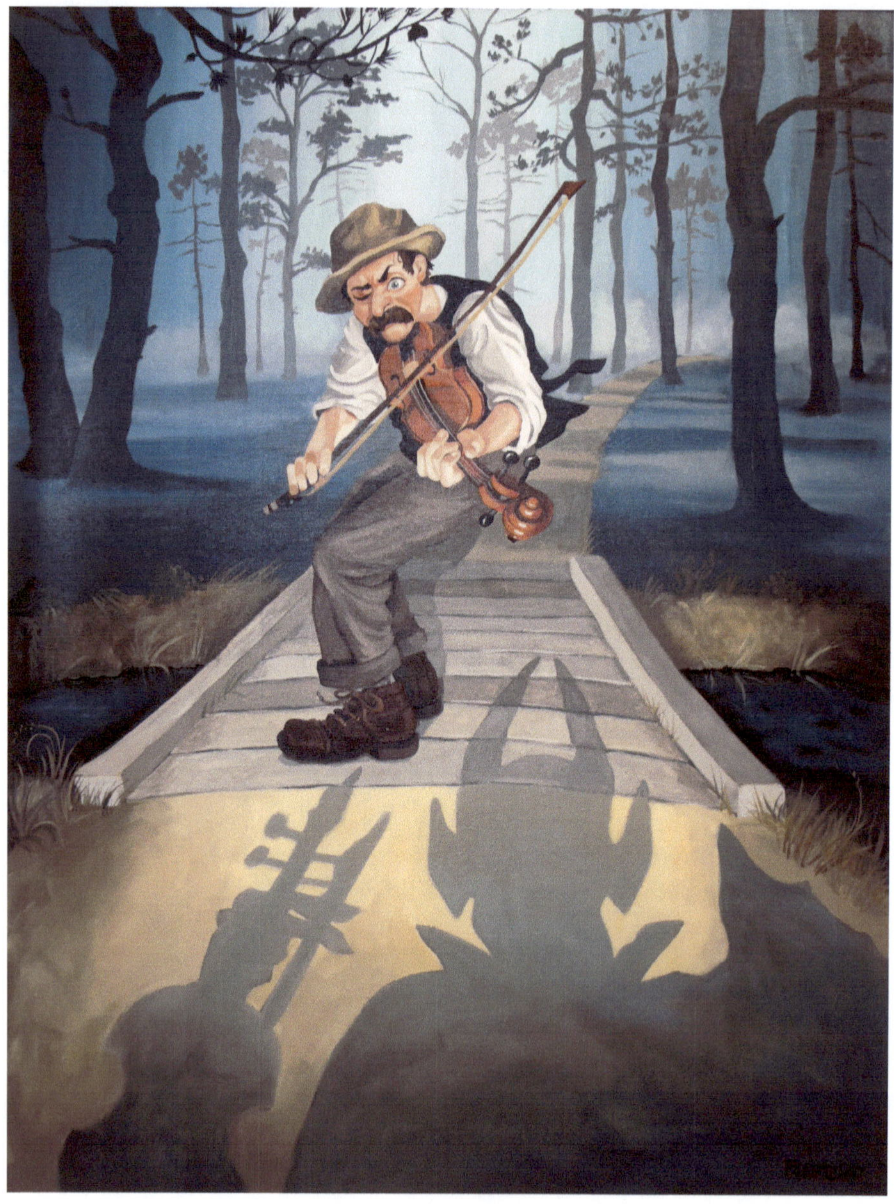

Sammy Giberson Meets the Jersey Devil, Nancy Palermo, 2015.

Acrylic on canvas

Sammy Giberson's Place, near Whiting, Ocean County, 1872.

Sammy Giberson's house was 2 miles southeast of Whiting. The E. W. Giberson up the road from Sammy was his son, Edward. Selection from *Topographical Map of Ocean Co.*, F. W. Beers, 1872.

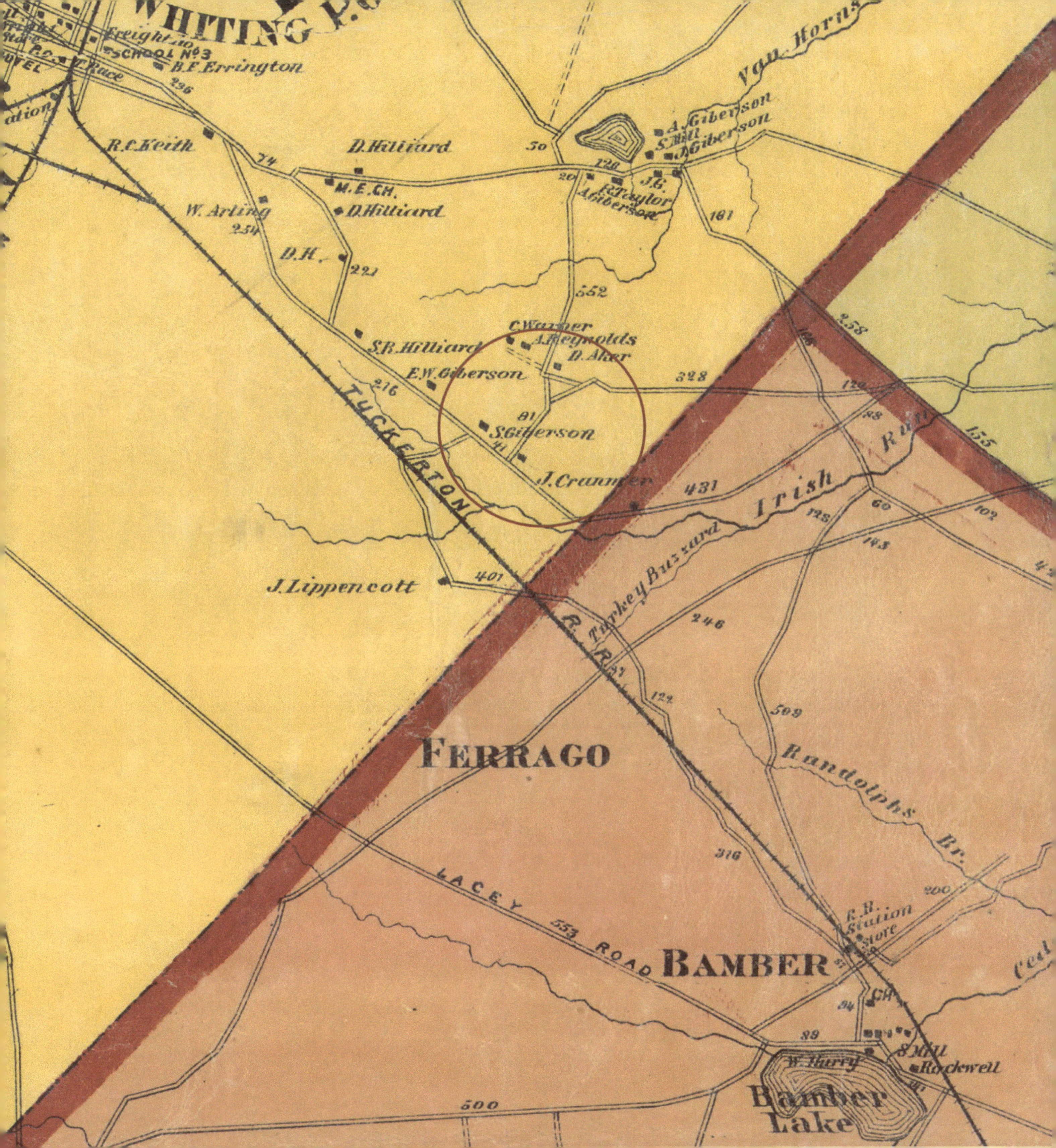

WHITING P.O.
Freight
SCHOOL No 3
B.F. Errington
R.C. Keith
D. Hilliard
M.E. CH.
D. Hilliard
W. Arling
D.H.
Van Horns
A. Giberson
S. Mill
J. Giberson
J.G.
F. Taylor
A. Giberson
C. Warner
A. Reynolds
D. Aker
S.B. Hilliard
E.W. Giberson
S. Giberson
J. Cranmer
J. Lippencott
TUCKERTON R. R.
Irish Run
Turkey Buzzard
FERRAGO
Randolphs Br.
LACEY 553 ROAD
BAMBER
R.R. Station
Store
CH.
S. Mill
W. Hurry
Rockwell
Bamber Lake

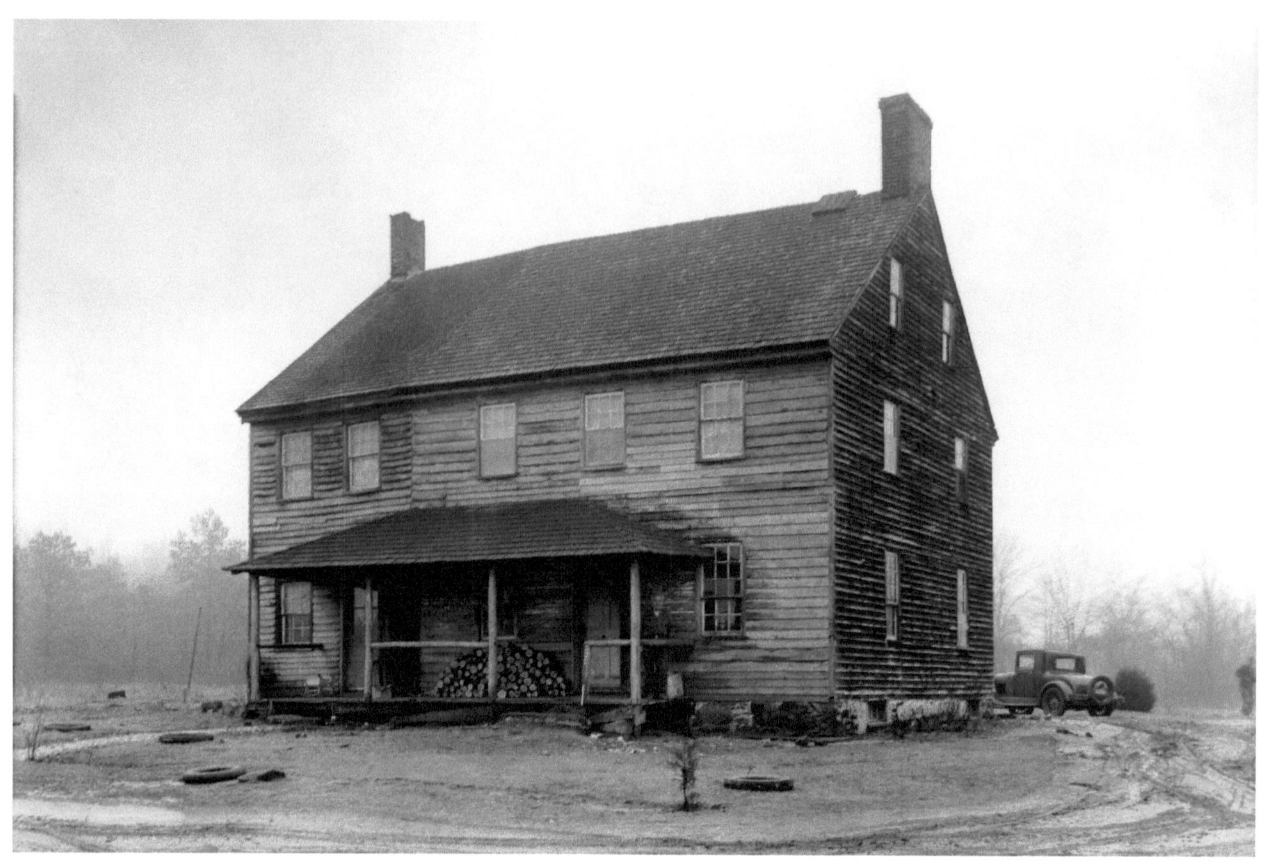

Cedar Bridge Tavern, Cedar Bridge, Ocean County, 1938.

The Cedar Bridge Tavern was about seven miles south of Sammy's house near Whiting. It is likely to have been a frequent location where he showcased his fiddle and dance skills. Nathaniel R. Ewan, photographer, January 22, 1938; from the Prints and Photographs Division, Library of Congress.

"I've heard the old fellows say that knew a lot of people played the violin, there never was anything like him; never heard anybody could play as good. And he could dance a jig with a glass of water on his head – and he wouldn't spill any of it either."

Frank H. Reynolds, Whiting, Ocean County, June 24, 1941

"They said when he died that fiddle they never could find."

Mrs. Betsy Bell, Colliers Mill, Ocean County, June 24, 1940

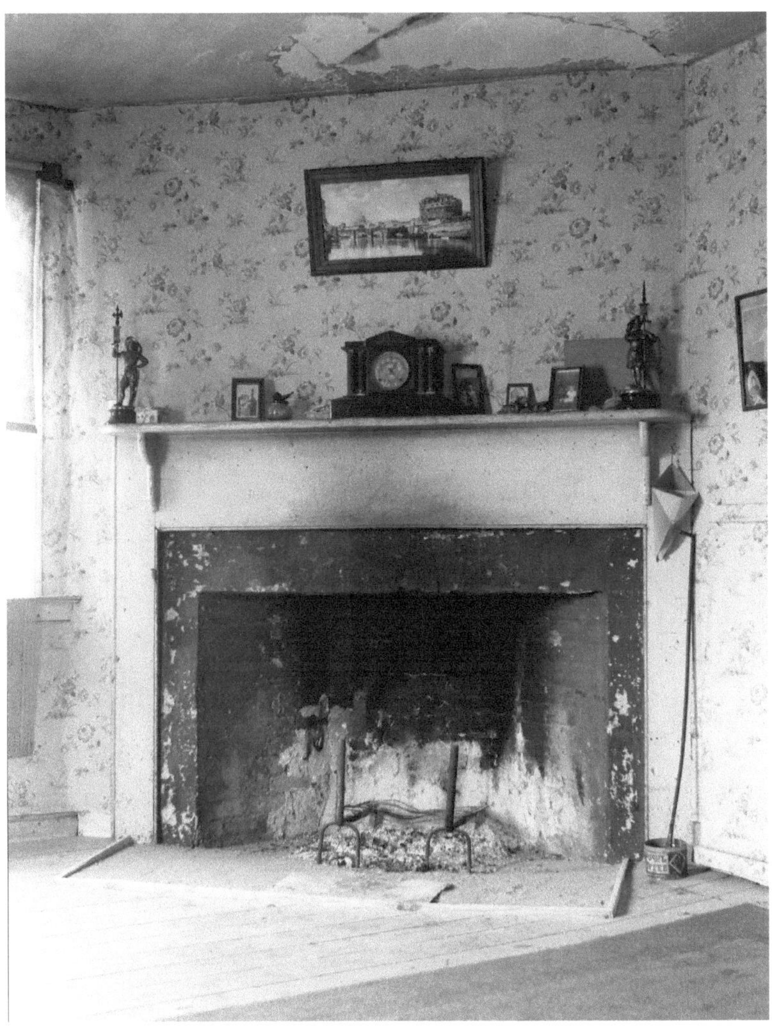

Living Room of the Cedar Bridge Tavern, Cedar Bridge, Ocean County, 1938.

At the date of this photograph, the Cedar Bridge Tavern was more than 120 years old; it was a homey, unassuming stopping place. The fire poker to the right is resting in a used tin of Boscul Coffee, a product of Camden-based William Scull & Co., importers of coffee from 1821 - 1960. Nathaniel R. Ewan, photographer, January 22, 1938; from the Prints and Photographs Division, Library of Congress.

Nathaniel R. Ewan

Local historian Nathaniel Rue Ewan was born on April 28, 1870 in Ewansville, Southampton Township, Burlington County. Nathaniel's father raised him in the family's cider and vinegar distillery business. In 1894, Nathaniel wedded Camden resident Ella L. Thomas and assumed control of the family distillery. Ewan's interest in local history began early in his life, and he gained great acclaim for his knowledge of Burlington County history. His local history prowess led to his work with the Historic American Building Survey during the Great Depression. Ewan retired from the distillery in 1936 and pursued a career in history, serving as president of the Burlington County Historical Society and curator, librarian, and treasurer of the Camden County Historical Society. Governor Edison appointed Ewan to the New Jersey Historic Sites Commission in November 1943. Ewan wrote many pamphlets, among them a work on early brickmaking. He died on January 10, 1961 at the Masonic Home in Burlington Township. His legacy lives on through his writings, photographs, and his scrapbook collection at the Burlington County Library, assembled in the old distillery account books.

Peggy Clevenger, the Witch of the Pines

WITCHES were a frequent subject of tales in the Pines, and Peggy Clevenger was the witch most often named. She could shape change into the form of animals, cast spells on her neighbors, and perpetrate evil in an assortment of ways. She was especially fond, it appears, of tormenting children:

> They'd get sick and wouldn't eat. She'd steal a lock of their hair when she was around. And she'd all the time borry [borrow]. If you didn't let her have anything, she couldn't get the best of you – so they said.
>
> Annie Goff, 1941

Peggy's husband, Bill, also had more than mortal abilities. The story goes that on his deathbed he made a promise to Peggy: If he landed in Hell after death and found it hot he would cause the family well to boil – and soon after his death, boil it did.

Witch tales at their core describe social outcasts – women on the margins of society who lived alone, who willingly cast spells against their neighbors, and who needed to be fended off with counter charms. People feared witches, but they were also fascinated by them. Mary Estelow Parker (b. 1879) admitted about Peggy, "I used to talk about her so much I dreamt about her." Peggy, of course, was particularly fascinating because she was real.

The Real Peggy Clevenger

MARGARET "PEGGY" CLEVENGER entered the world about 1786, the daughter of Thomas and Sarah Blake. She married William Dothey Clevenger during the first decade of the nineteenth century, probably in 1806 or 1807, based on the birth of presumably their first child, John R. Clevenger, about 1807. Two years later, the couple had Sarah Blake Clevenger, born December 27, 1810. Son Thomas Blake Clevenger was born circa 1818 and son Samuel Clevenger about 1825.

William and Peggy lived in a one-story cabin located within Pemberton Township, Burlington County, near Old Half Way, "situate on the Old Shore road, about half way between Mount Misery and Cedar Bridge." Bill died sometime between 1850 and 1857, leaving Peggy alone in the cabin. To earn extra money, she established a "jug tavern" in the cabin, selling liquor to travelers, local woodsmen and colliers. She became addicted to opiates, probably in the form of laudanum, and in all likelihood used the money raised through the sale of liquor to satisfy her habit.

In December 1857, fire consumed her cabin with her inside. Those who came to investigate only found her skull and ribs amid the ashes. Juliustown undertaker Joel Mount arranged to have the scant remains interred in Wrightstown at the Methodist Episcopal Church, the only burial ground in town.

Most folk tales contain a modicum of truth. It is likely that the derangement Peggy suffered from her addiction to opiates, exacerbated by the effects of a hard life and old age, made her babble and speak in ways that others thought to be crazy – even thought to be the behavior of a witch. From these circumstances tall tales arose, but in actuality it appears Mrs. Clevenger was just a woman who married, raised a family, and lived out in the woods until her husband died. Then, she continued her life alone, using opiates and liquor to numb her grief and the effects of a hard life in the Pines, until fire claimed the old woman's life.

A TERRIBLE AFFAIR

We learn that the dwelling of Mrs. Clevenger, situate on the Old Shore road, about half way between Mount Misery and Cedar Bridge, was destroyed by fire, one night last week, and sad to relate, Mrs. C. perished in the flames. She was a very old lady, lived entirely alone, and was known to travelers as "Old Mother Clevenger." – Her residence was a one-story Cabin, and was well known to persons in the habit of travelling the road.

Since the above was in type, we learn that it is generally believed the old lady was murdered, and her cabin then set on fire. The Coalings are near her residence, and those employed in them, frequently went there to obtain liquor, she being in the habit of keeping some for travelers. – Several times, recently, upon refusing it to persons who were intoxicated, she has been severely beaten.

She was known to be in possession of some money, and it is thought that the desire to get hold of it, in connection with the hatred existing against her, in refusing to supply the drunken brutes at the Coalings with liquor, was the cause of her sad and terrible death. The ruins were examined, but her skull and some few of her bones were found. She was about 80 years old. A night or two previous to the fire, her hogs were poisoned and her horse's throat was cut. We trust that the affair may be thoroughly investigated and the villains brought to justice.

New Jersey Mirror, December 10, 1857:3

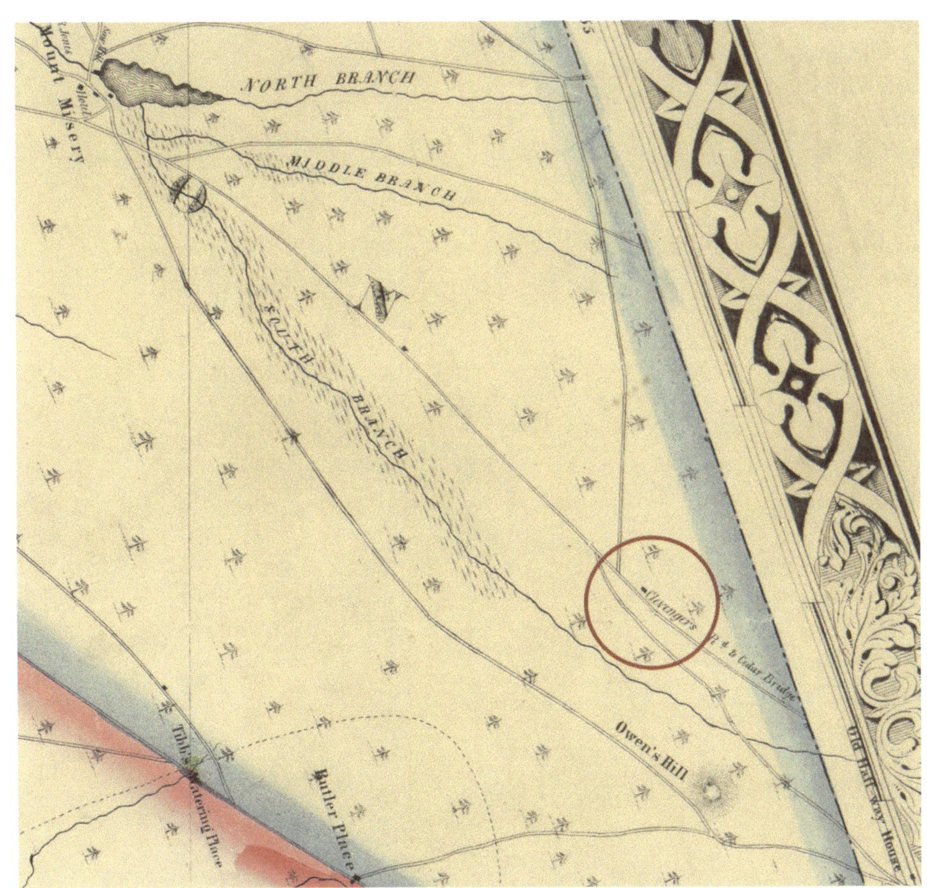

Clevenger's Place, Pemberton Township, Burlington County, 1849.

Peggy Clevenger's home is identified on this map about 5 miles southeast of Hanover Furnace on the road to Mount Misery, not far from the Old Half Way Tavern. Selection from *Map of Burlington County*, Smith & Wistar, 1849.

THE FIRE IN THE PINES

We are indebted to our friend, Joseph W. Cox, of Hanover Furnace, for the following correct account of the "Terrible Calamity" in the Pines, mentioned in our paper of last week. It will be seen that the intelligence we received was greatly exaggerated. We gave it as we received it, from persons who passed through the neighborhood, and was believed by them to be as near the truth as could be obtained at the time.

It gives us pleasure to learn that it is generally believed no person was implicated in the calamity, but that the fire was entirely an accident:

Mr. Carr – Dear Sir:—Permit me to correct you in some of the statements in your paper with regard to the death of Mrs. Clevenger. The parties to whom you refer being in my employ, on the Hanover Tract, I deem it but justice to them to send you more correct information with reference to the affair.

I have made as thorough an investigation as I could, and from the facts I gather from her children and others who were present, I am fully satisfied that no one was implicated in the matter – but that the fire originated from the chimney or fire-place.

The old lady was in the habit of providing a bountiful supply of fuel, and piling it up near the fire, when about retiring for the night. She was Providentially saved from the same calamity two weeks previous. A person living near, having occasion to apply for her stable to accommodate a friend's horse, went there after she had retired, and on entering the house, discovered the wood, contiguous to the fire-place, ignited, and in a short time the house would have been in flames.

And again, the old lady had, the day previous to the fire, provided herself with a quantity of opium, to the use of which she was much addicted. When under the influence of opium, she was frequently much deranged. From this cause, most probably, the fire took place.

The persons employed by me, this year, do not make use of liquor in the Coaling. She has not sold any liquor to my hands the present season, nor have they applied for any. The two head colliers do not use it at all themselves and they will not employ a drinking man.

Your paper states that the old lady was known to have had some money. The testimony of her son-in law, who brought her from Forked River, the day previous, was that she had no money, or not exceeding two or three cents, which were found with the clasp of her purse, amidst the ruins.

The poisoning of her hogs is misrepresented, also. She had a hog or pig given her last spring, but it died in a short time. Since then she has not had any hogs. – With reference to her horse, no person could inform me whether his throat was cut or not, and he was so decayed when I was there that it could not be ascertained. If it was the case, however, it was done by some one of her own family, to relieve the old horse from his misery, for they had to lift him up every morning.

The remains of the old lady, which consisted of the chest and skull, and what bones they could gather from the ruins, were taken charge of by the undertaker from Juliustown, Joel Mount, who accompanied me, and were properly interred at Wrightstown.

Your, &c,. J.W. COX.
Hanover Furnace, Dec. 12, 1857.

New Jersey Mirror December 17, 1857:3

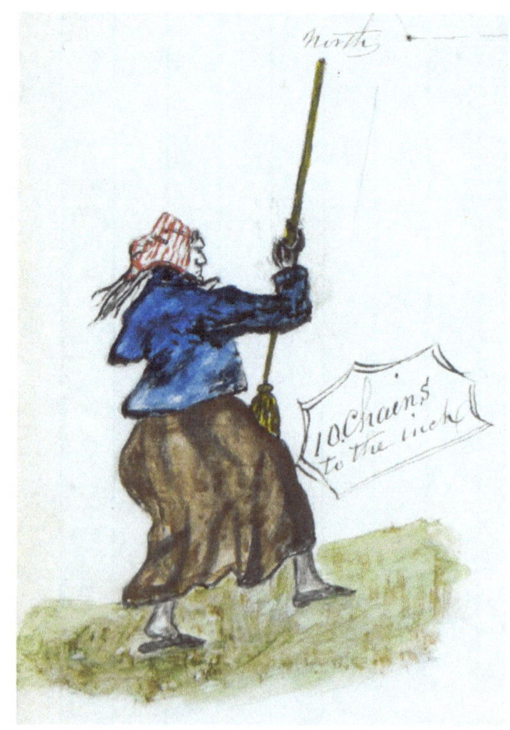

Peggy Clevenger Stories

"The boys was out a huntin' one day around Peggy Clevenger's house and this here rabbit come out, and the dog pretty near catched this rabbit. Then it went for Peggy's house just as hard as it could go. This rabbit jumped right in the window – and there was Peggy. Soon as the rabbit jumped in the window, there she was."

Mrs. Charles Parker, New Lisbon, Burlington County, June 18, 1941

"One time she bewitched a feller, and he was pretty angry and said he was gonna kill her. He drawed her picture, and then he cut up silver money and loaded his gun with this silver money. – They say that's only thing you can kill a witch with. – He aimed at this picture, and when he shot this picture, he shot it in the hand. And she come runnin' over to her neighbor with her hand all done up – all mangled – and she told the people that the hog had got her hand in its mouth and crunched it up. And this feller says, 'The old devil,' he says, 'if I'd only got her heart instead of her hand, I'd fix her.' "

Mrs. Annie Goff, Waretown, Ocean County, June 25, 1941

"This woman, her name was Alice – she was aunt by marriage – she had spells of some kind and she did out and run just like a horse. And they said she was crazy, but some person or other said she was bewitched – and she said something or other about she was gonna break the spell. And she went up on a hill and took these pins and drew her picture – old Peggy's picture – as near as she could on the sand, and stuck the pins into it. And that's the way she broke the spell and she didn't have the spells after that."

Mrs. Charles Parker, New Lisbon, Burlington County, June 18, 1941

Witch as Map Compass, Manuscript Map, undated.

Clever north arrow from a map of wood lots near Batsto. Undated, but map depicts two bridges through Mordicai's Swamp, including one for the "new straight road." Samuel L. Southard Collection, Firestone Library, Manuscript Division, Princeton University.

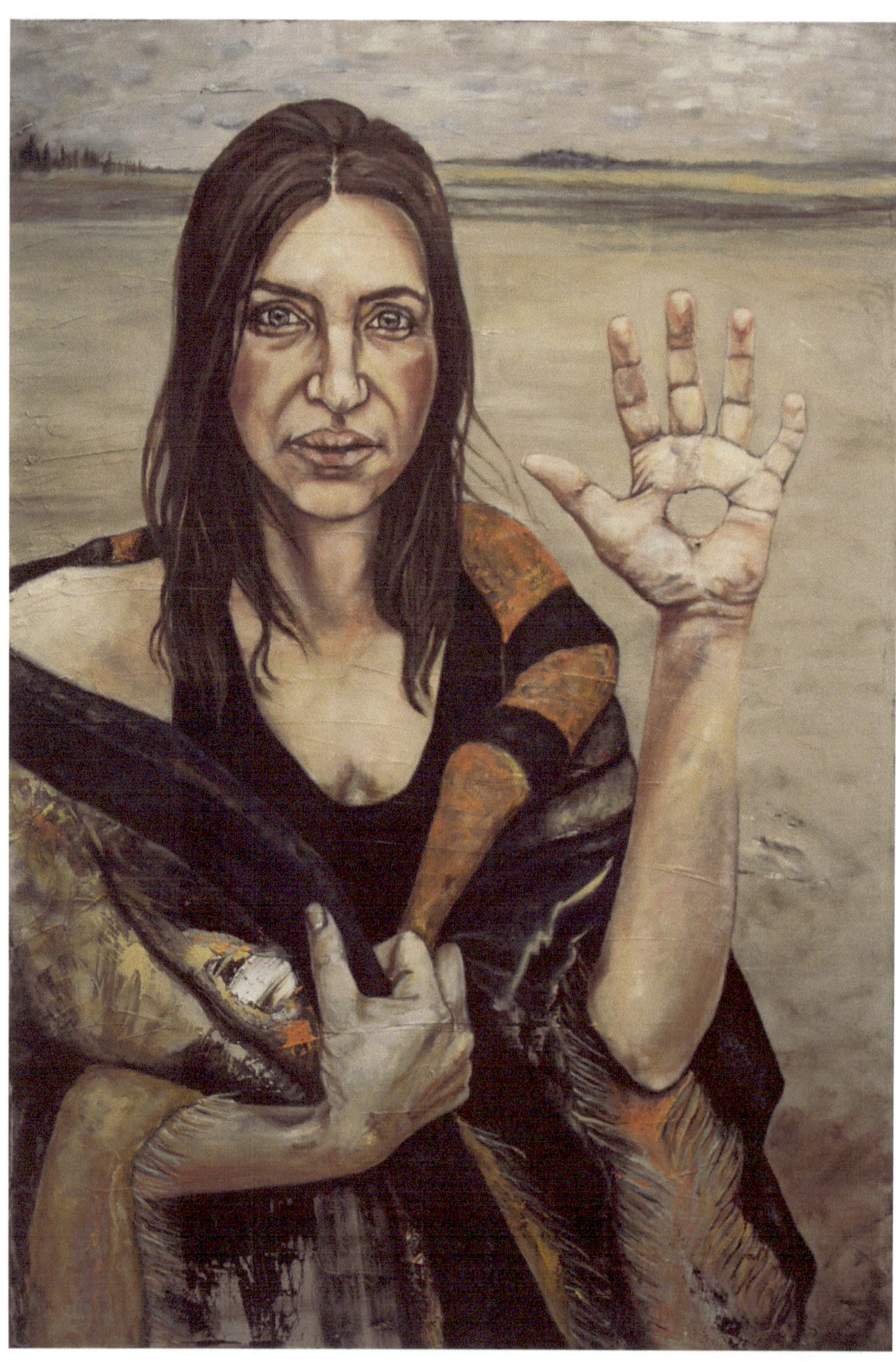

Peggy Clevenger, Witch of the Pines, Sara Gendlek, 2015.

Oil on canvas

Generic Witch Stories

"I was living up at the Four Mile. One morning Mike Genone come to me and said he couldn't work his horse. Wanted mine. I asked him what was the matter with his'n, and he said the witches had been ridin' him all night, and he was tired out. For proof of that he took me out to the stable and showed me that the horse had his tail platted – braided, and his mane too. He was scared about it."

Charles H. Grant, New Egypt, Ocean County, January 23, 1940

"Charlie's mother, Matilda Grant, was blind for seven years, and they said it was a witch put the spell on her. – She told me herself. – She put a sack of salt over each door and window, and she said at a certain time the doors all flew open and the windows rattled and banged. She says they made a terrible noise. And she got better after that, and it wasn't long before she could see out of one eye. She thought she broke the spell."

Mrs. Charles H. Grant, New Egypt, Ocean County, January 23, 1940

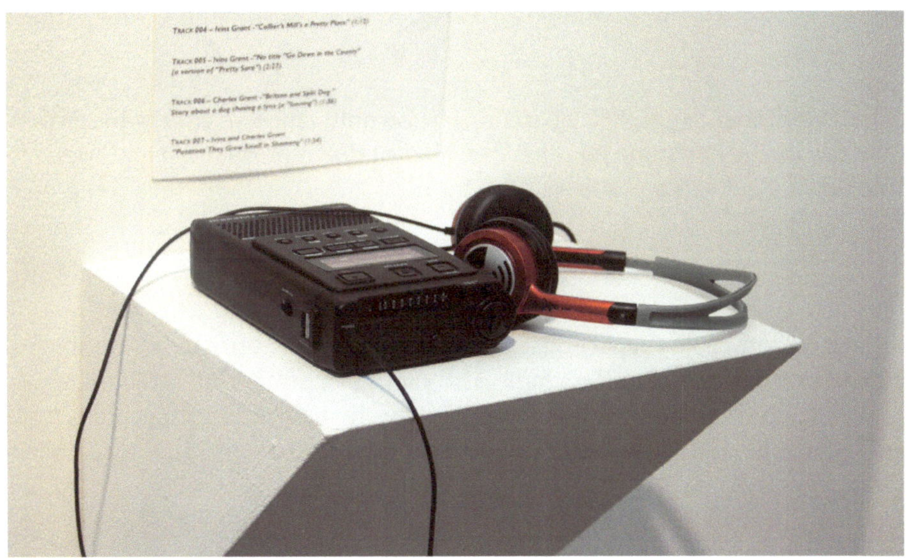

Jerry Munyhun: Wizard of the Pines

Stories told about Jerry Munyhun form the largest group of tales that survive from the heyday of storytelling in the Pines. According to Herbert Halpert, they are the earliest robust story cycle of wizard or magician lore in America. Munyhun's origins are unclear – some describe him as descended from Hessian refugees in the Pines, others identify him as an Irishman or an escaped slave. None of the storytellers had met him, though some believed that their grandparents had done so.

What is clear is that Jerry Munyhun was a wizard whose magic bordered on ventriloquism, illusionism, and sleight of hand and who insisted on having things his way. He enjoyed the discomfort or embarrassment of others. On occasion Old Jerry would use his magic in helpful ways, but most often he used it to selfish and even spiteful ends.

Jerry Munyhun Stories

"Said Jerry set there on Harry Shumar's store porch at Browns Mills, and Harry he had this little dog. These two girls was comin' down the path and this little dog was a-barkin' at 'em. The girls was a-playin' with the dog and said, 'Whose little black dog are you?' The dog said, 'I'm Harry Shumar's little black dog.' Jerry sat there on the porch laughin' at them. Frightened the girls though."

Mrs. Mary Parks, Retreat, Burlington County, June 26, 1940

"They had to cut timber to get their charcoal. Jerry would take two axes with him, and start one on one side the tree and one on the other. He'd sit down on a stump and watch the axes cut the tree down. That was a pretty easy job for him. Wasn't anybody else could do it."

Frank L. Harker, Browns Mills, Burlington County, June 17, 1941

"They was a-movin' this old furnace that they used at Hanover Furnace. And they had six mules hitched to it comin' up a little grade. And they got stuck with it – the mules couldn't pull it. And Jerry come along with this rooster under his arm and he told them to onhitch these mules – take 'em out of the way. And he jest tied this rooster to the cap o' the tongue and hollered, 'Shoo!' And away she went right up the hill."

Tom Test, Browns Mills, Burlington County, December 20, 1940

"Them days, you know, they used to have big set-outs like fox chases over here to Cookstown, and Jerry used to go there, and o' course, he wanted to be nice to his friends, and he would call 'em up and treat 'em. And he'd pay for the drinks, and after they'd gone out, they'd go to the drawer and there'd be full of clamshells."

Tom Test, Browns Mills, Burlington County, December 20, 1940

"Jerry Munyhun – this was old Hanover Furnace where he done these tricks. The Joneses run the place, and he used to hang around there – too. The Joneses were goin' away, had their matched team hitched to the post, and they was dressin', getting' ready to go away. He asked them for money – he just wanted money to sport around with. They refused him. And then when they come out to go away, their team was in the pond – in Hanover Lake. They had the men that worked for them on the place tryin' to get them out.

And he told the Joneses if they'd give him the money, he'd get 'em out. And when they paid him, the horses was tied to the post, right where they had left them. And when they examined the pond, the men was workin' at two old logs in the pond."

Albert Foulkes, near Whitesbog, Burlington County, June 24, 1940

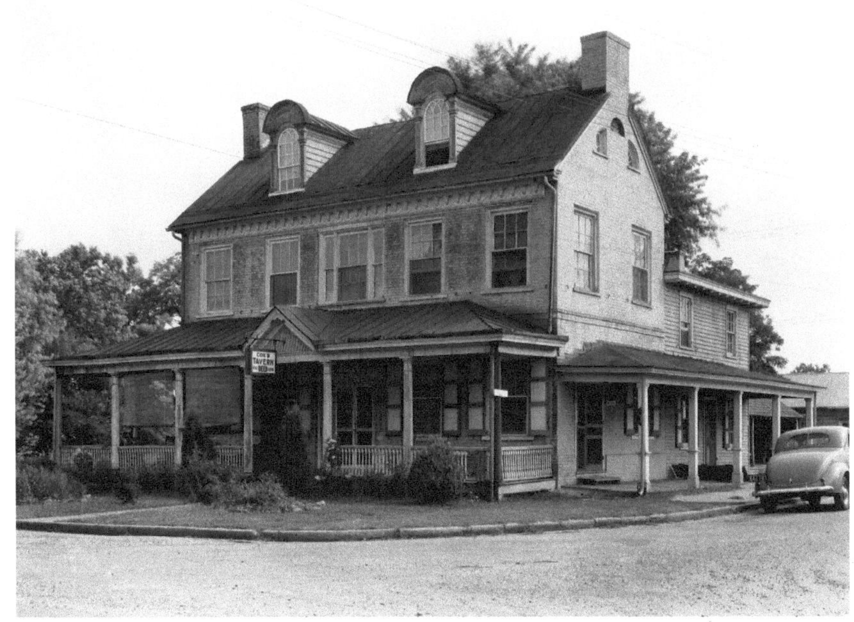

Cookstown Tavern, Main Street & Bunting Bridge Road, Cookstown, Burlington County, 1938.

The Cookstown Tavern was erected c. 1825. Nathaniel R. Ewan, photographer, September 7, 1938; from the Prints and Photographs Division, Library of Congress.

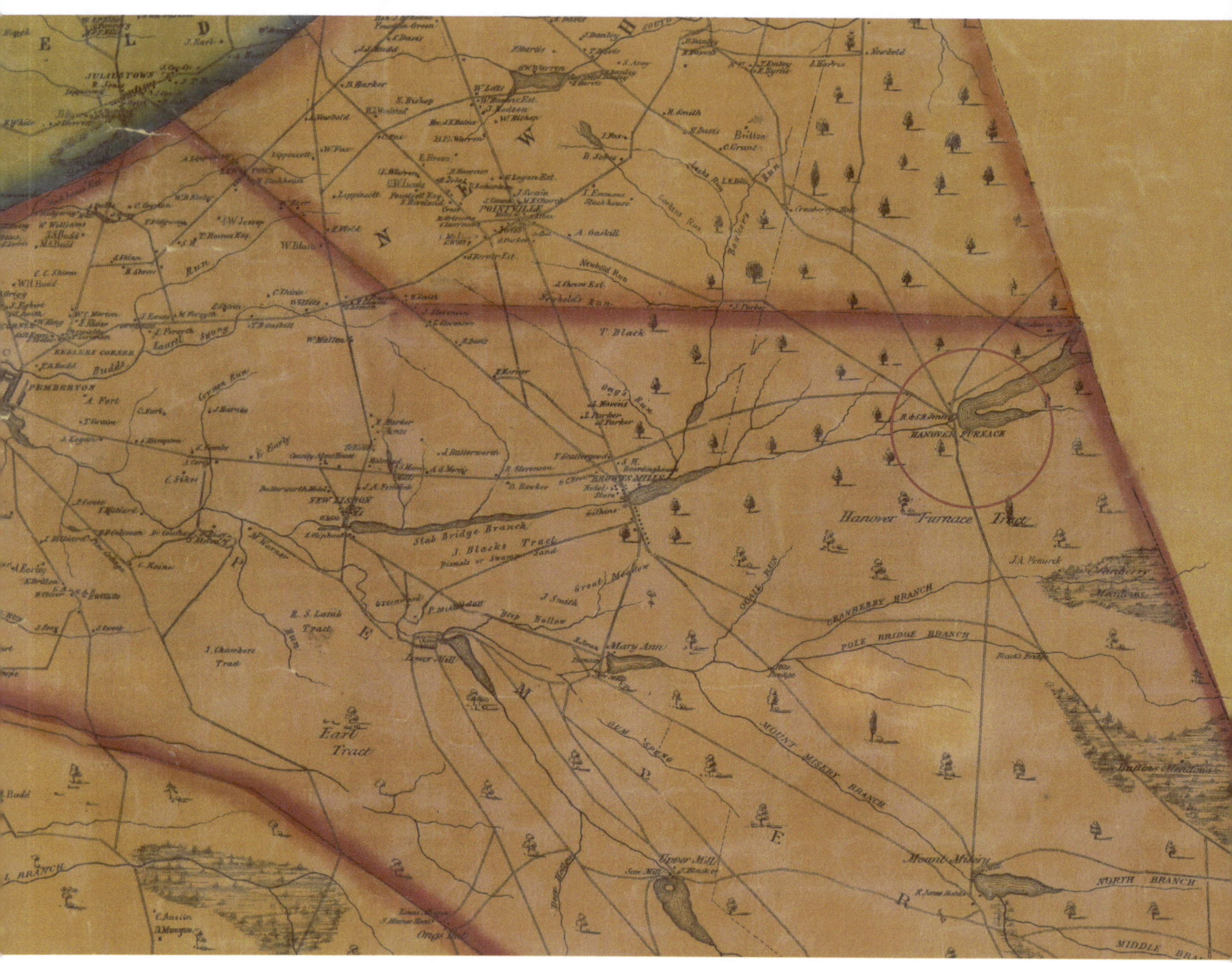

Pemberton, New Lisbon, Browns Mills, Hanover Furnace Area, Burlington County, 1859.

Note at the right R. & S. H. Jones are named at Hanover Furnace, the family that Jerry Munyhun bedeviled on more than one occasion. In the center you can see the hotel and boarding house at Browns Mills and to the left across the "Dismals or Swamp Sand," Greenwood. Selection from *New Map of Burlington County*, Wm. Parry, Geo. Sykes & F. W. Earl, 1859.

The Blue Hole

Any Piney knows not to expect crystal clear depths when it comes to bodies of water in the Pine Barrens. The norm is swampland and brown-tinted cedar water. So why is the Blue Hole of Winslow Township in Camden County – a body of water approximately seventy feet across – filled with still, beautiful, and clear (if not blue) water? And why do so many legends swirl around it?

Folklorist Henry Beck recorded locals telling stories of water that is ice cold and bottomless, of strong, swirling currents, of certain death by drowning or the more foreboding likelihood that the Jersey Devil will pull unsuspecting swimmers to its watery lair.

> "My father and others warned me and the boys I went around with not to hang around that bottomless pit. They used to say things about cramps but they meant more than that. It was as if there was something about that pool that had them scared, something they didn't want to understand, something that gave them the shakes."[1]
>
> Dave Dixon to Henry Charlton Beck, c. 1937

> "I remember John I. Brown . . . he was a big, heavy-set man. He laughed at their warnings one day and swam out to the middle. Just as he got there he let out a shout. We thought he was fooling, at first – he was a great one to cut up. Then we saw that he was going down for the last time. They managed to fish him out and he came to after they rolled him all over the place and bounced him up and down. He said the devil reached up and got him from deep in the pool."
>
> Dave Dixon to Henry Charlton Beck

> Mr. Anlage said that some years ago a party of scientists visited the Blue Hole, with the purpose of coming back with an explanation for it. They obtained a huge weight and a long line of cable. The weight was dropped in the middle of the pool and it kept going down until all the cable was paid out. More cable was obtained and the same thing happened again. There was no explanation, as far as we have been able to discover.
>
> Henry Charlton Beck

[1] This and the following selections are drawn from Henry Charlton Beck, *More Forgotten Towns of Southern New Jersey* (E. P. Dutton & Co, 1937).

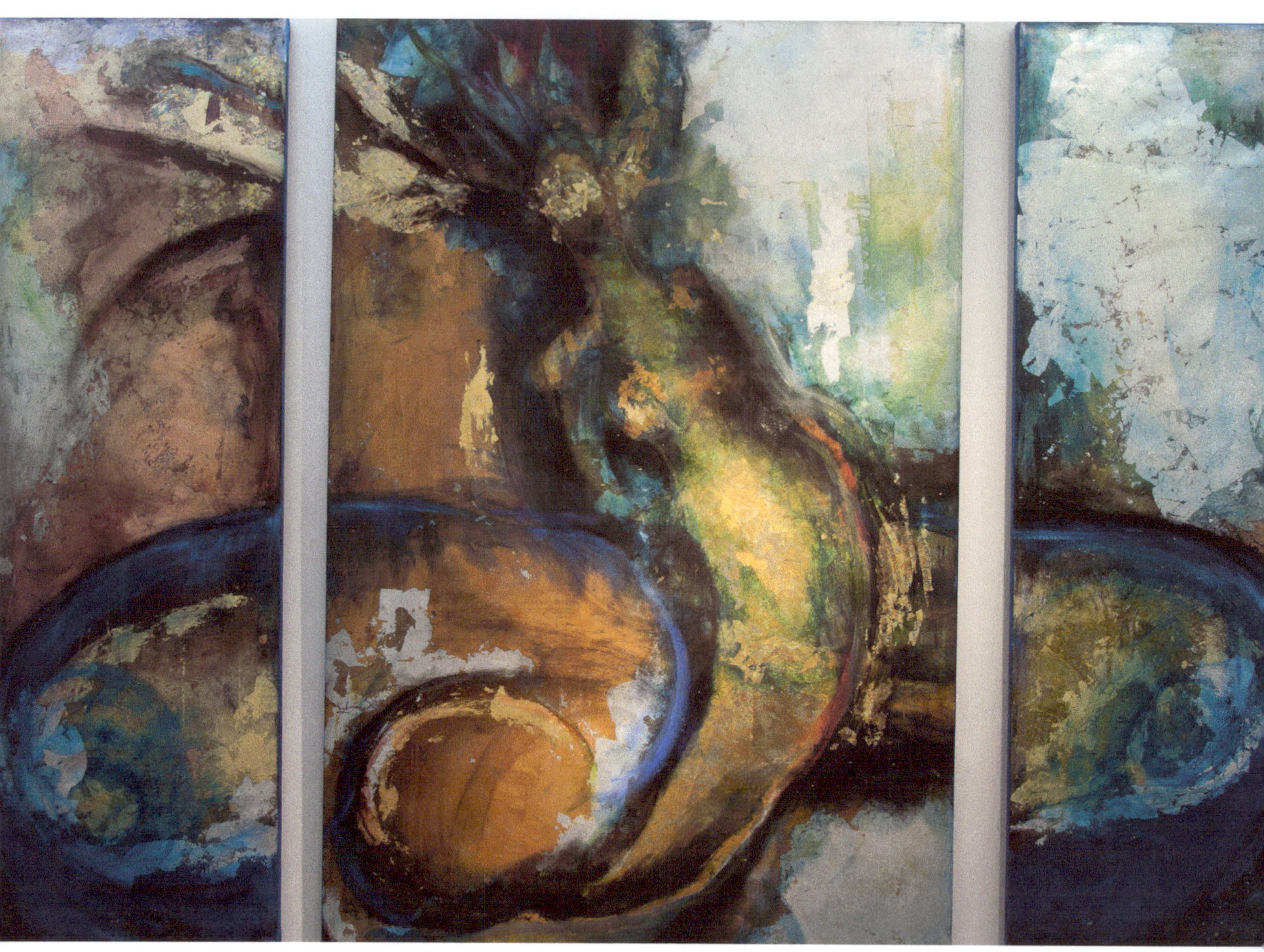

The Blue Hole, Suzanne Reese Horvitz, 2015.
Acrylic, gold and silver leaf

The Jersey Devil

ONE TALE from the Pines has made the leap to modern cultural relevance. The story of the Jersey or Leeds Devil is variously told, but it customarily begins with Mother Leeds who, sickened by seasonal pregnancies, curses her final confinement and gives birth to a monster.

Mentioned in print as early as 1859, the Devil captured national attention in 1909 with a rampage through South Jersey and southeastern Pennsylvania. Across the country, newspapers described the fear occasioned by sightings. That same year the Devil moved into the cultural slipstream as the title of a burlesque performed in Philadelphia theatres, a motor launch participating in races off the Jersey shore, and eventually as a small but memorable part of modern American folklore.

Today the Devil holds its greatest significance locally, having given its name to at least one pub, a surf shop, a local heavy metal band (*The Son of Leeds*), and a display in the Atlantic City *Ripley's Believe It or Not.* Although New Jersey's hockey team is located in the north, it has taken the Devil's name and engraved it three times on Lord Stanley's cup. There are numerous books on the Jersey Devil, including comic, cook, and children's books. One of the latest, Bill Sprouse's *The Domestic Life of the Jersey Devil*, wrestles with the beast's origins and, at the same time, presents a witty and insightful meditation on life.

Perhaps the Devil's current popularity should be attributed to crass commercialization. It does catch our attention, it's fun, and it apparently makes sales. But commerce does not explain the longevity of the story – and it is the story, joined with the joy of storytelling, that has survived and thrived over three centuries, not the Devil.

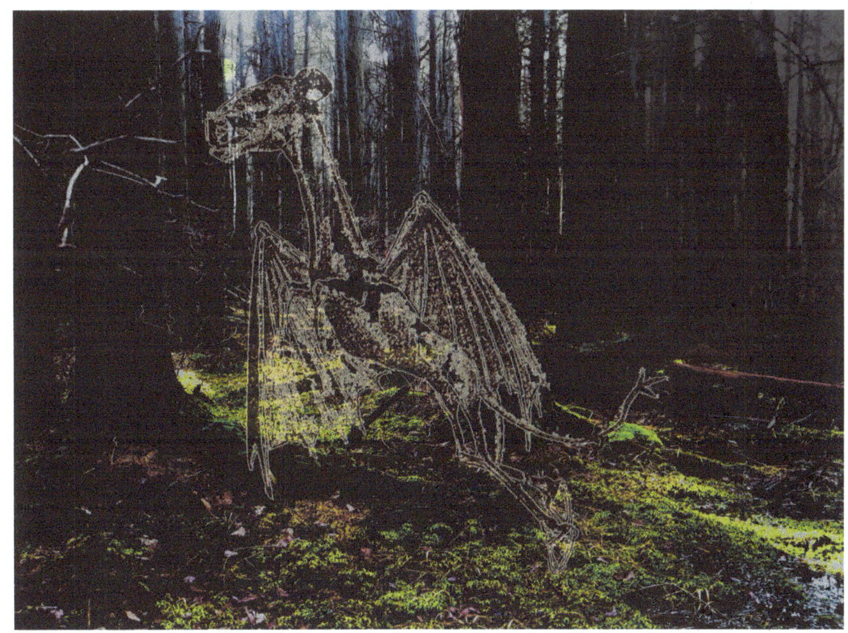

NIGHT FLIGHT, 2014.

The devil, from the *Philadelphia Evening Bulletin*, January 1909, flies over the cedar bog (Cedick Run) on the campus of Stockton University.

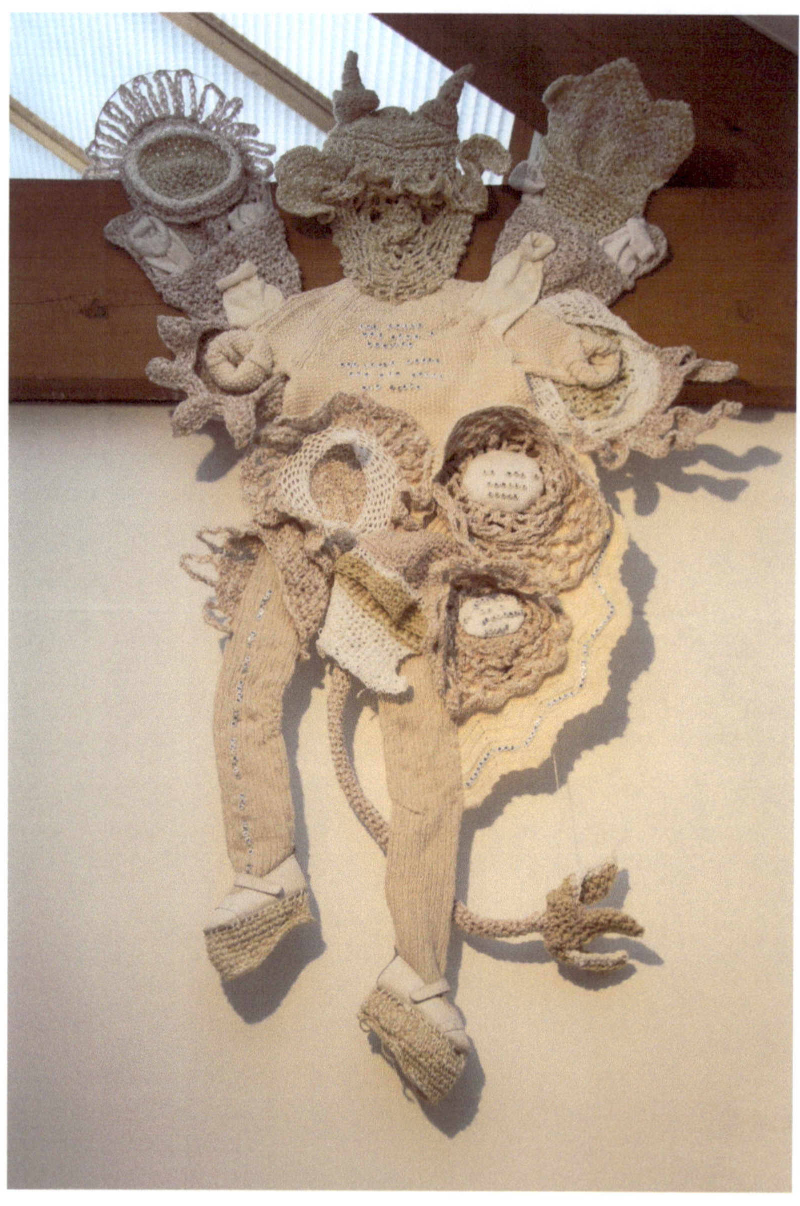

Dressing (the NJ Devil), Diane Savona in collaboration with Marisa DiPaolo, 2014.

Textile

The legend of the Jersey Devil is usually traced back to Mrs. Leeds of Atlantic County. After giving birth to 12 children, and pregnant with the 13th, she alleged her last child would be a devil. This legend has been translated into baby clothes by Marisa DiPaolo and Diane Savona.

Marisa DiPaolo crocheted the baby bonnets while breastfeeding. They represent those anxious preparations for a newborn that are made while unsure of what really awaits. Twelve of the bonnets are for the older siblings, the ones Mother Leeds *could* handle. Diane Savona added used baby sweaters, which she embellished with elements of the story.

Who Will Survive, and What Will be Left of Them?, Ray Nunzi, 2014.

Photography

“By combining the folklore of the Jersey Devil, a concept-album from the band *Murder by Death*, and the rough structure of a graphic novel, I have created this photographic story. Folklore is of great interest: it expresses beliefs and sometimes the morals of life, passed down from generation to generation, often getting misconstrued along the way.

My version is a bit different from the standard tale. It is the story of a man and the Devil battling until one of them dies. My small contribution to the folklore of the Jersey Devil is this story right here.”

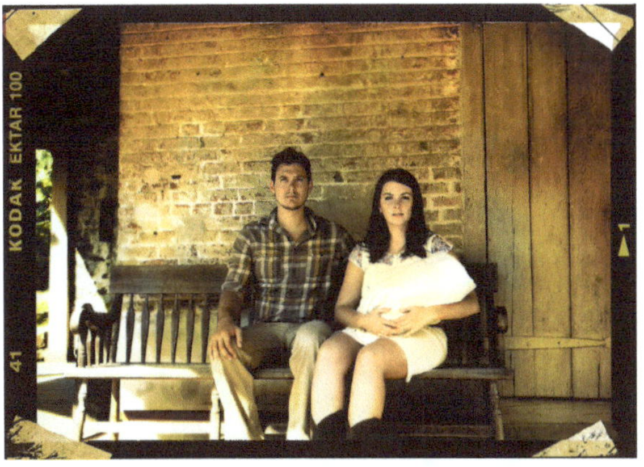

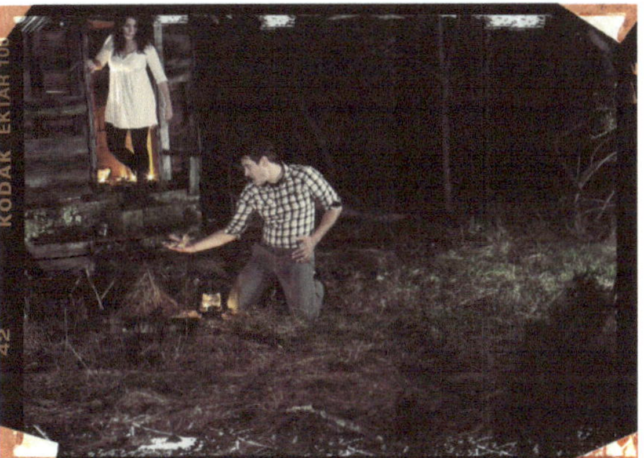

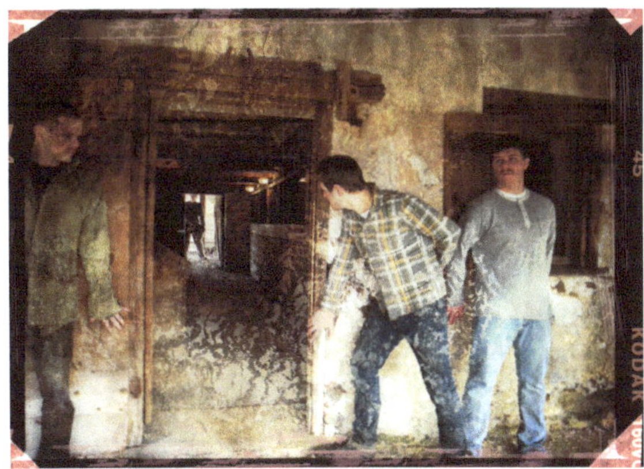

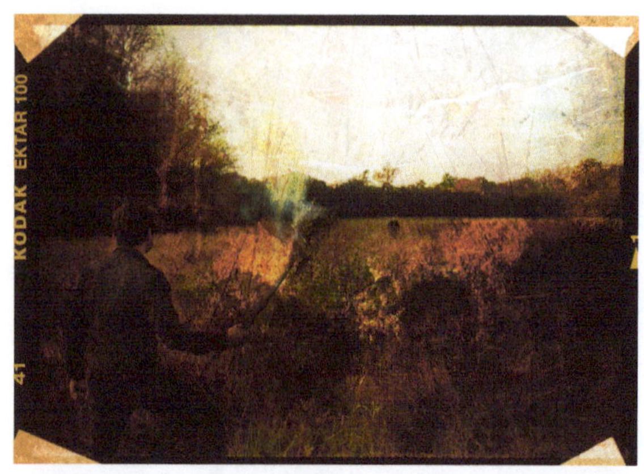
KODAK EKTAR 100
41

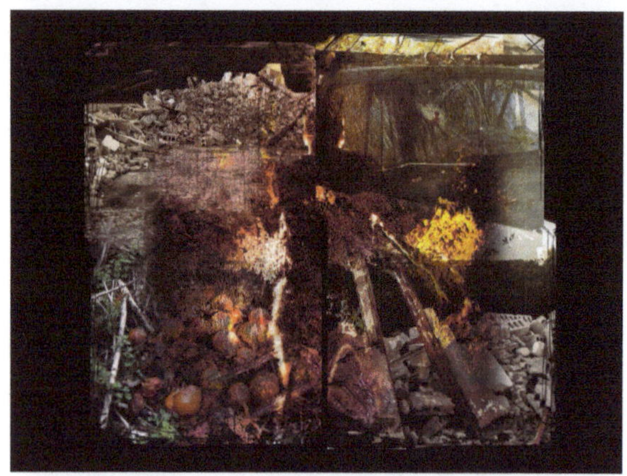

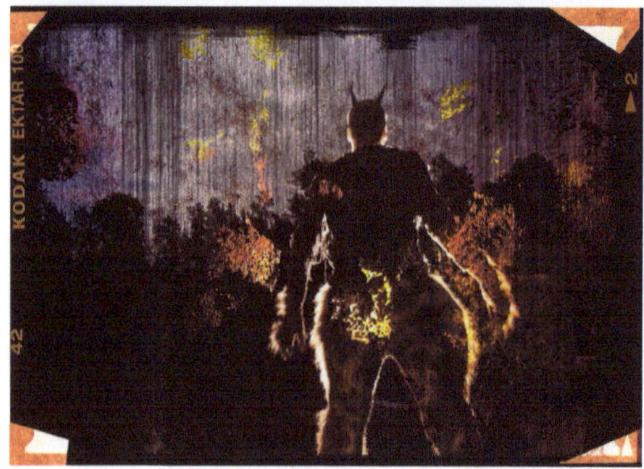
KODAK EKTAR
42

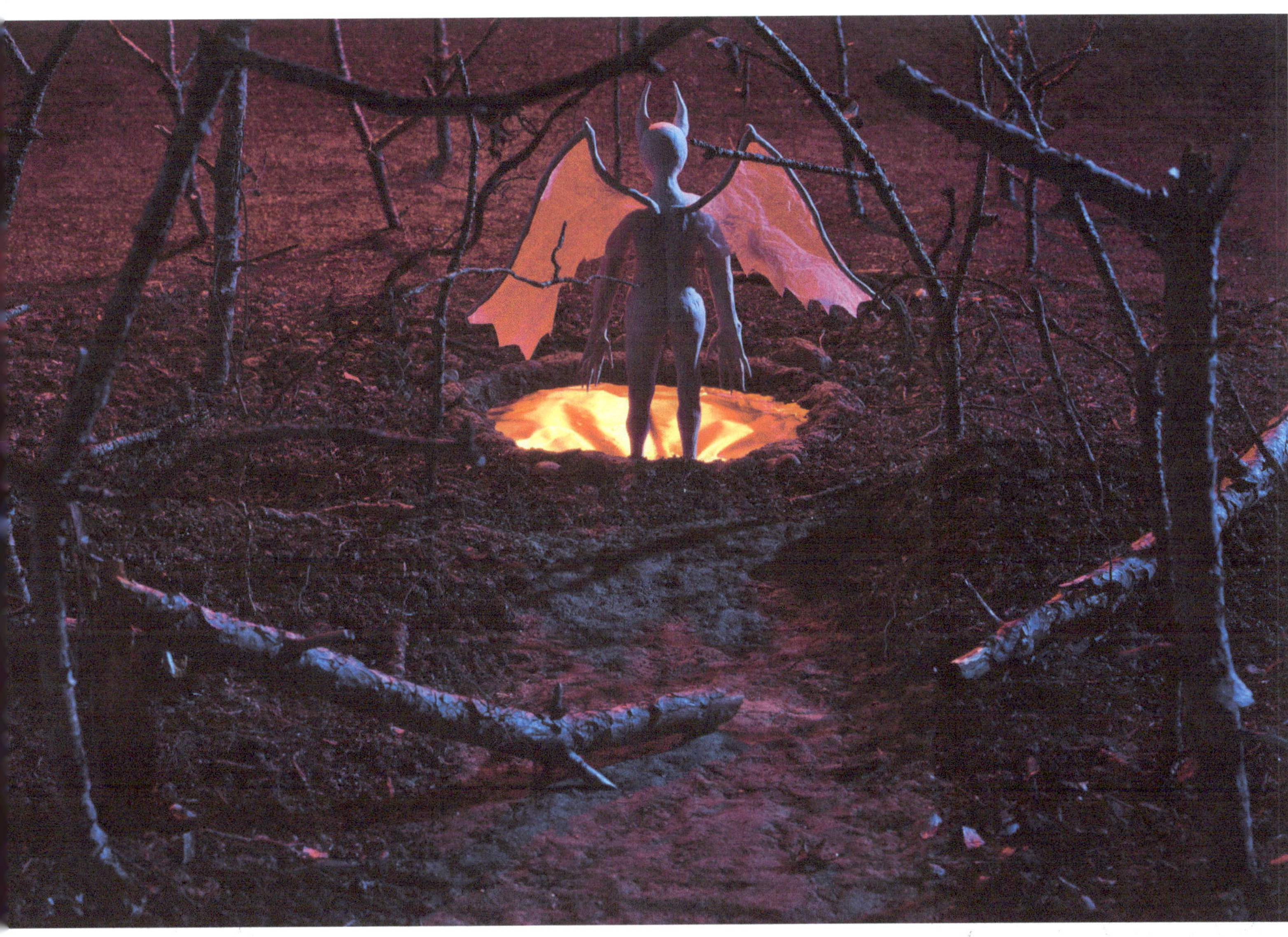

Devil of the Pines, Ian London, 2015.
Photograph of custom built diorama

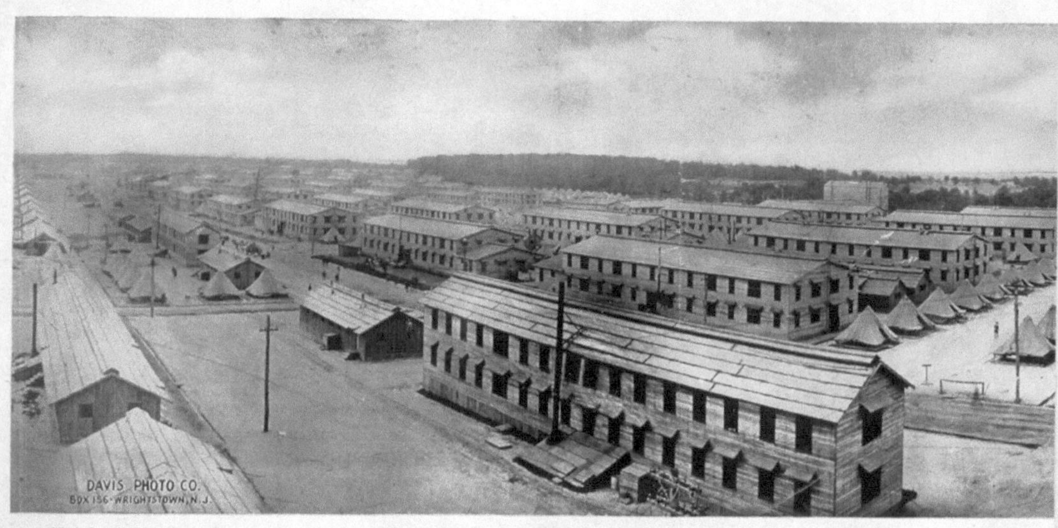

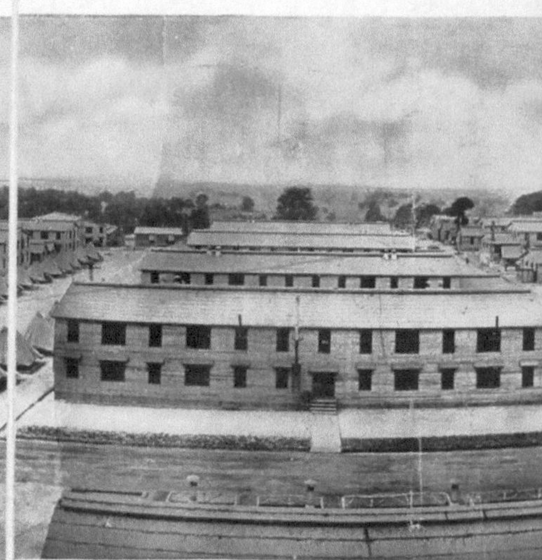

PANORAMIC VIEW OF CAMP DIX NE

The End of Storytelling

With America's entry into the First World War, construction began on Camp Dix in the Pine Barrens during June 1917. Completed with breathtaking speed, the camp covered almost 5,000 acres with another 3,500 acres set aside for the rifle range, subsuming the site of the old Hanover Furnace and occupying adjacent lands. It became a training and staging ground for over 55,000 troops during the war and afterwards served as a demobilization center, processing 300,000 men back into civilian life. Camp Dix was also ground zero for the Spanish Influenza epidemic, brought to American shores by the returning doughboys.

The camp remained in use by the military during the 1930s and throughout WWII; the name changed to Fort Dix in 1939. Indeed, it is still in use today. Two factories for producing military ordnance were also built during WWI in southern portions of the Pines. Amatol, four miles east of Hammonton, was a shell-loading facility that sprang up quickly in the early part of 1918. Belcoville (named for the Bethlehem Loading Company), a second shell-loading complex, was built just south of Mays Landing.

The influx of construction crews, military personnel, and the money that accompanied them, along with the gradual introduction of better roads, electricity, and phone lines deep into the Pines, brought about a fundamental shift in the life of its residents. The slow, seasonal pace of life that fostered storytelling was changing, and though Herbert Halpert completed his fieldwork during the 1930s through the early 1950s, it was the oldest residents who were his storytellers, not the youth.

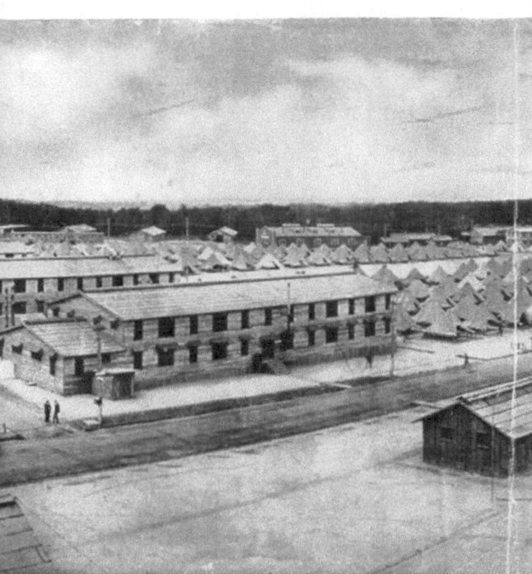

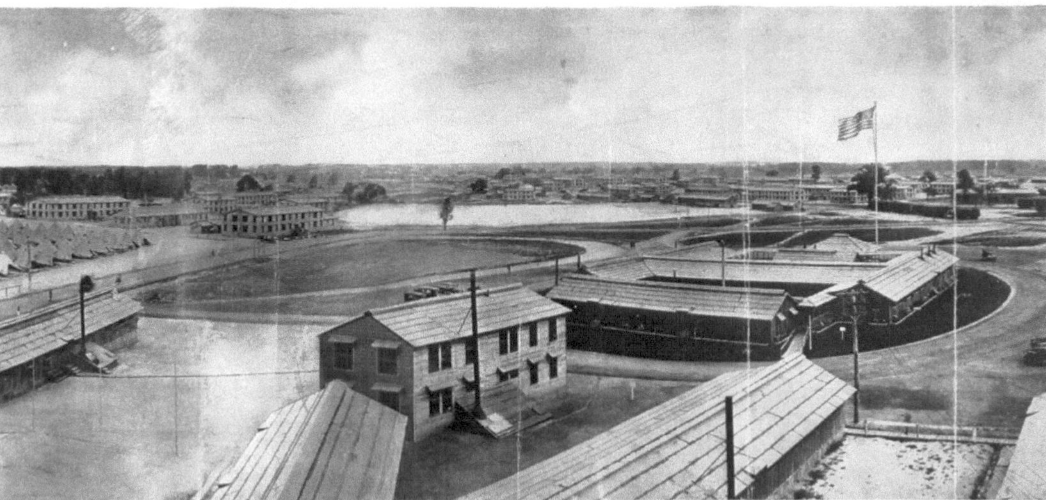

Camp Dix, c. 1918.

This panoramic view of Camp Dix attempts to portray the size of the training base. The Hament-Romans Company of Baltimore, Maryland, published this image for the Y.M.C.A. after receiving permission from censors. Covering almost 10,000 acres, including the rifle range, it is hard to comprehend the full scope of the cantonment comprising over 1,650 buildings, not including tents. Courtesy of the Paul W. Schopp Collection.

In Appreciation

THANKS TO Dorrie Papademetriou and Saskia Schmidt of the Noyes Museum, without whom the exhibition would not have occurred. Special thanks to Linda Stanton, Mark Demitroff, and Ted Gordon who each helped in important ways. We also received valuable assistance and encouragement from John Bunnell, Jack Connor, David Dimmerman, Christine Farina, Edward E. Fox III, Niki Giberson, Nicholas Halpert, Peter C. Hamilton, Lisa Honaker, Russel Juelg, Harvey Kesselman, David Scott Kessler, John Morsa, Carl Lindahl, Pat Martinelli, John Mattel, Ong's Hat Band, David Pinto, Ben Ruset, R. Marilyn Schmidt, Louise Tillstrom, Ken Tompkins, Deanna Tumas, Wendel White, J. D. A. Widdowson, Budd Wilson, and Dianne Wood.

Many Stockton students completed research and/or contributed to exhibition blurbs. We would like to thank Stephanie Allen, Ian Angotti, Eric Anglero, Samantha Baird, Kaylan Bini, Lauren Bork, Ian Brown, Kristen Callaghan, Carmen Capoferri, Tim Chivalette, Kirsten Corley, Taylor Coyle, Tricia Frechette, Lauren Goodfellow, Toyka Henderson, Edward Horan, Megan Jeffery, Kaleen Kern, Kevin Konrad, Samantha Levine, Andrea Manley, Bobby McGruther, Kaitlin Montague, Erik Nelson, Tania Rivera, Allison Shegda, and Ashley Vaccaro.

The Artists

Nancy Cohen ⁓ www.nancymcohen.com/

Janet Greco ⁓ www.frozenbay.com/

Albert Horner ⁓ www.pinelandsimagery.com/

Suzanne Horvitz ⁓ www.suzannehorvitz.com/

Rory Mahon ⁓ www.rorymahon.com/

Ray Nunzi ⁓ www.raynunzi.com/

Ian London

Nancy Palermo ⁓ www.nancypalermo.net

Diana Savona ⁓ www.dianesavonaart.com/

The Noyes Museum ⁓ www.noyesmuseum.org/

SJCHC ⁓ blogs.stockton.edu/sjchc/

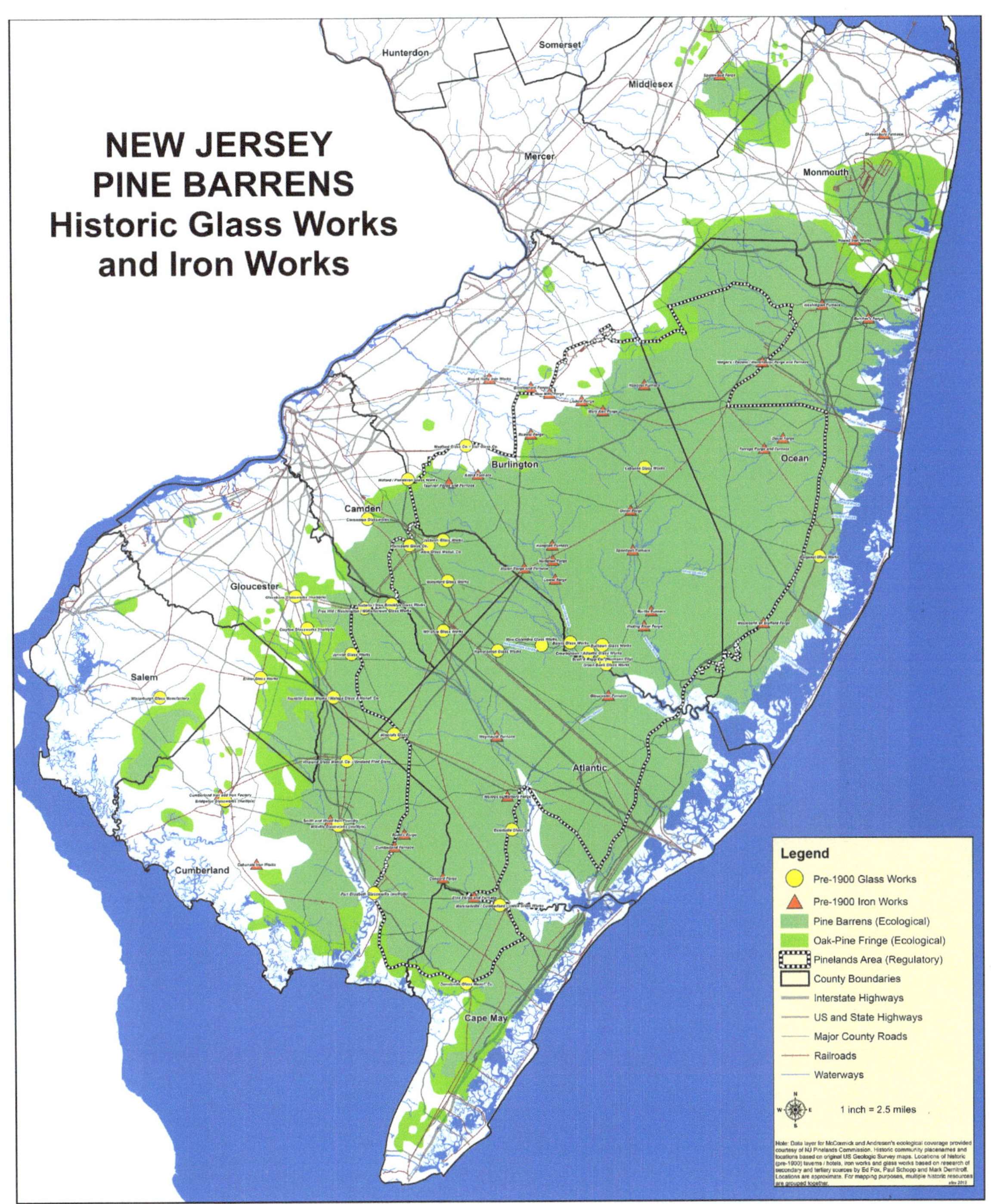
NEW JERSEY
PINE BARRENS
Historic Glass Works
and Iron Works
Hunterdon
Somerset
Middlesex
Mercer
Monmouth
Burlington
Ocean
Camden
Gloucester
Salem
Atlantic
Cumberland
Cape May
Legend
Pre-1900 Glass Works
Pre-1900 Iron Works
Pine Barrens (Ecological)
Oak-Pine Fringe (Ecological)
Pinelands Area (Regulatory)
County Boundaries
Interstate Highways
US and State Highways
Major County Roads
Railroads
Waterways
1 inch = 2.5 miles

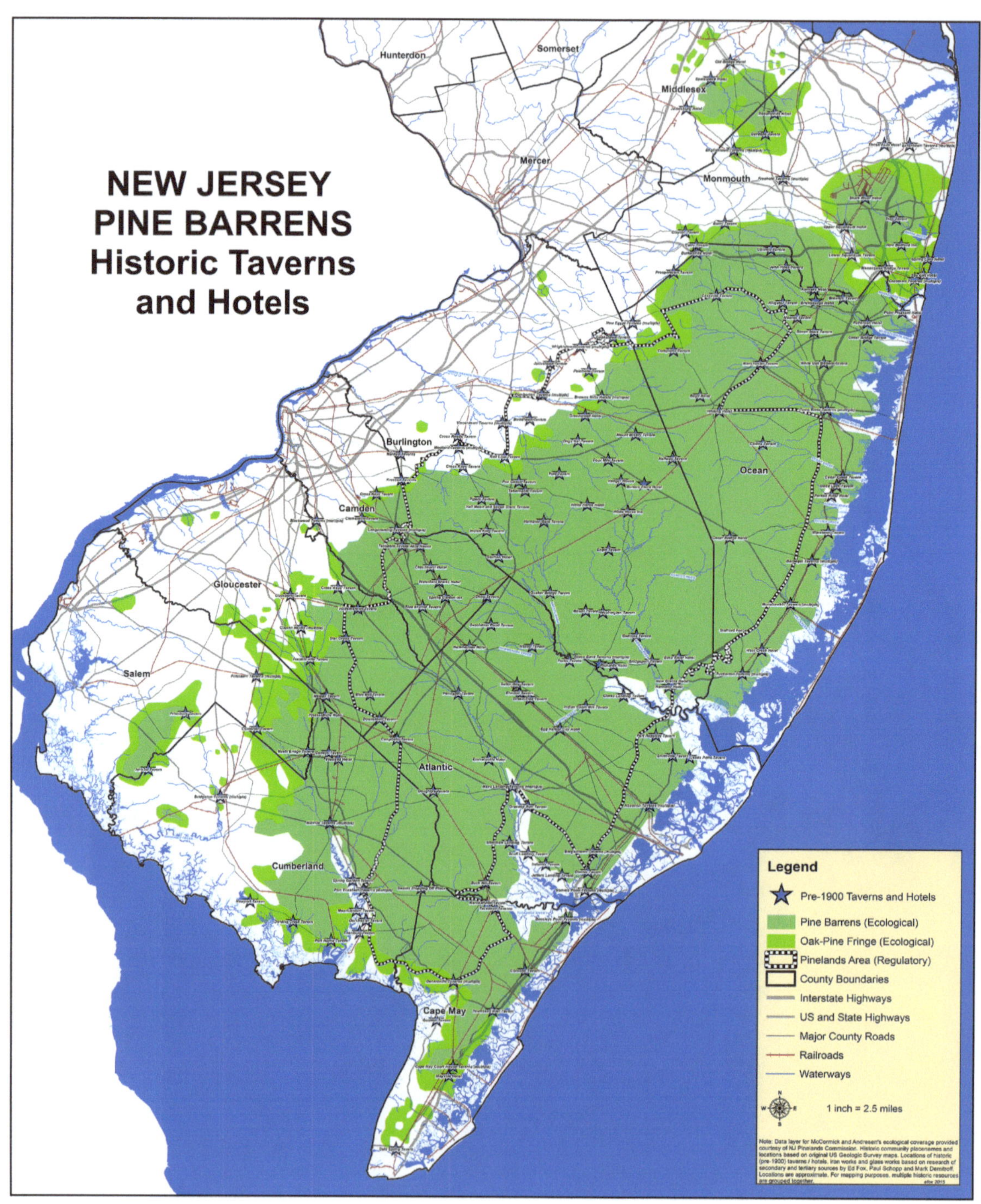
NEW JERSEY
PINE BARRENS
Historic Taverns
and Hotels
Hunterdon
Somerset
Middlesex
Mercer
Monmouth
Burlington
Ocean
Camden
Gloucester
Salem
Atlantic
Cumberland
Cape May
Legend
Pre-1900 Taverns and Hotels
Pine Barrens (Ecological)
Oak-Pine Fringe (Ecological)
Pinelands Area (Regulatory)
County Boundaries
Interstate Highways
US and State Highways
Major County Roads
Railroads
Waterways
1 inch = 2.5 miles
Note: Data layer for McCormick and Andresen's ecological coverage provided courtesy of NJ Pinelands Commission. Historic community placenames and locations based on original US Geologic Survey maps. Locations of historic (pre-1900) taverns / hotels, iron works and glass works based on research of secondary and tertiary sources by Ed Fox, Paul Schopp and Mark Demitroff. Locations are approximate. For mapping purposes, multiple historic resources are grouped together.
efox 2015

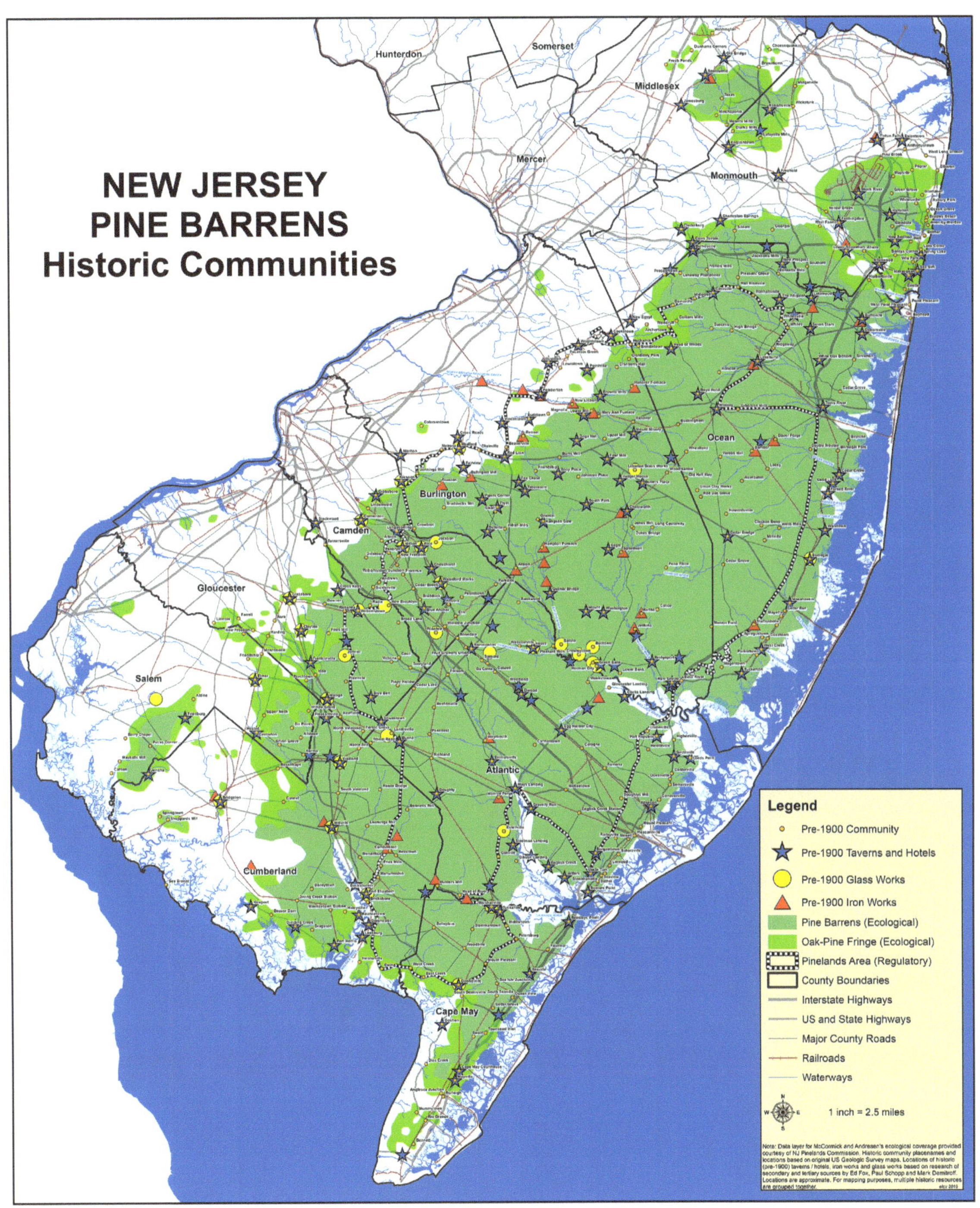
NEW JERSEY
PINE BARRENS
Historic Communities
Hunterdon
Somerset
Middlesex
Mercer
Monmouth
Ocean
Burlington
Camden
Gloucester
Salem
Atlantic
Cumberland
Cape May
Legend
Pre-1900 Community
Pre-1900 Taverns and Hotels
Pre-1900 Glass Works
Pre-1900 Iron Works
Pine Barrens (Ecological)
Oak-Pine Fringe (Ecological)
Pinelands Area (Regulatory)
County Boundaries
Interstate Highways
US and State Highways
Major County Roads
Railroads
Waterways
N
W
E
S
1 inch = 2.5 miles
Note: Data layer for McCormick and Andresen's ecological coverage provided courtesy of NJ Pinelands Commission. Historic community placenames and locations based on original US Geologic Survey maps. Locations of historic (pre-1900) taverns / hotels, iron works and glass works based on research of secondary and tertiary sources by Ed Fox, Paul Schopp and Mark Demitroff. Locations are approximate. For mapping purposes, multiple historic resources are grouped together.

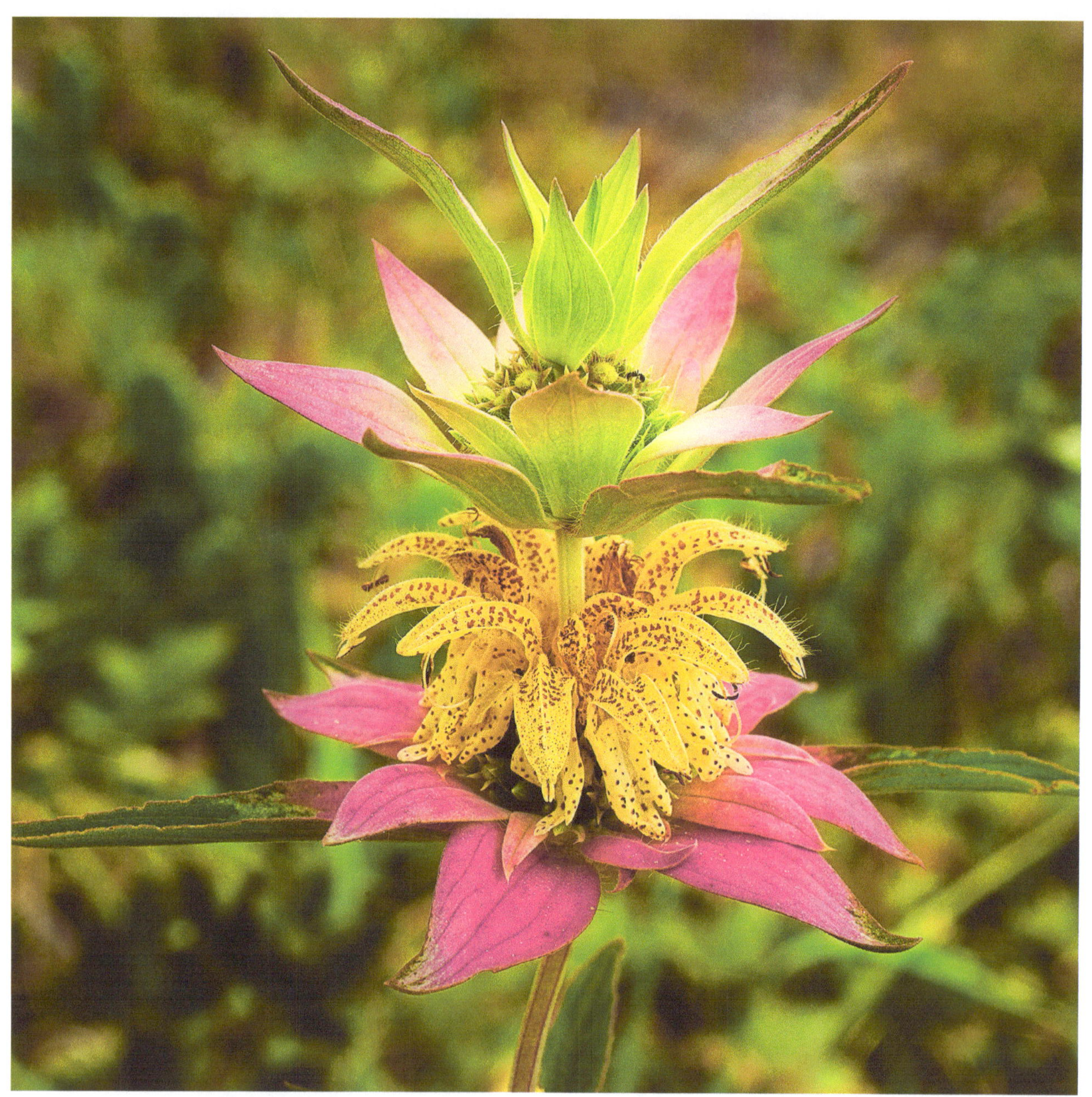

Horse Mint, Albert Horner, 2014.

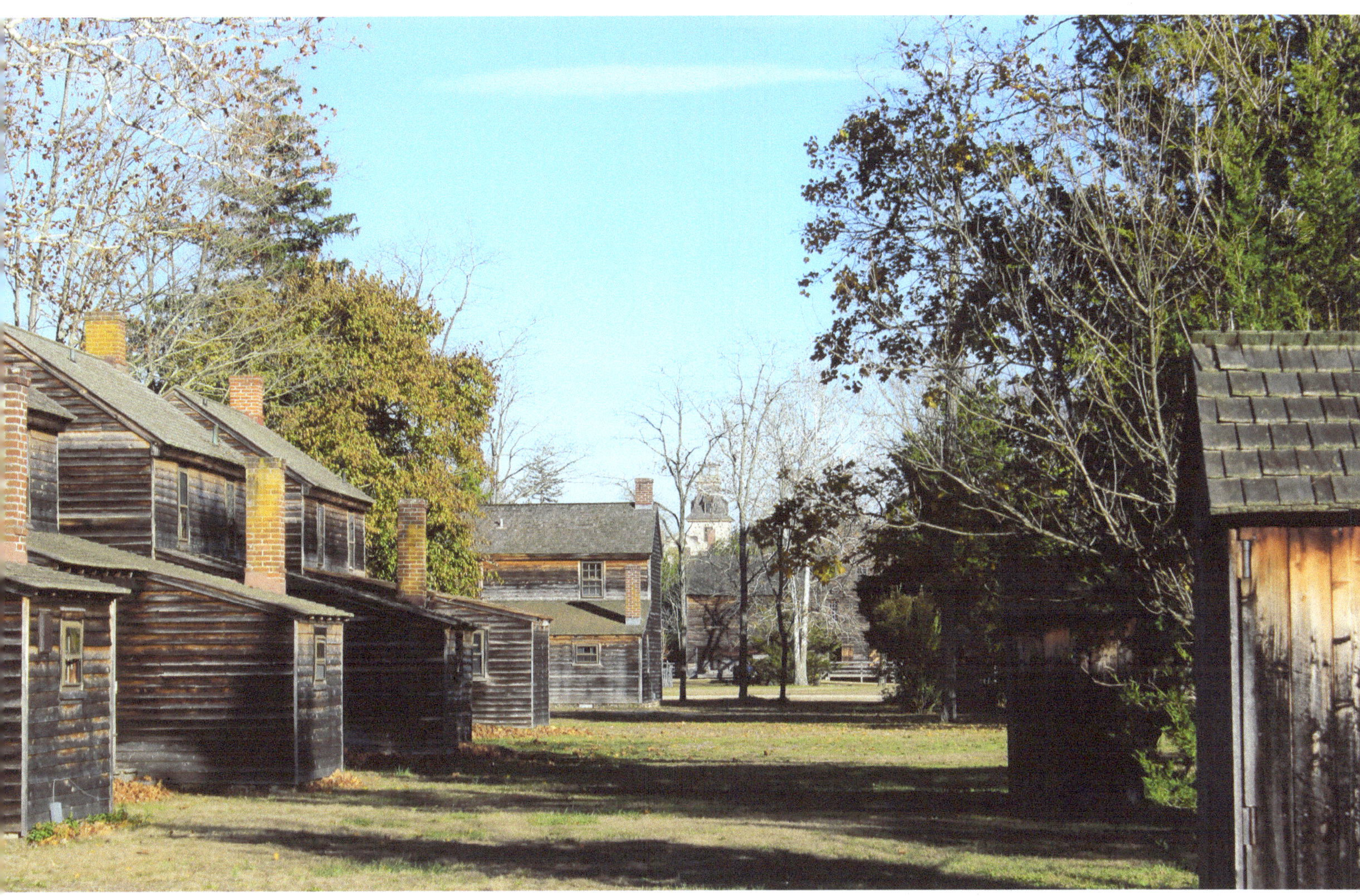

Workers Houses & Mansion, Batsto Village, Burlington County, 2014.

First an iron furnace and then a glass manufactory, Batsto Village provided housing and village services, such as a post office and general store, for its workers. The workers' dwellings, seen from the back, rented for $2 a month in 1878. In the background, dominating the village, is the Wharton mansion. Tim Chivalette, photographer, November 2, 2014.

Wood-Cutters wanted

At BATSTO FURNACE, in New-Jerſey, to whom good Wages will be given; the Wood to be cut is chiefly Pine.

For ſale or barter, for flour, midlings, pork, corn or molaſſes, either at the ſaid Furnace, or at the ſtore of CHARLES PETTIT, on Mr. Allen's Wharf.

CANNON SHOT of all ſizes, STOVES and other Caſtings, Rolled and Rod-IRON.

N. B. Guns, Howitz, or other particular Caſting, may be contracted for by applying as above.

Wood-Cutters Wanted, Batsto Furnace, Burlington County, 1781.

This eighteenth-century advertisement suggests the barter economy that was practiced at and around the iron furnaces in the Pines. Middlings are coarsely ground wheat mixed with bran and other by products; it was an important animal feed. *Pennsylvania Packet*, Philadelphia, March 20, 1781.

www.ingramcontent.com/pod-product-compliance
Lightning Source LLC
LaVergne TN
LVHW070130110826
845147LV00002B/226

9780988873148